TRUE SEX

True Sex

The Lives of Trans Men at the Turn
of the Twentieth Century

Emily Skidmore

NEW YORK UNIVERSITY PRESS

New York

NEW YORK UNIVERSITY PRESS
New York

www.nyupress.org
© 2017 by New York University

References to Internet websites (URLs) were accurate at the time of writing. Neither the author nor New York University Press is responsible for URLs that may have expired or changed since the manuscript was prepared.

ISBN: 978-1-4798-7063-9

For Library of Congress Cataloging-in-Publication data, please contact the Library of Congress.

New York University Press books are printed on acid-free paper, and their binding materials are chosen for strength and durability. We strive to use environmentally responsible suppliers and materials to the greatest extent possible in publishing our books.

Manufactured in the United States of America

10 9 8 7 6 5 4 3 2 1

Also available as an ebook

CONTENTS

Introduction

Harry Gorman's Buffalo

In 1902, thirty-three-year-old Harry Gorman was hospitalized in Buffalo, New York, after he suffered a serious fall that broke one of his legs. While on the surface this event sounds inconsequential, it prompted a firestorm of media coverage. Indeed, on his[1] hospital bed, it was revealed that Gorman lacked the anatomy generally associated with maleness—despite having lived as a man for more than twenty years. This revelation drew attention from newspapers across the nation, from Tucson to Boston and Fort Worth to New York City.

Gorman explained that his decision to dress as a man had been made in his youth, motivated by both a desire for freedom and a frustration with the limited opportunities available to women. He told the *New York World*, "I wanted to be a man, and since I reached my thirteenth birthday[,] I have worn male attire. I landed in New York twenty years ago. I have worked in all the large cities of the United States and Canada as a man. People think they are so smart. Why, I fooled them all, and if it had not been for my accident when I fell and broke a leg[,] I would still be a man." Gorman went on to explain that, as a man, he took advantage of all the opportunities with which men were provided, including getting married to a woman. He also voted, telling the *New York World*, "I'm a good democrat . . . and have voted the straight ticket for the last seven years."[2]

Perhaps most sensational of all, however, was Gorman's revelation that he was not the only trans man to call Buffalo home. In fact, he claimed that he knew at least "ten women right here in Buffalo who wear men's clothing and who hold men's positions."[3] He went on to explain, "Did we have an organization? No, hardly an organization, but we run across each other once in a while[,] and over our beer and cigars in saloons[,] we have had many a good hearty laughs at the expense of the

1

men."[4] In this way Gorman suggested to readers that though *his* "true sex" may have been discovered, there were many more individuals like him who still roamed the streets, undetected. Indeed, the headline of Indiana's *Logansport Journal* worried, "Ten Women Masquerade as Men." Furthermore, and perhaps more unsettling to some readers—especially cisgender[5] men—those undetected trans men were frequently in saloons, one of the most hallowed male institutions in the early twentieth century, mocking and having "many a good hearty laughs at the expense of the men."

Just as the brief story of Gorman initially may appear inconsequential, the revelation of Gorman's "true sex" might, at first glance, similarly seem unimportant to the history of the United States at the turn of the twentieth century. However, nothing could be further from the truth. Newspapers across the country discussed Gorman's case in articles under flashy headlines such as "She Was a Man for 20 Years."[6] The blitz of newspaper coverage about Harry Gorman illustrates that Americans at the beginning of that century were fascinated with gender—particularly its permeability, its elasticity, and the ways it intersected with race, class, and sexuality. Even though the disclosure of Gorman's "true sex" was described by some newspapers as "startling," it is likely that this was not the first story of a trans man that newspaper readers had encountered. In fact, newspapers around the country regularly reported stories of individuals who had been assigned female at birth but chose to live as male; at least sixty-five cases appeared in U.S. newspapers between the 1870s and 1930s.

For example, in 1883, Frank Dubois gained national attention when his "true sex" was discovered. Anatomically female (and the birth parent of two children), Dubois abandoned his family in Belvidere, Illinois, to start a new life in the small town of Waupun, Wisconsin. Once in Waupun, Dubois made a name for himself as a hardworking man, and he quickly settled down and married a young woman named Gertrude Fuller. Dubois fit so well within the small community that the townspeople only discovered his "true sex" when his former husband and their two children arrived in town searching for their departed wife and mother, attracting widespread attention in the nation's newspapers. And while Harry Gorman portrayed Buffalo's trans men in an antagonistic relationship with cisgender men, mocking them from the corners of saloons, it appears that many trans men sought to live normative lives—just as Frank Dubois had done in Waupun—supporting wives, earning respect as hard workers, and flying under the radar as much as possible.

The stories of Harry Gorman and Frank Dubois are illuminating in that they provide a far more complicated vision of the American past than the one historians have previously accepted. Gorman's comments about there being ten other trans men in Buffalo are suggestive not only in what they reveal about that city but also in what they imply about everywhere else in the United States at the turn of the twentieth century. His comments intimate that if Buffalo—a city not commonly thought of as the bedrock of the queer community—had at least eleven trans men in 1902, than surely so did Tulsa, Saint Paul, Jackson, and Reno. In short, his remarks reveal that our nation's past is far queerer than is generally discussed and that queer history penetrates beyond the coasts and into the nation's interior.

Furthermore, Gorman's depiction of the community of trans men is revealing. Rather than being part of a tight-knit community that shared an underground lifestyle, trans men existed out in the open, living and passing as normative men, and only on occasion encountered one another. While perhaps some urban enclaves did exist, Gorman's comments anticipate a great deal of what this book reveals: that trans men at the turn of the twentieth century were not always urban rebels who sought to overturn normative gender roles. On the contrary, they often sought to pass as conventional men, aligning themselves with the normative values of their communities. Additionally, when mixed-raced Milwaukee resident Ralph Kerwineo's "true sex" was revealed in 1914, the local papers were full of testimonies attesting to how conventional Kerwineo's life as a man had been. His neighbor Joseph Traudt told the *Evening Wisconsin*, "In the neighborhood it was frequently remarked what a nice married couple [Kerwineo and his wife] were. After having seen the 'husband' help his 'wife' across a muddy street[,] my mother said to me: 'How nice he is to his wife.'"[7]

Like many of the other trans men discussed in this book, Kerwineo, Gorman, and Dubois lived lives marked by movement. However, their trajectories challenge the dominant narratives about queer history. Although Gorman claimed that he had "worked in all the large cities of the United States and Canada as a man," many of his contemporaries chose to move not from large city to large city but rather from small town to small town, often living in rural outposts like Manhattan, Montana, and Ettrick, Virginia. For his part, Kerwineo's life as a man began once he had moved *away from* Chicago—a city with a burgeoning queer subculture—to the relatively sleepier city of Milwaukee. Frank Dubois also began his male life after a move; he had left his family in Belvidere, Illinois, to start over not in Chicago (the nearest large city) but in the tiny hamlet of Waupun, Wisconsin. Trans men seemingly chose these out-of-the-way places in order to make quite regular, maybe even ordinary, lives. They were, in a word, unexceptional.

True Sex explores the lives of Frank Dubois, Ralph Kerwineo, and many other trans men who lived in the United States in the decades around the turn of the twentieth century. More specifically, this book examines the newspaper narratives produced around the moment of "discovery" when a trans man's "true sex" was revealed to his community in the period between the 1870s and the 1930s. The reports published around these times of revelation are the focus here because they provide a unique window into the ways individuals and communities made sense of national discourses about proper gender embodiment and the emergent medical literature on homosexuality. Indeed, the period on which this study focuses witnessed the emergence of *sexology*, or the study of human sexuality, in the United States. A field of inquiry first established in Europe, sexology gained a foothold in the United States in the late nineteenth century with the publication of several important works, most notably Richard von Krafft-Ebing's 1886 *Psychopathia Sexualis* and Havelock Ellis's 1895 "Sexual Inversion in Women." Both of these works defined *homosexuality* as pathological and degenerative and argued that in women, same-sex desire was most often signified by *inversion*, or the predilection toward masculinity and cross-dressing.[8] Thus, one of the objectives of this book is to interrogate how the emergence of this new scientific discourse affected the ways communities responded to the trans men in their midst.

Scholars for three decades have been attempting to understand the relationship between sexological theories on gender and sexuality and popular understandings of the same. While Michel Foucault has famously argued that sexologists created the "species" of the homosexual, other scholars have been more tepid in their analyses. George

Chauncey warned in 1982 that "it would be wrong to assume . . . that doctors created and defined the identities of 'inverts' and 'homosexuals' at the turn of the century, that people uncritically internalized the new medical models, or even that homosexuality emerged as a fully defined category in the medical discourse itself in the 1870s."[9] However, one challenge scholars have faced is a methodological one: How can we recover the ways everyday Americans embraced or rejected medicalized understandings of sexuality and gender? Lisa Duggan's *Sapphic Slashers*, which focuses on Alice Mitchell's 1892 murder of her female lover, Freda Ward, provides useful insight in this arena by tracking the emergence of "a recognizable American type—the mannish lesbian or invert, a prosperous white woman whose desires threatened the comfortable hegemony of the white home."[10] Duggan argues that the emergence of this recognizable "type" occurred in the 1890s through the development of the cultural narrative of the "lesbian love murder"—a form that developed in sexology, the sensational press, and literature. These accounts portrayed lesbians as masculine women who were violent, dangerous, and a threat to white domesticity. However, even Duggan acknowledged that her study was limited and analyzed only one of the many cultural narratives of lesbian identity that had been circulating at the turn of the twentieth century.

True Sex takes a wider optic and depicts a world in which gender norms were subject to sustained debate. This book reveals that Americans, from small towns to big cities, often questioned proper "male" and "female" behavior and that the newspaper-reading public came face to face with stories of cross-dressers, "female husbands," and "sexual inverts" with surprising regularity. This discourse was not isolated to metropolitan areas but instead could be found within the most rural frontier outpost. For example, in the summer of 1901, newspapers nationwide breathlessly reported on the Parkersburg, West Virginia, trial of Ellis Glenn. The objective of the trial was to determine Glenn's "true" identity; an individual named Ellis Glenn had committed several crimes in West Virginia and Illinois, but upon arrest it was discovered that he was anatomically female. When asked to clarify this turn of events, the suspect explained that he was not actually Ellis Glenn but rather Glenn's twin sister—and that the pair had switched places just prior to the arrest. According to the story, a deep sisterly devotion motivated her to

[margin annotation: challenge]

take the fall for her persecuted brother.[11] Thus, a lengthy trial took place centered wholly on determining Glenn's true identity as either (as the *Chicago Tribune* described it) "a latter[-]day martyr or . . . an adventuress so exceptional as to lack a class."[12] In other words, the prosecution was charged with proving that the Glenn who had committed the forgeries—the Glenn previously known as a man—had actually been a woman posing as a man.

For several weeks in July 1901, Ellis Glenn's trial was featured in newspapers across the country, from Anaconda, Montana, to Montgomery, Alabama.[13] Therefore, in discussing Glenn's story, and those of many others, *True Sex* depicts a past during which gender norms were consistently challenged, questioned, and, most significant, in process. Whereas historians have traditionally credited only certain decades as being moments of "gender trouble" (the 1920s being the most common example), this book illustrates that gender is always in crisis and that cross-dressing figures have often been the site on which debate about gender norms has taken place.

True Sex also reveals that many trans men chose to live in small towns and farming communities rather than in the nation's burgeoning metropolises. Since its inception, queer history has been dominated by studies of individual communities that were often centered in large coastal cities, such as George Chauncey's *Gay New York* and Marc Stein's Philadelphia-based study *City of Sisterly and Brotherly Loves*.[14] This historiographical trend (which Jack Halberstam has referred to as "metronormativity," defined as the notion that queerness and urban centers have a particular, and unique, relationship) was also long a guiding force in queer studies more broadly. Since the early 2000s, scholars in both LGBT history and queer studies have begun to explore queer life in rural areas, adding depth to our understanding of queer lives beyond the coasts and major cities. However, most of the historical work that exists covers the period beginning in the mid-twentieth century and focuses on male sexuality and cisgender bodies, leaving big questions about earlier periods and other bodies.[15] *True Sex* begins to answer those questions and, in so doing, reminds us that urban queer communities are just the tip of the iceberg of queer history.

This book not only looks beyond the confines of coastal cities but also looks closely at the affiliations trans men developed within their chosen hometowns. Whereas the studies of urban queer subcultures have long been the preferred format for LGBT histories, the approach used here is far different. *True Sex* reveals that not only did trans men at the turn of the twentieth century often choose to live in small towns and rural outposts, but they also often sought to pass as normative men, aligning themselves with the values of their chosen communities rather than seeking consolation in the presence of other queer individuals. As Harry Gorman's remarks suggest, even trans men who lived in urban areas did not always choose to live in those locations because of the existence of queer subcultures there. This book presents a critical evaluation of the meaning of "community" for trans men; in doing so, it offers an alternative perspective from the near-universal embrace of the framework of community within LGBT history.[16]

In addition, *True Sex* tracks the ways in which the narratives produced around trans men changed as their stories circulated from local newspapers and courtrooms to national newspapers and sexological literature. For example, Ralph Kerwineo's story was narrated far differently on the pages of his hometown papers than it was in the pages of widely circulating metropolitan newspapers like the *Washington Post* or the *New York World*. Whereas Milwaukee's *Evening Wisconsin* reported that Kerwineo "adopted the disguise for moral and financial reasons and led an exemplary life while posing as a man," the *New York World* depicted him as a dangerous deviant whose marriage to a woman constituted a threat to national security.[17] By highlighting the distinctions between local and national iterations of stories about trans men, *True Sex* explores the ways that local communities negotiated with national discourses in order to forge their own boundaries of social membership. Recognizing the operation of this dynamic is a key insight because this process is precisely what escapes studies that seek to elucidate purely local or purely national accounts of queer history.

shifting discourses in media

Lastly, *True Sex* articulates the uncomfortable insight that trans men at the turn of the twentieth century were not always "queer" as scholars use the term today—that is, dissenting, nonnormative, and critical of heteronormativity. Upon the revelation of their "true sex," trans men often articulated their acceptability through their adherence to the norms of U.S. male citizenship. This tactic should be understood as an early example of "homonormativity," which Lisa Duggan has defined as "a politics that does not contest dominant heteronormative assumptions and institutions, but upholds and sustains them."[18] Although homonormativity is most often thought of as being a formation specific to neoliberalism, this book lays bare the deep roots of this current phenomenon.

Archives and Methods

By utilizing both the traditional methods of social and cultural historians and the latest advancements in digitization, *True Sex* brings together a breadth of sources that would have been nearly impossible to accumulate only ten years ago. The primary sources for this book are newspapers—sources that over the past decade have been digitized and made available to researchers at an astonishing rate. I made use of these recent innovations and utilized several online databases, including America's Historical Newspapers, the Library of Congress's Chronicling America, Readex's Early American Newspapers, and the Google News Archive. These resources enabled me to quickly search thousands of newspapers—many of which had been published in small cities and towns. Largely by using keyword searches such as "masquerade" or "as a man," I identified sixty-five individuals assigned female at birth who lived as men during the sixty-year period of this study—many of whom have never been discussed in previous scholarship. Additionally, these resources enabled me to track the circulation of narratives in a way never possible before; whereas previous scholars who have looked at newspaper articles about gender or sexual deviance have generally focused either on one city or on the sensational press,[19] digital resources have enabled me to use a much wider optic, tracking the circulation of stories from the local to the national context.

Indeed, using the methods of cultural history, I carefully tracked the ways that stories of revelation morphed as they circulated and how representations of trans men changed as they moved from the local to the national context. I noted whose voices were present in the articles and paid attention to what the national accounts left out or added to the local iterations of the stories. For example, were the trans men able to explain themselves in their own words or did journalists (or police officers) speak for them? I then combed through sexological publications to compare medical narratives of gender deviance with the stories that were written for popular audiences. This process—tracking narratives from local newspapers to national ones and then into medical literature—allowed me to read the narratives against one another and to think deliberately about the ways gender and sexual norms were being produced at the local and national levels as well as within the medical community.

In addition to reviewing newspapers and sexological literature, I also searched through census data, city directories, and marriage/divorce records to illuminate the ways the historical subjects of this book performed their identity to various institutions and what role(s) they played in their communities. Whenever possible, I also sought out court records and trial transcripts. These documents proved to be important resources to help determine the veracity of the newspaper narratives, both local and national, that were produced about the queer bodies discussed in this book. Taken together, the sources composing the breadth of research in *True Sex* illustrate the tremendous potential that digital archives hold for transforming the ways that scholars of queer history imagine the past. This method of carefully tracking the circulation of narratives clearly demonstrates the uneven history of gender and sexuality in this period and shows that this history is far more complicated— and interesting—than was previously thought.

Use of Terminology

This work is heavily indebted to, and in many ways is made possible by, the field of transgender studies. Transgender studies scholars such as Susan Stryker and David Valentine have shown how bodies are changeable and how the meanings attached to bodies are not the inherent result of the bodies themselves.[20] Transgender theory has provided a method of inquiry that is evident throughout this book and that has profoundly shaped the way I approach the past and the individuals discussed in the subsequent pages. As Scott Larson explains, "Engaging in historical work from a transgender perspective opens up new modes of analyzing gender as broadly unstable and mutable, particularly by taking seriously the possibility that gender gets crossed, changed, destabilized, and remade in ways that are not restricted to two genders."[21] In carrying forward the insights of transgender studies, I have made conscientious choices regarding the names and pronouns used to refer to the subjects of this book.

I believe that these individuals should be considered within the rubric of "transgender history" as they provide clear examples of the ways gender has been made, remade, and transgressed in the past.[22] This book provides clear evidence of the diverse range of gender expressions present at the turn of the twentieth century and explores how individuals and communities negotiated the porous boundaries of the gender binary. I refer to the historical subjects of this book with male pronouns because each of the subjects herein chose to live as a man for many years prior to his appearance within the public record, and many continued to live as men even after their queer embodiment resulted in arrest, incarceration, or other hardship. Additionally, I have chosen to prioritize the names chosen by the historical subjects discussed herein rather than the names assigned to them at birth as a way of honoring their self-identification.[23]

Furthermore, I refer to my historical subjects as "trans men" because they chose to live their lives as male even though they had been assigned female at birth. Thus, *trans* here suggests the ways in which the subjects of this book transitioned from the gender assigned to them at birth to the one with which they identified. I refer to them as "men" because they all expressed the sentiment that they were men despite their anatomy.[24] Additionally, I chose to use the prefix or term "trans" rather than "transgender" since the latter as a category did not emerge until the late twentieth century and as such was not an identity category available to the subjects of this book. Also, I am wary that the use of today's terminology would render less visible the historical specificities of the lives of the subjects discussed in this work. Of course, the term "trans" was similarly not available to the subjects of this book, but I have chosen to use it instead of "transgender" in hopes of conveying the open-ended nature of gender being made and remade.

In addition to the term "trans men," throughout this book I also use the terms "true sex" and "queer embodiment." I use "true sex" to refer to the sex an individual was assigned at birth. I place this term in quotes throughout the text to trouble the assumed connection between the sex assigned at birth and gender identity, and to make clear that I am *not* suggesting that biology is (or should be) destiny. Additionally, I use the term "queer embodiment" to refer to nonnormative forms of gender

embodiment. This term also signals the dissonance between the sex assigned to the historical subjects at birth and their gender presentation
(i.e., the gender their community took for granted). I find the term "queer
embodiment" particularly useful because it helps to register the nonnormative quality of certain bodies yet refuses to fix them in the strict identity categories. The term, therefore, exists in productive tension with
"trans men," and it suggests the impossibility of any modern term conveying the historical reality of the subjects of this book. Of course, these
choices are contentious, as a great deal of scholarly debate has occurred
within queer and transgender studies regarding the "true" identities of
historical cross-dressers, with some scholars arguing that they should be
considered butches, and others maintaining that they represent transgender men.[25] My terminology choices of "trans men" and "queer embodiment" therefore attempt to thread the needle, highlighting gender
transgression and utilizing the insights of transgender studies while also
being cautious about applying modern terms to people and situations
in the past.

Organization of the Book

Chapter 1, "The Last Female Husband: New Boundaries of Identity
in the Late Nineteenth Century," centers on the 1870s and 1880s, the
period during which sexology first emerged in the United States. This
chapter analyzes the impact that the emergent discourse had on popular understandings of sexuality, embodiment, and gender. It argues
that this period marked a new awareness of the possibility of same-sex
intimacy but that no one framework became hegemonic to replace the
"romantic friendship" model that had been dominant in the early and
mid-nineteenth century. Chapter 1 discusses the cases of Joseph Lobdell
and Frank Dubois, two trans men who gained newspaper attention in
the 1870s and 1880s. Both of these individuals are notable in their own
way: Lobdell was the first individual to be referred to as a "lesbian" in
an American publication, and Dubois has the dubious distinction of
being the last person referred to as a "female husband" in the mainstream, mass-circulation press. Through an analysis of the popular and
medical representations of Lobdell and Dubois, this chapter reveals that
the mass-circulation press of this period was far less squeamish when it

came to discussing female sexuality than has previously been described. Additionally, the chapter analyzes the demise of the notion of the "female husband" and argues that after the 1890s newspapers (both local and national) were far less apt to describe trans men as a singular, definable group—even in light of the invention of the new term "lesbian."

Chapter 2, "Beyond Community: Rural Lives of Trans Men," discusses the cases of four trans men who deliberately chose to live their lives in rural communities in the late nineteenth and early twentieth centuries: George Green, William C. Howard, Willie Ray, and Joe Monahan. Whereas most of the existing historiography on queer history has portrayed rural areas as inherently repressive, this chapter illustrates that, at the turn of twentieth century, many trans men did not seek refuge in the bustling anonymity of large cities but chose instead to live within the nation's small towns and rural communities. As such, this chapter's subjects provide a means to meditate on the meaning of community for trans men during this historical period. Rather than seeking the community of other queer individuals in urban enclaves, these trans men were able to find support, tolerance, and, at times, acceptance from their rural neighbors. This chapter asserts that the structure of small-town communities, wherein community standards were policed through regimes of familiarity, provided tolerance for the gender transgressions of trans men in ways that urban communities, wherein behavior is more often policed through impersonal means, could not. On the whole, this chapter explores what queer history can look like when the framework of queer community is abandoned.

Chapter 3, "'The Trouble That Clothes Make': Whiteness and Acceptability," tackles an issue that the historiography of the LGBT past has been hesitant to take on thus far: the power of whiteness in transferring acceptability to all individuals perceived as white—even queer ones. This chapter looks at four of the most widely circulating stories of trans men in the early twentieth century (Murray Hall, Frank Woodhull, Eugene De Forest, and Ellis Glenn) and notes not only that each trans man was white but also that he was lauded in the press for his successful mastery of the tenets of white masculinity. "The Trouble That Clothes Make" contends that stories of white trans men became a means through which newspapers could extol the virtues of normative citizenship—to celebrate the importance of hard work, economic productivity, independence, and service to the community. In a context in which much was changing, newspaper editors mobilized stories of trans men to assure their readers that patriarchy, citizenship, and white supremacy still regulated who had access to the power of self-determination.

Chapter 4, "Gender Transgressions in the Age of U.S. Empire," moves from examining local responses to trans men to meditating on the impact that global phenomenon had on national representations of trans men at the turn of the twentieth century—a period of rapid U.S. expansion abroad. This chapter argues that the context of the growing U.S. empire provided national newspapers with a ready-made discourse to pathologize gender transgressors: the notion of "foreignness." "Gender Transgressions in an Age of U.S. Empire" focuses on four trans men who were either nonwhite or immigrant or who were otherwise associated with "foreign" elements such as non-Western religion: Jack Garland, Ralph Kerwineo, Nicolai De Raylan, and Peter Stratford. In each case, the individual's alleged "foreignness" proved to be a liability. This chapter reminds readers of the power of empire in shaping perceptions of gender and argues that acceptance of one's queer embodiment is all too often a privilege of whiteness.

The final chapter, "To Have and to Hold: Trans Husbands in the Early Twentieth Century," circles back to a topic discussed in the first chapter: "female husbands." Though the mass-circulation press had ceased using the phrase in the 1880s, trans men persisted in marrying women into the 1920s and beyond. Indeed, between 1890 and 1930, almost half of the newspaper articles about trans men mentioned the fact that the individual was married (or planned to marry). This chapter finds that many trans men sought marriage as a means to illustrate their status as "good men" in their communities—a commonality that illustrates their distance from the growing urban queer subcultures. In addition, this chapter finds that, in most cases, local newspapers (and courts) responded with indifference when a trans man's marriage became public knowledge. However, as the story circulated away from the local context, the act of getting married was increasingly portrayed as pathological, and the stories became overtly sensationalized. For example, national headlines published after the 1929 arrest of Los Angeles resident Kenneth Lisonbee included "Suave, Trouser-Clad Barber Turns Out to Be Damsel," "Posing as Man, Girl Weds Two," and "Trousered Tomboy Bleats in Bastille."[26] This chapter highlights how accounts produced around cross-dressing figures were by no means uniform in the early twentieth century and how the precise nature of the narratives' meaning was acutely dependent on context.

Overall, *True Sex* reveals a deep history of gender transgression in the United States. This book suggests that trans men lived in every region of the United States in the decades around the turn of the twentieth century—within even the most remote hamlet and within spaces long thought to be dominated by religious conservatism. What is more, this book reveals that trans men fought hard to create livable lives for themselves, often utilizing surprising tactics, such as deploying the tropes of normative male citizenship or risking the revelation of their "true sex" by seeking legal marriage. These tactics were only available to trans men who were, or who could pass as, white, as they depended on the subjugation of nonwhite or foreign peoples. In this way, this book is a testament to the deep roots both of queer and trans history, but also of the long tradition of white homonormativity.

1

The Last Female Husband

New Boundaries of Identity in the Late Nineteenth Century

In late October 1883, a salacious story emerged out of Wisconsin that captivated readers nationwide and that tells us a great deal about how Americans perceived the porous boundaries between masculinity and femininity in the late nineteenth century. Newspapers reported that Samuel Hudson had arrived in the small town[1] of Waupun with his two children in search of his wife, who had deserted the family in northern Illinois several months earlier. To his surprise, he found his wife posing as newlywed Frank Dubois, husband to Gertrude (née Fuller) Dubois. Frank and Gertrude Dubois then quickly fled Waupun, prompting a manhunt that lasted several weeks, and which was covered with great interest in newspapers throughout Wisconsin and the nation. These newspaper narratives divulge a great deal about the ways gender deviance, same-sex desire, and pathology were constructed in the 1880s. Sexology was still an emerging science in this period, and newspaper editors had very few authorities to turn to if they wanted "expert" opinions on the significance of "female husbands" such as Frank Dubois. In the void of plausible scientific rationale, newspaper editors around the nation crafted their own explanations of the case; some viewed Dubois's case as relatively harmless, whereas others mobilized Dubois's marriage to ridicule the notion of women fulfilling the role of husband. Collectively, the newspaper accounts published about and around Frank Dubois show that there was no single coherent national narrative that explained the phenomenon of gender transgressors in the early 1880s.

This lack of cohesion is surprising, given the fact that this period witnessed a clear shift in the language used to describe gender transgression and relationships between individuals perceived as women. In fact, Frank Dubois is the last individual to be described in the mass-circulation press as a "female husband"—a term that had appeared with some frequency in both British and American works since the mid-eighteenth century.[2] Additionally, the same year that Dubois appeared on the pages of newspapers nationwide, the first utterance of the term "lesbian" appeared in an American publication.[3]

Thus, given that 1883 witnessed the emergence of the term "lesbian" *and* the disappearance of the term "female husband," one might assume that the early 1880s ushered in a new era in understandings of gender and sexuality. This assumption is supported by the existing historiography, which suggests that the late nineteenth century witnessed a dramatic shift from the "romantic friendship" model of same-sex intimacy to the heterosexual/homosexual binary.[4] According to Lillian Faderman, this process (spearheaded by sexologists) resulted in the "morbidification" of relationships between women.[5] However, despite the introduction or disappearance of terminology used to describe gender transgression or same-sex intimacy, the 1880s should not be heralded as a sea change moment wherein everyday Americans embraced a new paradigm of gender and sexuality. Instead, Americans were slow to accept the homosexual/heterosexual binary, and even as sexological writing appeared with greater frequency in the mass-circulation press, sexological theories had little influence on popular understandings of gender and sexuality in this period. Collectively, the newspaper accounts produced around Frank Dubois and other gender transgressors in the 1880s show that, despite the fact that this decade might seem like one in which there was great transformation, there was, in fact, no single coherent national narrative that explained gender and/or sexual deviance.

This chapter will challenge the ways we have traditionally thought of this period—questioning the ways nineteenth-century female gender and sexuality were conceived, as well as how these formations were viewed *after* the purported shift at the end of the century. As scholars such as Carroll Smith-Rosenberg have argued, in the nineteenth century, women were allowed to pursue intimate connections with other women because sexual desire without a male partner was allegedly inconceivable, or at least unmentionable.[6] Additionally, the social structure of middle-class life in the nineteenth century meant that many women lived in what Smith-Rosenberg famously referred to as a "female world." In this world, homosocial networks "accompanied virtually every important event in a woman's life, from birth to death . . . Within such a world of emotional richness and complexity, devotion to and love of women became a plausible and socially accepted form of human interaction."[7] Coupled with Victorian notions of female passionlessness, the pervasiveness of close relationships between women allowed for these relationships to appear innocent and, at times, compatible with heterosexual marriages.

However, scholars such as Rachel Hope Cleves and April Haynes are beginning to acknowledge that Americans were not quite so naïve about female sexuality as historians have previously assumed.[8] As this chapter will discuss, newspapers readily made illusions to female desire. Additionally, as we move beyond 1870, the year in which Foucault famously argued that sexologists "invented" the homosexual, sexual desire and relationships between trans men and biological women continued to be discussed as relatively benign in the nation's newspapers—an observation that is surprising given that the rise of sexology is often associated with the increasing pathologization of intimacy between individuals perceived to be the same biological sex.[9] Thus, as this chapter will show, the late nineteenth century witnessed more continuity than change.

"A Truant Wife"

Before moving into a discussion of the specifics of Frank Dubois's story, it is first important to pause to consider the world in which Dubois emerged. Life in the United States in the early 1880s was both exciting and terrifying, depending on where you stood and who you were. Reconstruction had been brought to a halt, although the nation was still fractured in significant ways between North and South, and racial tensions continued to drive American politics. The lynching of African American men still constituted a national crisis, though few in power acknowledged it as such. Many elites *were* vocalizing concern, however, about another purported social problem: the "New Woman." This decade witnessed a growing number of white, middle-class women entering professions and political activism, and the mainstream national press regularly gave voice to those who expressed concern that such "New Women" might destabilize the social order by stepping outside their traditional roles.[10]

In the West, the encroachment of both the national boundaries of the United States and white settlers continued, resulting in sustained conflicts with Native people. In East, the "Gilded Age" was in full swing. Immigrants were flooding into cities at a record number, drawn by the perception of employment opportunities provided by the nation's nascent industries. Business moguls such as Jay Gould, John D. Rockefeller, and Andrew Carnegie were transforming the nation's economy, landscape, and skylines. The combination of immigration and industrialization led to rapid growth of the nation's cities, but the majority of the nation's population remained in rural areas. Despite the rural populace, the nation was increasingly interconnected. Advances in communication technology meant that even the most remote outpost was connected to the nation's burgeoning metropolises through an ever-growing network of telegraph wires, railroad lines, and, most relevant to our purposes here, newspapers.[11]

In fact, when Frank Dubois's story emerged in Waupun, Wisconsin, in 1883, the United States was home to about one thousand daily newspapers nationally, and a greater number of weekly or biweekly papers. In fact, the Census Bureau reported in 1880 that newspapers were published in 2,073 of the nation's 2,605 counties.[12] Papers around the country shared content through wire services such as the Associated Press, and around one-third of small-town papers purchased "readyprint" pages of news stories from metropolitan suppliers.[13] Improved transportation networks (especially the railroad) facilitated the circulation of metropolitan newspapers to hinterland subscribers and enabled the editors of small-town newspapers to gather and present to their readers news from around the country.

Despite these indications of standardization of content, most newspapers retained their local flavor. Most were focused on local issues, and editors selected which elements of national stories to reproduce, adding or subtracting components of wire dispatches to appeal to local audiences and to reflect local print cultures.[14] Most large cities had numerous competing dailies, and editors sought to differentiate their paper from the competition in order to gain readers. While editors of small-town papers may not have had the same competition, they nonetheless selected content and framed stories in ways that revealed regional or local flavor and reflected the editorial biases of the staff. These advances in the processes of newspaper publication allowed Frank Dubois's story to spread very quickly in 1883, and yet the continued influence of local print cultures assured that the story would not be packaged in the same way as it circulated.

Indeed, Dubois's story appeared almost immediately in national newspapers. The same day that Dubois's local paper, the *Waupun Times*, reported the revelation of his "true sex," the story also appeared in newspapers around the nation, from New York City to Grand Forks, North Dakota. The wire dispatch read:

> A Waupun special to the Sentinel[15] says: "S. J. Hudson of Belvidere, Ills., who came here recently with two children in search of his runaway wife, found her masquerading in male attire under the name of Frank Dubois. She was living with Gertrude Fuller, having been married to her early last spring by Rev. H. L. Morrison, at the home of the bride's mother. The deception had not been suspected, but many thought Frank Dubois had many characteristics of a woman. Under this name she had solicited odd jobs of painting, and was earning enough to support them both."[16]

In most cases, the above dispatch was published on an interior page within a column relaying other brief stories from around the nation, likely provided to the papers by the Associated Press.[17] The remarkably unsensational account presented the details of the story in a matter-of-fact way and provided very little in the way of a framework through which readers could make sense of the story; there is no suggestion as to why Dubois began dressing as man, or what motivated him to marry Fuller. However, newspaper editors stepped in to fill the void and presented the dispatch under a wide range of titles, including "A Truant Wife" in the *Helena Independent*, and "An Insane Freak" in the *Grand Forks Daily Herald*. While such titles did not provide much framing, they did suggest to readers how they should think about the story. Additionally, they reflect a range of understandings regarding gender transgressions: the "truant wife" of Helena was the "insane freak" of Grand Forks.

One term that was used by the press with regularity to describe Frank Dubois, however, was "female husband."[18] The term was originally coined by English novelist Henry Fielding in his 1746 criminal biography

The Female Husband.[19] Fielding's novel was based on newspaper stories, which had appeared in England the same year, about the arrest of a fraudulent doctor and "female husband" Mary/Charles Hamilton.[20] After the publication of Fielding's work, the term "female husband" would go on to appear with relative frequency in the British and U.S. press, most often to describe women who lived as men or who partnered with other women and took on "masculine" occupations.[21] While female husbands were by no means celebrated in the mass-circulation press, they were not denigrated as insane, as sexologists were beginning to do with their figure of the "female invert." As Jennifer Manion has argued, "If representations of female husbands in the eighteenth-century press appear to mock their protagonists at first glance, they also serve to make the category real."[22] The utterance of the term "female husband" in the press animated in the minds of some readers the possibility of women serving the function of husband, a prospect that some readers likely found appealing. Indeed, as Rachel Hope Cleves has observed, the term "female husband" had a long tenure in the U.S. press, and yet its meaning was by no means stable. She writes, "The diversity and longevity of stories about female husbands leads to the conclusion that this form of same-sex union, in particular, had cultural legibility within American society despite its routine description as singular and astonishing."[23] As Cleves explains, the term "female husband" appeared with great regularity in the press in the eighteenth and nineteenth centuries. Significantly, it was often used to discuss cases that the press deemed remarkable but not pathological.

Additionally, newspaper coverage of female husbands consistently conveyed an understanding of the boundaries of gender as porous and incomplete. It appears that a great deal of public interest in stories such as that of female husband Frank Dubois was provoked precisely by their illustration of how permeable gender boundaries really were. American audiences had a powerful desire for such stories, and newspaper editors did not shy away from them. As such, by referring to Dubois as a "female husband," newspaper editors rendered his case legible as a familiar social phenomenon to American readers and helped to ensure interest in the case. Furthermore, while the term itself was likely familiar to readers, they also likely had seen it used in a variety of ways; "female husband" is ambiguous (or is an oxymoron, as Susan Clayton has argued), allowing for it to be interpreted and utilized in a variety of ways, which likely added to its appeal to newspaper editors nationwide.[24]

"He Is a Woman"

Journalists in Milwaukee were seemingly aware of the potential national interest in the Frank Dubois story and pounced on the case as a means of earning national recognition for their papers. Indeed, Milwaukee was the closest big city to Waupun, and its newspapers (mainly the *Milwaukee Sentinel* and *Milwaukee Journal*) possessed many more resources than did Waupun's. However, the journalists' drive to produce an exclusive story that would be reprinted nationally apparently led to some violations of ethical journalism. For example, on November 1, 1883, the *Milwaukee Journal* published a front-page article titled "He Is a Woman," which was supposedly the first interview with Frank Dubois and Gertie Fuller after the revelation of Dubois's "true sex." This story appeared to be quite the scoop, as no other paper had yet reached the pair. The article began with a lengthy description of the *Journal* reporter's long chase of Dubois and Fuller, which brought him "seven miles into the country."[25] The reporter found the pair taking refuge in the house of a local farmer, where Dubois and Fuller allegedly agreed to an interview.

The reporter painted a dramatic scene, wherein both parties appeared distressed. Dubois "cast nervous glances toward the door, and his small hands worked and twisted in apparent mental agony," while Fuller "was in tears, and appeared greatly distressed when the question of her husband's sex was mentioned." The reporter also offered detailed physical descriptions of both Dubois, who appeared as "a slightly built effeminate personage," and Fuller, who is depicted as a "rather pretty blonde with dark hair." The article goes on to reproduce the reporter's interview with Dubois, wherein Dubois initially insists on his maleness:

"Mr. Dubois, you, of course, know the stories which have been circulated concerning you"

"I do," hesitantly and in a voice which could not be mistaken for a man's.

"You are married to Gertrude Fuller, are you not?"

"I am; the ceremony was performed by Rev. H. L. Morrison, in Waupun."

"You insist you are a man?"

"I do—I am. As long as my wife is satisfied it's nobody's business."

"Mr. Dubois, you look like a woman, act like a woman, and there are dozens of reasons to suppose you are not Frank Dubois, but Mrs. Hudson—a woman. Do you refuse to reveal yourself?"

"There is nothing to reveal."

"If you are caught in this disguise you will be arrested! You should place yourself in the proper light at once and thus avoid punishment."

Apparently this line of questioning got to be too much for Fuller, who then cried:

"O Frank, Frank, for God's sake tell all and have it over," at this moment exclaimed the young and pretty wife, tears streaming down her face.

Dubois looked toward her, his lips trembled, and he burst into tears, sobs choking him for a time. Finally he said: "It's true," and endeavored to leave the room. He was restrained and finally was induced to tell his story.[26]

In this account, Dubois is presented as wholly effeminate, and the notion that he could have successfully passed as a man is presented as absurd. His innate femininity is highlighted at the end of the above quote, where he bursts into (feminine) tears. For her part, Fuller is presented as a heartbroken young woman. She is characterized here, and in other press coverage of the Dubois case, as a "normal" woman; later in the interview, Dubois reveals that Fuller did not know his "true sex" before their wedding night. However, the precise nature of her relationship with Dubois is cast in vague terms, and the possibility of sexual intimacy is at least tacitly suggested. For example, Dubois's flippant line about how "as long as my wife is satisfied it's nobody's business" assuredly reflects a certain understanding that biological women could sexually satisfy one another and, furthermore, that biological women *had* (contrary to Victorian notion of female passionlessness) sexual desire.

Significantly, this interview later proved to be entirely contrived. Many of the details provided in the *Journal*'s "scoop" were contradicted in the days following the article's initial publication. Both the *Milwaukee Sentinel* and the *Waupun Times* reported that the story was a forgery, and the *Sentinel* went so far as to report that the interview had been fabricated by a "swarthy young gentleman" who was seen at a hotel during the time the interview was supposedly taking place.[27] And yet, despite multiple reports that the interview was fictitious, it went on to be reproduced as truth in newspapers nationwide, from the *Chicago Daily Tribune* to the *New York Times*, from the *Boston Globe* to Illinois's *Decatur Review*.[28] Thus, the representations within this article are noteworthy because they embody a narrative that was deliberately constructed to appeal to a wide audience.

Contrary to the interview published in the *Milwaukee Journal*, neither Dubois nor Fuller admitted Dubois's "true sex" for several weeks, even after interviews with Dubois's former husband and stepmother were published in which they both stated emphatically that Dubois was biologically female.[29] Initially, Fuller explained the misunderstanding by arguing that the news of Dubois's "true sex" was merely a malicious rumor started by her sister, who wanted Dubois for herself. In response to her mother's pleas to come home, Fuller reportedly mailed a letter that explained, "I and Frank intend to stick together until the last cat is hung."[30] However, Fuller eventually *was* compelled to return to Waupun, where she remained loyal to her husband, telling reporters, "I ain't quite such a big greenhorn that I wouldn't know [his 'true sex'] after living with him for pretty near a year. I am positive that he is a man."[31] While such statements were (anatomically speaking) false, their inclusion in the press coverage of the Dubois case reveals that newspapers throughout the country were comfortable with frank discussions of female sexuality and were capable of acknowledging women's capacity for sexual desire—and, perhaps most significant, they reveal an acknowledgment of female desire for a "female husband."

Dubois himself was not apprehended by law officials until late November 1883, and in the month between the first reports of his "true sex" and his final admission, many different theories regarding the rationale behind his marriage to Fuller circulated in newspapers. No doubt, readers wondered about the nature of their relationship. However, standards of decorum prevented newspaper journalists from explicitly discussing (or pondering) the level of intimacy shared by the pair. Nonetheless, the stories contained frequent allusions to romantic or sexual contact. For example, the *Milwaukee Journal* reported, "Mrs. Hudson [Frank Dubois], the husband, wields a powerful influence over the young girl who is wedded but not a wife—an influence far more powerful than would be possible for one woman to wield over another without ties stronger than are known to exist between the Hudson woman and Gertrude Fuller."[32] Even more suggestive, the *Milwaukee Sentinel* reported that, prior to the revelation of Dubois's "true sex," the pair "as far as appearances indicated was reveling in the full enjoyment of connubial bliss and enjoyment."[33] Such statements appeared throughout the local and national coverage of Dubois's case. While references to "full connubial bliss" didn't explicitly state that Dubois and Fuller had a sexual relationship, they did nonetheless leave the possibility open to readers and suggested that perhaps the pair were more than simply friends. Indeed, newspapers refused to state emphatically what the nature of their relationship was; the *Milwaukee Sentinel*, for example, reported four days after its reference to "connubial bliss" that "the mysterious link of sympathy which must exist between the pair is still a mystery."[34]

The nineteenth-century boom in newspaper publishing and wire service technologies allowed for the Dubois's story to circulate to papers throughout the nation quickly. However, the availability of information did not mean that all newspapers presented the story in the same way; instead, Dubois and his relationship with Fuller were produced differently according to the logics of local print cultures. In fact, local coverage of the case in Waupun, Wisconsin, was substantively different from coverage that appeared elsewhere.[35]

"The Wonderful Pair"

The *Waupun Times* covered the story with great consistency between late October and mid-December 1883; only twice was Dubois *not* mentioned in issues published during this period. Due to the paper's weekly publication schedule, editors had the opportunity to provide commentary on the stories that had appeared in other publications since their last edition. For example, the opening to their second article on the story stated, "There is not much new in regard to Frank Dubois and his would-be-wife since our last issue. The subject has been pretty thoroughly advertised throughout the state, and even to the Atlantic coast, and no one has yet advanced any plausible reason for the strange conduct of the wonderful pair."[36] In preparation for subsequent issues, the editors looked for other examples of trans men to contextualize Dubois's story. This contextualization is one of the things that marks the Waupun coverage as distinct—whereas virtually all other coverage of the story depicted Dubois as a singular individual without precedent, the local press sought to find Dubois's antecedents in order to make sense of the case.

The first analogue that the *Waupun Times* reported was the "Case of Betty John," from Birmingham, England.[37] The case involved a suit against an individual who had been known as both Elizabeth and John Haywood, and much of the published excerpt described the difficulty the Birmingham court had determining the individual's "true sex." Elizabeth/John was described thusly:

> It appeared from undoubted evidence that while dressed like a man, she was suspected to be a woman; but in both dresses was strongly suspected to be a man. The common opinion of the ignorant was that she was a hermaphrodite, partaking of both sexes. When she carried a male dress, she spent the evening at the public houses with her male companions, and could like them, swear with a tolerable rate, get drunk, smoke tobacco, kiss the girls, and now and then kick a bully. Though she pleaded being a wife, she had really been a husband, for she courted a young woman, married her, and they lived in wedlock until the young woman died, which was some years after and without issue.[38]

This excerpt seems to serve dual purposes; it suggests that gender deviants are spectacles but also assures readers that the Frank Dubois case was not wholly unprecedented. However, in highlighting Dubois's historical precedent, the editors of the *Waupun Times* produced his body as potentially intersex. Indeed, in the above quote, the subject discussed is not a gender transgressor but a "hermaphrodite."

As John Howard and Lisa Duggan have illustrated, the relaying of analogues when discussing sex or gender transgression was a relatively common way for late nineteenth-century newspapers to make meaning. For example, in "The Talk of the Country," Howard discusses how the trial of Oscar Wilde provided a reference point for discussions of a case of alleged sexual misconduct and describes it as a "referential idiom—a Victorian-era tendency to connote homosexuality only through references to prior cases."[39] Even within the discussions of the Wilde trial itself, newspapers did not explicitly discuss the sexual charges made against the Irish author. As Jonathan Ned Katz has argued, "This ambiguity left readers quite in the dark about Wilde's transgressions, or forced them to use their imaginations to make sense of the reports."[40] Thus, subsequent references to Wilde's case created a situation wherein, as Howard has described, "the referential idiom, it seems, had no concrete referent."[41] As such, readers were provided with an analogue, and yet the precise meaning they drew from the reference was subjective and, as Katz has noted, up to one's "imagination." Indeed, newspaper editors relied heavily on readers' "imaginations" to fill in the blanks regarding sexuality.

Perhaps such references went over the head of some readers, but assuredly *some* readers understood that sexual intimacy was possible between Frank Dubois and Gertie Fuller (and Elizabeth/John and their love interest, as well). Assuming otherwise would be to fall into the same trap that befell nineteenth-century sexologists, wherein sexual innocence was believed to be the hallmark of all but the perverted. Indeed, individuals in the nineteenth century most often lived in close quarters with one another, making sexual prudery virtually impossible (or at the very least, possible only to the upper middle class). Furthermore, those individuals who were raised in rural areas or in close proximity to livestock were similarly well acquainted with reproductive activities and therefore no strangers to sexuality in many manifestations. In this context, it is foolish to dismiss the power in such "referential idioms" as the "Case of Betty John" that the *Waupun Times* published, as such references were powerful framing devices that provided context for audiences to interpret the Frank Dubois case. However, the *Waupun Times* did not stop at the "Case of Betty John" and instead went on to publish another analogue that perhaps provided a clearer referential idiom for readers.

Two weeks after the publication of the "Betty John" case, the *Waupun Times* again published a "counterpart" to Dubois, this time drawn from the medical journal *Alienist and Neurologist*. The paper introduced the

example with the following preface: "The sensation produced by the attempt of Mrs. Hudson [Frank Dubois] to play the role of husband has
attracted a good deal of attention, but other similar cases have been
known before. In a recent . . . *Alienist and Neurologist*, Dr. P. M. Wise,
of the William [*sic*] Lunatic Asylum, described a woman now in that
institution who for some years passed as 'husband' and was acknowledged as such by the 'wife,' although it does not appear that any marriage
ceremony was ever performed. The following is an abstract of Dr. Wise's
paper."[42] Significantly, Wise's article was a pathbreaking piece within the
realm of sexology, as up to this point sexologists had primarily been
interested in exploring gender and sexual deviance in men. Thus, Wise's
study was one of the first to be entirely devoted to a patient with female anatomy. What's more, Wise's article contained the first usage of
the term "lesbian" in an American publication. The individual featured
in Wise's article was Joseph Lobdell, a gender transgressor who gained
notoriety in the national mass-circulation press in the 1870s and 1880s. I
will return to discuss Lobdell's appearance in the *Waupun Times* shortly,
but given the great importance of Lobdell's case history as the first "lesbian," it is worth pausing to discuss his life previous to his mention in
the rural Wisconsin paper (and for that matter, prior to his incarceration
in the Willard Asylum for the Insane).

"Romantic Paupers"

Joseph Israel Lobdell was born Lucy Ann Lobdell around 1829 in Westerlo, New York.[43] According to an autobiography published in 1855,
Lobdell was different from the start, desiring pursuits such as school-
ing and hunting that were unconventional for young girls. He endured
an unhappy marriage to a man (George Slater), who eventually abandoned Lobdell and their young daughter.[44] At that point, faced with few
opportunities to support himself as a woman, Lobdell began dressing
as a man.[45] He lived a transient life for many years, working in various
rural communities in upstate New York, Pennsylvania, and even as far
west as Minnesota. In most of these locations, he presented himself publicly as a man and earned a living through hunting or working in other
rural industries, such as lumbering.[46] By the mid-1860s, Lobdell fell on
hard times and sought refuge in the almshouse of Delaware County,

New York. It was here that Lobdell met a woman named Mary Louise Perry, and the pair developed a relationship that would last many years. The couple left the almshouse in the late 1860s and traveled throughout the rural areas of Pennsylvania.

Although there are few records related to the early years of their relationship, it appears that by 1871 the pair had become somewhat notorious in the region of southeastern Pennsylvania. One local paper reported, "Much has been said and written about lately concerning two dilapidated specimens of humanity, who have been wandering about through this region of country for nearly three years, and who have been representing themselves as man and wife, and call themselves Joseph Israel Lobdell and Mrs. Lobdell."[47] The story proved to be of interest beyond southeastern Pennsylvania, and it appeared in newspapers across the country, often under the title "Romantic Paupers."[48] This article established a standard narrative about Lobdell and Perry that circulated in the mass-circulation press as they continued to receive attention throughout the 1870s and 1880s.

Notably, just like the press coverage of Frank Dubois, "Romantic Paupers" reveals the relatively fluid and nonbinary way both gender and sexuality were described in the late nineteenth century. While historians for a generation have embraced the "romantic friendship" model as a means of understanding nineteenth-century same-sex intimacy, a close reading of "Romantic Paupers" and subsequent iterations of Lobdell's story suggests that Americans were not so innocent concerning the idea of same-sex love as previously believed. Similar to newspaper discussions of the relationship between Frank Dubois and Gertie Fuller, papers did not *explicitly* mention the nature of Lobdell and Perry's partnership, yet they did repeatedly suggest that it went beyond a platonic friendship, often describing it as "strange," or as a "mutual affection so strong they refused to be separated."[49] Such descriptions may not have signaled sexual connotations to all audience members, but the vague language certainly left much to readers to interpret for themselves and cracked open room to imagine sexual possibilities. Certainly the combination of phrases such as "female husband" and references to the "strong affection" that had "sprung up between the two women" were enough to suggest to some readers that Lobdell and Perry's relationship was similar to other marriages, including their erotic components.[50] Just as some have written about the closet being more of an "open secret" rather than the absence of knowledge, one of the remarkable aspects of newspaper coverage of their relationship is the silence that enveloped it.[51] Indeed, journalists allowed Lobdell and Perry to keep their "open secret" by not discussing explicitly the nature of their relationship—and yet some readers no doubt filled this silence with their own interpretations of the sexual possibilities therein.

Lobdell and Perry cycled in and out of various state institutions and almshouses throughout the 1870s. They generally escaped lengthy sentences and were relatively free to wander the rural counties of western New York and eastern Pennsylvania. At some point in 1877, Lobdell purchased a small plot of land in Wayne County, Pennsylvania—a plot his brother later characterized as "four or five acres situated near Narrowsburgh in Wayne County Pennsylvania. I don't think it is worth more than $10. Is a very rocky[,] poor place."[52] Although this may be read as a sign of the couple's increasing stability, their legal troubles continued, and in 1880 Lobdell's brother ordered that Lobdell be tried in an insanity hearing at Delaware County Court.

During the hearing, fourteen men from the surrounding community testified, and each swore that Lobdell was not of sound mind. William M. Main, for example, stated, "I am acquainted with Lucy Ann Slater and have known her for about twenty years. On one subject her mind is not sound but on other matters [I] have heard her talk quite sensibly. I have never had an intimate acquaintance with her habits and customs. I know that she sometimes dresses in men's clothes and it is on that subject that I think her of unsound mind."[53] In Main's testimony and several others recorded in the Delaware County Court, Lobdell's insanity was specific to his desire to wear men's clothing. However, as many of the testimonies made clear, Lobdell's mode of dress was nothing new for him. In fact, several of the witnesses testified that they had known of Lobdell's predilection for men's clothes for twenty years or longer. This revelation suggests something quite powerful: that Lobdell's neighbors were, for many years, willing to accept his queer embodiment *and* his partnership with a woman, and that they did not undertake any effort to modify his behavior or interfere with his relationship. While those actions would occasionally make Lobdell the subject of sensational newspaper articles, these courtroom revelations suggest a more mundane component of Lobdell's story: that his behavior was condoned by his neighbors, except in instances when he appeared to be a threat to himself or the community. Indeed, the court testimonies reveal that neither Lobdell's gender transgressions nor his relationship with Mary Perry was considered threatening.

Furthermore, such testimony suggests that it was *not* simply Lobdell's queer embodiment that brought about the insanity hearing, because otherwise the hearing would have been called years before. The testimony makes clear that there were more factors involved than simply Lobdell's dress, particularly his ability to support a household financially. Neighbor Harry Walsh, for example, testified, "She is insane without doubt and incapable of governing herself or of managing her property."[54] As Christine Stansell has shown, by the late nineteenth century in the North, mainstream attitudes about poverty had shifted from those widely held in the Revolutionary era. Whereas earlier, poor people were pitied, by the mid-nineteenth century, poor people were vilified as bringing poverty on themselves through laziness.[55] In this way, Lobdell's inability to properly care for himself, Perry, or his land was understood by those in his 1880 court hearing to be the result of personal pathology.

Another aspect of Lobdell's identity that prompted some to view him as a nuisance to the community was his public articulations of religion. Lobdell's brother made an explicit connection between Lobdell's strange faith and his supposed insanity in his testimony, stating, "I think her insanity was to some extent caused by excitement in religious matters."[56] Newspapers had long remarked on Lobdell's public expressions of religion, often noting that while traveling, he and Perry would present themselves as "Rev. Joseph Israel Lobdell and wife."[57] Furthermore, it was in Lobdell's expression of religion that he was most often described as insane. For example, the *New Haven Register* reported that in the 1870s, when living in Monroe County, Pennsylvania, the pair would make frequent appearances in "the village, where the man would deliver wild and incoherent harangues on religion, and both would beg for food and shelter."[58] Similarly, the *New York Herald* wrote in 1877, "They were preaching, they said, the gospel of a new dispensation. The man delivered meaningless harangues, until the strange pair were driven from the place."[59] Over and over, Lobdell's "incoherent" articulations of religious philosophy were deployed in newspapers as a means of conveying Lobdell as an outsider, someone who did not share the same values as the community he was attempting to enter. Thus, Lobdell was seen as a public nuisance not only (or perhaps even primarily) because of his queer embodiment, but also because of the ways he disrupted community life in other ways—his inability to provide for himself or his wife (and hence his reliance on the charity of others), and his religious provocations. These factors combined led to his incarceration at the Ovid Asylum in Seneca County, New York, and later the Willard Asylum for the Insane.[60]

This notion that Lobdell was strange, but what made him a danger was not his queer embodiment or his relationship with Perry per se, but rather their unconventional and undomestic lifestyle, is evident in the various contemporary newspaper narratives about the couple. Newspaper articles written about Lobdell and Perry in the 1870s conveyed a surprisingly fluid understanding of sexuality. Articles such as "Romantic Paupers" and "A Mountain Romance" suggested the possibility of a long-term "romantic" and "singular" attachment between the individuals. This relationship was consistently described as "strange," and yet it was not depicted as dangerous or pathological. Indeed, newspapers throughout the nation occasionally used the term "female husband," with all the ambiguities it contained, to refer to Lobdell.[61]

"A Case of Sexual Perversion"

Once Lobdell was institutionalized, however, he was placed under the medical gaze and his queer embodiment was interpreted much differently than it had been by his neighbors and in newspaper accounts. At Willard Psychiatric Center, Lobdell was put in the care of Dr. P. M. Wise, a sexologist who had studied under the prolific James Kiernan (who himself had studied under the influential German sexologist Richard von Krafft-Ebing). At the time, sexology was still in its infancy. In fact, Krafft-Ebing's pathbreaking *Psychopathia Sexualis* would not be published for several more years, and most studies of deviant sexuality remained focused on biological men. However, theories were circulating within European medical journals about women—specifically, the "sexual inversion" model of homosexuality was thought to apply to both men and women. Krafft-Ebing created a taxonomy of female gender and sexual deviance, dividing "abnormal" women into four categories, depending on their level of expressed masculinity.[62] This focus on gender rather than sexuality illustrates that sexologists (perhaps even more than newspaper editors) embraced the Victorian-era belief that women were passionless and asexual, which made erotic relationships between two women difficult to imagine. Indeed, as George Chauncey glibly noted in his canonical article "From Sexual Inversion to Homosexuality," "In the context of female passionlessness, there was no place for lesbianism as it is currently understood: if women could not even respond with sexual enthusiasm to the advances of men, how could they possibly stimulate sexual excitement between themselves?"[63] Although many Americans in the nineteenth century understood sexual desire in women to be a natural element of the human experience, sexologists viewed female sexual passion as pathological and "unnatural." In Krafft-Ebing's theories and elsewhere in early sexological thought, sexual inversion in women was a condition caused by the complete reversal of one's gender role. And because gender was believed to be an innate part of one's identity, sexual inversion was thus articulated in Krafft-Ebing's theories as a psychological disorder, likely congenital in origin. P. M. Wise wholly embraced this vision of sexual inversion, and the influence of Krafft-Ebing's theories is plainly evident in Wise's description of Joseph Lobdell in his article "A Case of Sexual Perversion."

Though it was published in a regional medical journal and written about an individual housed at a mental institution for patients whose families could no longer financially support or physically care for them, Wise's article was trailblazing in the field of American sexology. "A Case of Sexual Perversion" is historically significant because Lobdell was one of the first cases of "sexual inversion" in a biological woman to be discussed in the U.S. press.[64] Other American sexologists took interest in Lobdell's case, as did journalists in the mass-circulation press. Lobdell quickly became a measuring stick against which other gender and sexual deviants were compared and the theory of sexual inversion tested. Indeed, this was the same article that the *Waupun Times* reprinted in its analysis of the Frank Dubois case in late 1883—just months after the article first appeared in the *Alienist and Neurologist*. Before returning to the Dubois case, however, it is worthwhile to explore the ways in which

Dr. P.M. Wise described Joseph Lobdell and his purported sexual and gender deviance.

In "A Case of Sexual Perversion," Wise describes sexual inversion first and foremost as a mental disease; he remarks that "it is reasonable to consider true sexual perversion as always a pathological condition and a peculiar manifestation of insanity."[65] According to Wise, this "mental disease" was the cause of Lobdell's queer embodiment, his repeated assertions that he was a man, and his "deviant" sexuality. Wise suggests that Lobdell's case upholds the then-conventional sexological wisdom that insanity (and therefore homosexuality) could be passed from one generation to the next. He argues that Lobdell was genetically predisposed to this disease because he "inherited an insane history from her mother's antecedents."[66]

In Wise's account, Lobdell's claims of masculinity and his deviant sexuality are intimately connected. Wise's case description opens with the following remarks:

CASE.—Lucy Ann Slater, *alias*, Rev. Joseph Lobdell, was admitted to the Willard Asylum, October 12th, 1880; aged 56, widow, without occupation and a declared vagrant. Her voice was coarse and her features were masculine. She was dressed in male attire throughout and declared herself to be a man, giving her name as Joseph Lobdell, a Methodist minister; said she was married and had a wife living. She appeared in good physical health; when admitted, she was in a state of turbulent excitement, but was not confused and gave responsive answers to questions. Her excitement was of an erotic nature and her sexual inclination was perverted. In passing to the ward, she embraced the female attendant in a lewd manner and came near overpowering her before she received assistance. Her conduct on the ward was characterized by the same lascivious conduct, and she made efforts at various times to have sexual intercourse with her associates.[67]

In this account, Lobdell's assertion of masculinity and his "perverted" sexual inclinations are manifestations of the same pathology. This production is characteristic of the sexological conception of inversion as a theory of homosexuality, which, as Jack Halberstam explains, "folded gender variance and sexual preference into one economic package and attempted to explain all deviant behavior in terms of a firm and almost intuitive belief in a binary system of sexual stratification in which the stability of the terms 'male' and 'female' depended on the stability of the homosexual-heterosexual binary."[68] In Wise's estimation, Lobdell's sexual behavior was intimately connected to his masculinity—a connection that both testified to his pathology as well as validated the "naturalness" of the emergent heterosexual/homosexual binary and the bi-gender system on which it depended.

While much of Wise's article reads as very similar to the newspaper narratives about Lobdell that had been circulating in the press since the early 1870s, one arena where Wise's account diverges is his frank discussion of sexuality. While nineteenth-century standards of decorum prevented newspaper journalists from doing more than simply hinting at the intimate nature of Lobdell and Perry's relationship, the context of a medical journal allowed Wise to be explicit in his descriptions of Lobdell's desire for sexual gratification with women. Wise mentions how the pair met in the Delaware County almshouse—in prose strikingly similar to the "Romantic Paupers" article that circulated in 1871, suggesting that he used newspaper accounts of Lobdell's life to bolster his clinical observations, and thereby illustrating that some of Wise's observations were based on his reading of sensational newspapers, not on clinical evaluation. Nonetheless, Wise quickly moves on to discuss the sexual nature of Lobdell and Perry's relationship. Whereas earlier newspaper reports suggested that the pair posed as husband and wife to protect themselves while traveling, Wise makes clear that Lobdell assumed the sexual responsibilities of a husband and had "a vivid recollection of her late 'married life.' From this statement it appears that she made frequent attempts at sexual intercourse with her companion and believed them successful; that she believed herself to posses virility and the coaptation [sic] of a male; that she had not experienced connubial content with her husband, but with her late companion nuptial satisfaction was complete."[69] Wise then goes on to discuss Lobdell's claim that he possessed a "peculiar organ that make me more a man than a woman," which "had the power to erect . . . in the same way a turtle protrudes its head."[70] Although Wise explains that he had never seen this organ, he did confirm that Lobdell's clitoris was larger than normal—an observation which would come to be standard within sexological definitions of lesbianism.[71] Wise's descriptions of Lobdell's sexual relationship are significant here because they are written in such a way that seems to confirm that Lobdell's deviant sexuality was caused by a mental disease; descriptions of Lobdell's actions are prefaced by the phrase "she believed," and sexual relations with Perry are referred to as "attempts" rather than definitive actions.[72]

Additionally, Wise's inclusion of Lobdell's claim of a "peculiar organ" gave rise to the suggestion that he was perhaps intersex, which was another hotly debated issue within the medical community in the late nineteenth century. As Elizabeth Reis has observed, the last decades of the nineteenth century witnessed a transition in the ways intersex bodies were viewed by the medical profession (and American society more broadly). Previously, intersex individuals were thought to be physically monstrous creatures; by the nineteenth century, however, Americans increasingly viewed an intersex individual as human, although "a repulsive and duplicitous one."[73] As the nineteenth century progressed, intersex bodies were increasingly associated with homosexuality and other forms of sexual "deviance" defined by the medical profession as immoral and perverse.[74] Thus, Wise's decision to include a description of Lobdell's anatomy (regardless of whether it was accurate) was likely deliberate in that it aided in Wise's depiction of Lobdell as deviant and pathological.

Wise's "A Case of Sexual Perversion" was the first study of female sexual inversion published in an American medical journal, and he played a critical role in formulating American medical definitions of gender and sexual deviance (and normativity). Indeed, although the *Alienist and Neurologist* was a St. Louis medical journal with a relatively small circulation, its articles were frequently noticed by local newspaper editors, who reproduced or summarized them in columns compiling news items of interest.[75] Such was the case with the *Waupun Times* in their reproduction of Wise's study, but this reproduction should not be interpreted as acceptance of his sexological theories. Indeed, the general public did not immediately embrace the new concepts introduced by sexologists— they were deployed skeptically rather than embraced enthusiastically.

"A Case of Sexual Perversion" appeared in the *Waupun Times* in substantially edited form. Many of the details that would have been considered salacious were removed; there was no mention of Lobdell's description of his "special organ," for example, and no reference to his repeated advances toward female staff members at the hospital. Instead, the only portions that the *Waupun Times* reproduced were those that described Lobdell's early life, his marriage to Henry Slater, and his decision to don male clothes to facilitate hunting, along with a brief description of his relationship with Mary Perry. On this last point, the excerpt explained, "The attachment became mutual which led to their leaving their temporary home and commencing life in the woods in the relation of 'husband and wife.' In 1876 she was arrested as a vagrant and lodged in jail in Pennsylvania. A petition is now on record there from the wife for the release of her husband Joseph Israel Lobdell from prison because of failing health. In compliance with this petition he (or she) was released, and for three years they lived quietly together until she had a maniacal attack that resulted in her committal to the Willard Insane Asylum."[76] Although this description of Lobdell's relationship with Perry appears somewhat benign, it is followed immediately with the concluding sentence (which, significantly, was not included in Wise's original article): "Several similar cases of 'perverted sexual instinct' have been reported in Germany, male as well as female."[77]

The inclusion of Wise's article within the *Waupun Times* reveals several important insights into popular understandings of gender and sexuality in the late nineteenth century. First, it illustrates that newspaper editors—even those in small towns such as Waupun—were aware of sexology from its earliest days in the United States. As was mentioned earlier in this chapter, Wise's article on Lobdell was one of the first studies of sexual inversion in women published in the United States, and the article contains the very first usage of the term "lesbian" in a U.S. publication. The fact that within a few months of its initial appearance in the *Alienist and Neurologist* Wise's article would go on to appear within a small-town newspaper like the *Waupun Times* illustrates that sexological theories did not remain isolated within elite publications, and that they very quickly began to circulate within the mass-circulation press, flowing to and from rural areas. However, the fact that readers and newspaper editors in rural areas were aware of sexological theories on sexual and gender deviance did not mean that they necessarily believed them.

Subsequent articles published in the *Waupun Times* suggest that the editors were unwilling to accept sexological theories on "perverted sexual instinct" as the final word on the Dubois case. On December

18, 1883, at the conclusion of an article republished from the *Fond du Lac Commonwealth*, the *Times* editors wrote, "The Dubois matter is getting tiresome. We have published many articles on the subject because the whole thing is so marvelously strange and without much plausible reason. We hope the article published today from the *Commonwealth* is the last chapter."[78] Thus, while the newspaper narratives produced around Frank Dubois in 1883 suggest some of the ways sexology was beginning to influence popular discourse on gender and sexuality, they also provide evidence that sexology was looked to as providing *a* possible explanation, but not *the only* one. Indeed, the *Waupun Times*, unlike virtually all the other newspapers nationwide, went out of its way to provide readers with antecedents to makes sense of Dubois's story. This likely displays how much more invested Dubois's friends, neighbors, and fellow citizens of Waupun were in the story than were typical readers of newspapers elsewhere in the nation. They desired not just to be titillated by the tale of an eccentric individual but also to *understand* the story and the possible rationale behind Dubois's unusual decisions. Editors of the *Waupun Times* understood this but came up short in terms of being able to provide local readers with a definitive explanation because there was no definitive explanation for gender transgression or "female husbands" in 1883.

"Female Husbands"

As was mentioned above, the national press consistently used the ambiguous term "female husband" when discussing Frank Dubois's case. This phrase was by no means new, but its resurfacing in relation to the Dubois case prompted some newspapers to ruminate on its meaning. For example, on November 4, 1883, the *New York Times* published a multivalent editorial titled "Female Husbands." It began by reminding readers of the details of the Dubois case, and it almost mournfully reported that "public opinion will not tolerate the marriage of two women."[79] The paper then went on to carefully consider the potential benefit that such marriages might pose:

> If Mrs. Dubois chose to marry a woman, whose business was it? Such a marriage concerns the general public less than the normal sort of marriage,

since it does not involve the promise and potency of children. It has been well established that if a woman chooses to wear trousers she has a right to wear them, and no one will venture to deny the right of any two women to live together if they prefer one another to solitude. Why, then, has not Mrs. Dubois the right to live with another woman who wears lawful trousers, and why should so much indignation be lavished upon Mrs. Dubois's female husband?

There are many women who, if they had the opportunity, would select other women as husbands rather than marry men. The women who regard men as dull, tiresome creatures, incapable of understanding women, would find sympathy and pleasure in the society of female husbands.[80]

While up to this point the anonymously published editorial appears to be an earnest endorsement of same-sex marriage, it quickly takes a satirical turn:

The marriage of women would solve the problem which renders wretched the superfluous women of New England. Those unhappy women cannot marry because there are not enough men in New England to be divided fairly among them. The New England men, to a large extent, abstain from marrying their fellow New England women, and prefer to seek wives in other states. If half of these neglected women were to put on trousers and marry the other half, the painful spectacle of a hundred thousand lonely spinsters would forever disappear. The female husbands and their wives could read Emerson's essays to each other, and thus completely satisfy the wildest longings of the female New England heart. What more could a New England spinster desire than a husband who never smokes, swears, or slams the door; who keeps his clothes in order, and does not stay out of the house until late at night, and who reads Emerson, understands the nature of women, and can discuss feminine dress with intelligence and appreciation?[81]

A sense of anxiety is palpable in the article, and it is clear that for some readers, news of the Dubois story provoked fears about the sanctity of marriage and its future in American society. This anxiety is articulated more clearly in an editorial published in the Milwaukee *Peck's Sun*, penned by editor and eventual Wisconsin governor George W. Peck. He argues that "the marriage relation is an excellent thing for the world at large but if it is tooled with in this way by amateurs it will be brought into discredit and will become very unpopular. The idea of a woman playing husband and trying to split wood or drive team is absurd. The best woman in the world could not take the place of a man, and do chores around the house and go down town nights and come home full of election whisky without giving herself away."[82] Of course, several fictions are required both here and in the *New York Times* in order for the narrative to operate on the level of satire and/or ridicule. Although the national press had flirted with illusions of the sexual attraction between Dubois and Fuller—using vague language to suggest a "mysterious link" joining the married couple—in the *New York Times* editorial, women are depicted according to the Victorian model of female passionlessness. As such, it is suggested that the "wildest longings of the female New England heart" could be satisfied by poetry—not sexual activity. Additionally, while Peck claims authoritatively that "the best woman in the world could not take the place of a man," he ignores the fact that Frank Dubois *had* successfully passed as a man for many months, adeptly performing all the manly chores that were expected of a husband.

Furthermore, while most coverage of the Dubois affair portrayed Gertrude Fuller as a "normal" woman—young, conventionally attractive, and, had it not been for Dubois, a suitable partner for a middle-class man—in the *New York Times* editorial, same-sex marriage is portrayed as a solution to the "problem" of spinsters (or, as the author refers to them, the "wretched . . . superfluous women of New England"). Americans had long been anxious about the troublesome figure of the "spinster," as rates of unmarried women had climbed throughout the nineteenth century, at times reaching near 10 percent.[83] The spinster was a queer figure, as she rejected convention by remaining unmarried, and yet the popular image of the spinster—old and unattractive—suggested that she was unmarried not by choice, but because she was undesirable to men. Thus, in the *New York Times* "Female Husbands" editorial, same-sex marriage was evacuated of its radical potential to serve as an alternative to heterosexual marriage, because it was positioned simply as a solution to a problem that plagued heterosexual men—unattractive women. Thus, rather than acknowledging the facts of the Dubois case—

that a "normal" biological woman chose to marry a trans man—the *New York Times* ridiculed the practice by associating it with a group that was universally derided.

Furthermore, these editorials differ substantially from coverage of the Dubois case elsewhere in the mass-circulation press in another important way: they portray the boundaries between men and women as inflexible and impermeable. As Peck writes, "The idea of a woman playing husband and trying to split wood or drive team is absurd." This conveys the notion that women are inherently so distinct from men that the suggestion that they could complete the same tasks was laughable. However, elsewhere in the mass-circulation press, journalists were not so quick to dismiss the idea of women successfully embodying masculinity. The editorials published in the *Peck's Sun* and *New York Times* reveal the anxiety provoked not simply by the facts surrounding Frank Dubois's marriage, but also by the tepid response to the marriage evident in the nation's newspapers. If individuals assigned female at birth could successfully woo "normal" women, and if their actions were condoned, then the romantic future of heterosexual cisgender men could be in peril.

Although George Peck and the author of the "Female Husbands" editorial likely sought to delegitimate same-sex marriage and trans men, neither the authors, nor the papers that published their editorials, could control the ways that readers interpreted their work. No doubt, some individuals who read the line "If Mrs. Dubois chose to marry a woman, whose business was it?" agreed with the sentiment. Some, perhaps even were themselves engaged in some sort of queer domestic arrangement. As subsequent chapters will illustrate, queer households peppered communities throughout the nation, and trans men lived in towns large and small from coast to coast. These individuals assuredly read editorials like "Female Husbands" with a smirk, perhaps before heading out and splitting wood or performing some other "manly" chore with ease.

Conclusion

The newspaper coverage of Dubois's story in 1883 marked a turning point in representations of trans men and relationships between individuals assigned female at birth; it was within coverage of Dubois that many of the last utterances of the term "female husband" appeared in metropolitan newspapers such as the *New York Times*.[84] Although the phenomenon of women posing as husbands did not disappear, the label of "female husband" did. This shift was likely caused by growing anxiety (palpable in the editorials discussed above) about the term itself. Indeed, the term "female husband" could serve dual purposes. At once, it registered the absurdity of the notion of women serving as "husband," as women in the late nineteenth century were constructed as being the opposite of that which is implied by the term. On the other hand, however, the term "female husband" could also provide same-sex relationships with a certain amount of legitimacy. Husbands in the nineteenth century carried a great deal of legal and social authority; male privilege was enshrined in large part through coverture laws that conferred authority to "husbands" in unique and important ways. As such, the term rendered respect such that the phrase "female husband" was jarring—too jarring, it seems, for newspaper writers to employ after 1890.

In the 1870s and 1880s, however, newspapers *were* willing to discuss "female husbands," and what's more, they were willing to make vague references to same-sex desire. Indeed, even in Victorian-era America, there appeared to be an understanding of biological women as sexual entities. In the coverage of both Joseph Lobdell and Frank Dubois, newspapers consistently made open-ended statements about their "mysterious" relationships with women, leaving readers to imagine the possibilities of same-sex intimacies. Furthermore, the relationships themselves were not portrayed as inherently deviant. Instead, Lobdell's failure to live up to the expectations of a "husband" (i.e., his inability to provide a stable home for Mary Perry) rendered him a nuisance—not his queer embodiment. Similarly, Frank Dubois was seen as strange because he abandoned a normative household where he was a wife and mother in order to serve as a husband to another biological woman. Such behavior was considered strange, but not in and of itself dangerous. Even as sexological writing began to infiltrate popular discussions of gender and sexuality, it was not immediately embraced as gospel. Newspaper editors, particularly those who wrote for the community wherein a trans man was "discovered," continued to do what they did in the Dubois case: they looked to sexology to provide one possible explanation, but they also sought out local experts—people who knew the individuals personally and could attest to their character and their standing in the community. It continued to be the case that the opinions of neighbors, coworkers, and wives mattered much more on the local level when it came to determining the reaction to trans men than did the "expert" opinion of sexologists.

On the national level, however, sexologists *did* come to have greater explanatory power after the 1890s. The sexological model of the "female sexual invert"—a dangerous and pathological individual who threatened to seduce "normal" white women—became an increasingly familiar figure in the national press broadly, and the sensational press in particular. Sensational journalism, referred to at the time as "yellow journalism," gained influence in the 1890s under the auspices of Joseph Pulitzer's *New York World* and William Randolph Hearst's *New York Journal*. Although Pulitzer and Hearst were critiqued by their competitors for exploiting violence, sex, and crime in order to appeal to mass audiences, the genre caught on. This growing popularity was helped in part, no doubt, by Pulitzer and Hearst's increasing roles as media moguls, which they used to exert influence beyond New York City by the purchasing of newspapers and, in Hearst's case, creating wire services, each of which bore the mark of sensationalism.[85]

In this marketplace—wherein journalists were expected to exploit difference in order to create morality tales in which "good" and "dangerous" were easily identifiable from each other—there was no room for ambiguous terms like "female husbands," as they left too much space for reader interpretation. As the genre of sensationalism increasingly marked metropolitan newspapers, trans men were figured as deviant in nationalizing discourse, and therefore little room was left for a term that conveyed some level of legitimacy to those figures whom sensational journalists sought to portray as freaks. Previous scholars have noted this identifiable shift in national representations of gender and sexuality, and the 1890s have been heralded as a period in which understandings of gender and sexuality underwent substantial change.[86] However, once you scratch beneath the surface and interrogate the dissonance between local and national discussions of trans men, tremendous continuity can be seen between the 1870s and the twentieth century.

2

Beyond Community

Rural Lives of Trans Men

In his recent work, Colin Johnson writes, "It still feels safe to many people to assume that rural Americans simply didn't talk about same-sex sexual behavior or gender nonconformity during the late nineteenth and early twentieth centuries. Or, if they did, what they had to say about these matters was probably more similar than not to what comparably situated people would say today." Johnson goes on to refute this truism—which he refers to as the "rural repressive hypothesis"—because it "assumes incorrectly that nothing ever changes in rural America."[1] This chapter picks up Johnson's insights and considers their applicability to the lives of trans men at the turn of the twentieth century. As such, this chapter follows a spate of recent work comprising the "rural turn" in queer studies—Johnson's as well as that of John Howard, Peter Boag, Brock Thompson, Rachel Hope Cleves, and Nayan Shah—taking a fresh look at non-metropolitan areas and challenging much of what scholars (and society more broadly) have long assumed about queer history in rural spaces. Looking beyond the coastal cities that once dominated the field of LGBT history, this chapter takes an in-depth look at the lives of trans men who chose to live in rural (or at least non-metropolitan) areas in the decades around the turn of the twentieth century. This chapter questions why, in a period when the nation as a whole was undergoing rapid urbanization and queer subcultures were beginning to emerge in the nation's cities, many trans men chose to remain in (or relocate to) small towns and rural spaces in the nation's interior.

While finding comprehensive statistical data on gender transgressors in this period is impossible, the available evidence suggests that many trans men chose to live in small towns. Between 1876 and 1936, newspapers discussed sixty-five unique cases of individuals who were assigned female at birth but who lived as men.[2] Of those sixty-five cases, twenty-two (or close to 35 percent) lived in non-metropolitan areas. Many others lived in small cities not commonly associated with large queer communities, such as Omaha, Salt Lake City, Milwaukee, Lincoln, and Bangor. In fact, at a time when the nation's cities were growing at a breakneck pace, a majority of the documented cases of trans men lived *outside of* large cities. In this way, the stories of Joseph Lobdell and Frank Dubois discussed in the previous chapter do not represent a prehistory to the urban migration of trans men that the 1890s would usher in; rather, they suggest patterns that gender-transgressive individuals would continue to express well into the twentieth century.

Whereas the metronormative logic that has guided much of queer history to this point suggests that individuals need to move to large cities in order to lead queer lives, this chapter suggests otherwise. What makes the fact that so many trans men lived in rural areas and small towns so remarkable is that it appears as though this was their choice. Like most individuals in the late nineteenth and early twentieth centuries, the trans men in this book were fairly transient, moving several times in their adult lives. Beginning in the 1890s, for example, a trans man named Ellis Glenn repeatedly chose to live in towns with populations under five thousand, such as Lapeer, Michigan; Hillsboro, Illinois; and Williamstown, West Virginia. And, as court testimony bore out, he was able to lead an active social (and romantic) life in each of these locales.[3] This movement (from small town to small town, not small town to large city) paints a very different trajectory for queer lives than queer history has traditionally presented. This chapter will ruminate on such movement: Why did trans men like Ellis Glenn choose to live in small towns? What did these spaces offer that larger cities might not? How might these deliberate choices shift the way we think about queer history? In answering these questions, this chapter will argue that rural spaces and small towns presented trans men with surprising opportunities. While large cities might afford their queer residents the benefit of anonymity, non-metropolitan areas offered their own set of advantages, which some queers found preferable to the ones offered by larger cities. Specifically, non-metropolitan spaces assured trans men that as long as they lived their lives as normative men, their gender transgressions would be tolerated due to the structures of familiarity that regulate life in small towns. Indeed, trans men were protected both by the nature of small town life as well as by the value placed on masculinity in such environments. Because trans men preformed vital functions within their communities (serving as farmers, husbands, and neighbors), their lives as men were often seen in a positive light.

Beyond rethinking the notion that rural areas and small towns are inherently dangerous spaces for queer individuals, this chapter will also challenge the notion that these spaces are "backward." It might appear on the surface that rural spaces were less likely to pathologize queer individuals at the turn of the twentieth century because they were "behind," or unaware of the emergent sexological discourse on sexual inversion or homosexuality. However, this is not what I wish to argue. I do not mean to suggest in any way that the inhabitants of rural areas were any less savvy about sexuality or gender than their urban counterparts, nor were they ignorant of the emergent discourse of sexology. In fact, individuals in small towns *were* aware of the emergent sexological discourse of the day, as illustrated by the *Waupun Times* reproduction of Dr. P. M. Wise's article "A Case of Sexual Perversion." The fact that within a year of its initial appearance in the *Alienist and Neurologist* Wise's paradigm-setting article would go on to appear in a small-town newspaper like the *Waupun Times* disproves the idea that rural communities were isolated from the emergent scientific discourse on sexual and gender deviance. Just as significantly, the *Waupun Times* editorial staff did not reproduce Wise's article to serve as the last word on the Dubois case; instead, they offered the article alongside accounts from Dubois's mother-in-law, neighbors, and other family members, and the testimonies from community members were granted just as much weight as the theories of sexual and gender deviance articulated by Wise.

This example suggests the utility of Martin Manalansan's notion of "alternative modernity" in thinking through the realities of gender and sexuality in rural areas, rather than the "backward" framework that all too often colors discussions of small towns and rural spaces.[4] Brock Thompson has deployed Manalansan's notion in his work on Arkansas, in which he explains, "Arkansas was never behind; Arkansas never played catch-up to modern alternatives found elsewhere in the nation. Rather, Arkansas offered and operated under specific social and cultural conditions that shaped it as an alternative modernity . . . Arkansas . . . operated within its own framework of modernity, buttressed by and defined within specific cultural circumstances found in the rural South."[5] Thompson's notion of Arkansas as an "alternative modernity" allows him to debunk the "rural is to urban as backward is to progressive" framework that has all too often guided work in queer history. This chapter will argue that Manalansan's "alternative modernity" can help us rethink rural spaces throughout the nation as well. Indeed, rural Waupun, Wisconsin, was not isolated from the rest of the country, nor were its inhabitants ignorant of the theories being presented by sexologists. Sexological theories circulated, and were combined with more colloquial ways of defining normative behavior, to create alternative means of regulating social membership, in ways that should not be considered "behind" or "backward" but rather "alternative." This alternative means of boundary definition, as this chapter will show, provided opportunities for trans men to gain acceptance and/or toleration in rural spaces at the turn of the twentieth century.

This formulation is dependent on a widening of Thompson's application of "alternative modernity" from a state-specific application to refer instead to rural spaces and small towns more broadly. This is a significant shift in the historiography within the "rural turn" of queer studies. With the notable exception of Colin Johnson's scholarship, much of the work within rural queer studies has been regional in its approach. For example, Peter Boag's *Re-dressing America's Frontier Past* investigates cross-dressing in the American frontier and argues that the specific historical realities of the frontier allowed for greater acceptance of gender transgressions than elsewhere in the nation. Boag correctly identifies the acceptance of cross-dressing in frontier communities, as well as common tropes through which Western cases of cross-dressing were discussed in national newspapers ("nineteenth-century sources typically found reasons for these female-to-male masquerades in the exigencies of western American settlement").[6] While this observation is absolutely true—national newspapers did commonly utilize tropes of the mythic West when discussing frontier cases of cross-dressing—the tolerance that cross-dressers found in frontier communities was actually quite similar to the tolerance that trans men were able to negotiate and build for themselves in rural communities throughout the nation.[7] Indeed, as this chapter will illustrate, trans men were able to find tolerance in rural communities throughout the United States, from Virginia to Montana, from New York to Mississippi.

George Green

In the mid-to-late 1860s, a trans man who went by the name of George Green married Mary Biddle in Erie, Pennsylvania. There is little trace of the details of how they met, or the nature of their relationship, but we can glean something of their lives together from extant census records. It appears that George Green was born in England in 1833 and immigrated to the United States in 1865 at the age of thirty-two.[8] Less is known about George's wife; newspaper reports published upon George's death suggested that she was married once before her marriage to George, but the veracity of those accounts cannot be determined. However, what is clear is that when Mary and George tied the knot around 1867, they both were above the average age of first marriage (Mary being twenty-six and George being thirty-four).

It is unclear where George and Mary lived immediately following their Pennsylvania marriage, but at some point in the 1870s the couple moved to the rural countryside seventy miles outside of Raleigh, North Carolina.[9] The couple lived in this poor, racially mixed area for about twenty years, and by 1900 they were listed as having a mortgage on their own farm.[10] At some point between 1900 and 1902, the couple moved 140 miles to the north, to the small town of Ettrick, Virginia, likely to be with family who lived in the area.[11] Once they arrived in Ettrick, the couple blended in with their rural neighbors. Despite the fact that George was approaching seventy by this time, he worked as a farmhand. No one, from the neighbors to the men George worked with, suspected that anything was amiss. However, in the spring of 1902, George passed away after a brief illness. Given how seamlessly the couple had blended into the Ettrick community, their neighbors and friends were very surprised when they arrived to help prepare George's body for burial, as it was only then that they realized his body lacked the anatomical components generally associated with masculinity.

Local newspapers[12] suggest that the revelation of Green's "true sex" was met not with condemnation, but rather with support for the fact that Green had been an honest and hardworking individual during his life. In fact, the *Index-Appeal* of nearby Petersburg, Virginia, suggested that any sensation elicited by the story was due not to the case itself, but rather was entirely driven by newspaper correspondents and editors of big-city papers who descended on the small town once word of the story had gotten out. The *Index-Appeal* reported, "The quiet and orderly community of Ettrick is about the last place that a newsmonger would look for a sensation, but as usual as it is the unexpected that has happened. Ettrick will wake up this morning to find itself famous all over the country wherever the Associated Press reaches and the enterprising correspondent has access. Ettrick has a genuine sensation."[13] Tellingly, the *Index-Appeal* chose to publish the story not on the front page, but rather in the "local news" section at the back of the paper, thereby suggesting that the widespread attention Green's story was receiving was not entirely warranted.

Newspapers in Richmond devoted a bit more attention to Green's story, and as with Petersburg's *Index-Appeal*, this coverage was marked by sympathy rather than sensationalism. Richmond's *Times* and *Dispatch* both emphasized how well Green played the part of a man. The *Times* remarked, "Daily has Green worked with men, and never [was there a] suspicion that their companion was a woman."[14] Additionally, both papers emphasized how devoted Green's wife had been. The first article published in the *Richmond Dispatch* reported, "Mrs. Green is overcome with grief and her sorrow at parting with her husband is as sincere and as genuine as has ever been witnessed." The *Times* observed that "the wife is almost overcome with grief. No sorrow more profound or deeper was ever seen."[15] Such statements presented Green's life as valuable in that he was sorely missed, and his widow's grief was presented as sincere and understandable—not deviant or strange. These superlative statements describing Mary's genuine grief and sincere sorrow had the additional effect of ensuring that she could go on living in the community without any negative repercussions.

As the coverage of Green's case continued in the Richmond press, more details emerged about the nature of his marriage—details that helped to depict his life as laudable rather than abnormal. For example, in its second story on the case, the *Times* published an interview with Green's widow wherein she explained the circumstances surrounding her marriage. Mary Green made clear that she did not know of her husband's anatomy before they married, and once she learned of it, she decided to keep the secret to avoid embarrassing her husband. Since that day, she said, "we lived together as brother and sister." Significantly, rather than criticize Mary Green's choice as evidence of a pathology or sexual deviance, the *Times* endorsed her decision, writing, "Those who at first censured, now pity the woman, and recognize the nobility of character she has shown in carrying untold a sorrow, because it gave happiness to another. Her course is commended by everyone now, and those who dared offer suggestion against her, are repentant."[16] In this quote, the *Times* characterized Green's marriage as one that no one else had the right to judge, despite its unconventional nature. Phrases such as "her course is commended by everyone now" suggest the universality of the paper's assessment, making any further speculation of the motives behind the marriage—such as sexual deviance—seem foolish.

Despite its laudatory assessment of Mary Green as a self-sacrificing individual, the *Times* also made clear that she should not be considered a martyr, as George Green himself had been an honorable man. The paper quoted her as saying, "He was the noblest soul that ever lived. He has worked so hard through his life, and has been all I had to cheer me. No man can say he ever wronged him. He was a Christian and I believe he is now with Christ."[17] Apparently others in the community also shared this opinion of Green, as Petersburg's *Index-Appeal* reported that Green's funeral was held at St. Joseph's Catholic church, conducted by Rev. J. T. O'Ferrell and that Green's body was buried in the Catholic cemetery in Petersburg.[18]

As Green's story circulated outside the local context to the pages of large metropolitan newspapers such as the *San Francisco Call*, the *New York World*, the *Chicago Daily Tribune*, and the *Philadelphia Inquirer*, it remained much the same as it appeared within the local press. This national coverage shared several common trends: most mentioned how well Green had played the part of a man, how contented his marriage had seemed, and rarely was any hypothesis offered as to why Green began living as a man.[19]

I will return to the implications of the national coverage of Green's case later in this chapter. For now, I would like to suggest that the local newspaper accounts of George Green's death can tell us a great deal about queer history in rural spaces. For one thing, the local reports are overwhelmingly supportive of Green and his life choices. While they present Green as a curiosity, at no point do they suggest that he was a deviant individual. Instead, they describe his life in male clothing in entirely normative terms—he was a hard worker, a good husband, and an altogether productive member of society. Furthermore, the fact that his funeral was held in the local Catholic church and his body buried in the parish cemetery supports the notion that the rural community of Ettrick was willing to stand by its queer citizen.

Additionally, the trajectory of Green's life suggests to us a new way of conceiving of queer history. Most works on queer history focus on the urban lives of queer individuals, as well as the formation of urban subcultures. In his now-classic essay "Capitalism and Gay Identity," John D'Emilio argued that the formation of the identity category of homosexuality was created out of the shifts that took place in the late nineteenth century from family-based household economies to modern capitalism. The movement from rural family units to urban enclaves of similar individuals was a crucial part of this shift. As D'Emilio explains, "By the end of the century, a class of men and women existed who recognized their erotic interest in their own sex, saw it as a trait that set them apart from the majority, and sought others like themselves . . . it has made possible the formation of urban communities of lesbians and gay men and, more recently, of a politics based on sexual identity."[20] Although some have quibbled with the particulars over the years, D'Emilio's essay remains an extremely important text, and in fact, it can be credited with shaping much of the historiography of LGBT history in the 1990s and beyond. Indeed, with its focus on rural to urban migration, D'Emilio implicitly suggests that the city is *the* place for historians to look for queer history.

In this way, George Green's case can be useful for several reasons. One, it seems to provide clear evidence that rural communities could be supportive environs for trans men in the late nineteenth and early twentieth centuries. In addition, George and Mary Green's choice to continually live in rural spaces, perhaps in isolation from other queer individuals, runs counter to the ways that historians have imagined queer history and suggests the need to reevaluate how portable the insights about gays and lesbians can be in understanding the historical lives of trans men and other gender transgressors. Indeed, not only did the Greens choose to live in rural North Carolina and Virginia, they seemingly chose to live outside of queer communities. Thus, even though much about the

Figure 2.1. William C. Howard, 1902. Image from the *Chicago Tribune*.

Greens' lives together is unrecoverable (Were they in a physical relationship? Was it true that Mary did not know George's "true sex" before their marriage? etc.), the things we *do* know about them should prompt us to reconsider what we think we know about queer history.

Similarly, we don't know what precisely the Greens' friends and neighbors thought about their relationship—whether, for instance, they presumed it to be asexual and therefore simply eccentric rather than queer. However, to assume that *everyone* in Ettrick presumed that George and Mary's relationship was (and had always been) nonsexual ignores clear evidence that ideas about same-sex intimacy had been circulating in even the most remote corners of the nation for decades.[21] Additionally, sexological theories of sexual inversion that connected cross-gender identification with sexual deviance (and, more broadly, pathology) had been circulating throughout the national press since at least the 1890s, and yet those ideas appeared irrelevant in the ways that the Ettrick community responded to the news that George Green lacked the anatomy traditionally associated with masculinity. He was not depicted as a deviant individual who had pathologically manipulated the public for years, but rather as a respected community member whose positive contributions were remembered fondly. Furthermore, it is worth noting that George Green was by no means the only trans man to choose to live in a rural area in the late nineteenth and early twentieth centuries. In fact, the day after newspapers nationwide reported George Green's "deathbed discovery," another very similar story appeared from Canandaigua, New York.

William C. Howard

Alice Howard was born in upstate New York in the 1860s. According to Howard's half brothers, as a child, Alice would often wear "men's attire, and showed fondness for boy's and men's work. This tendency grew till when still quite young she adopted male clothing and men's mode of life."[22] By the time Howard was twenty, he had taken the name William and was living full-time as a man. Perhaps surprisingly, this transition did not happen once he moved to a city or even upon moving away from his family home. Instead, the 1880 federal census lists twenty-year-old William Howard (male) as living in the same household as his mother, sister Minnie, as well as an aunt and uncle.[23] Although it seems that Howard's family wasn't thrilled with his choice (the Rochester *Democrat-Chronicle* later reported "though the family had known of the strange predilection . . . for many years, they had been unable to induce her to array herself in the proper garb for a member of her sex"), Howard clearly compelled them to reevaluate.[24]

As a man, William Howard became well-known within the small towns of western New York State. According to the Syracuse *Evening Telegram*, "'William' was quite a favorite with the girls, whom he frequently took riding in his rig, as many other 'young fellow' was wont to do on a Sunday afternoon."[25] Similarly, the *Ontario County Journal* reported that Howard was "a frail but good-looking young man, who enjoyed the company of girls. He spent his money freely and the rivalry for his exclusive attention was participated in by almost all the young women in the neighborhood."[26] As for Howard's family, the paper reported, they "had tolerated the secret [of William's 'true sex'] so long that when they discovered the fearful limit to which the girl was going—the marriage to another woman—they seemed almost unable to break the secret."[27] These newspaper accounts are revealing in what they suggest about queer possibilities in rural spaces. Indeed, not only do they portray William Howard as successfully dating several young women, but they also reveal that these relationships took place under the watchful eye of Howard's family.

As the *Ontario County Journal* article quoted above suggests, Howard not only courted young women but also ultimately married.[28] In 1892, Howard married Edith Dyer, a local woman twelve years his junior, at the Wellsville Methodist Episcopal church; the officiating minister was Rv. E. P. Hubbell.[29] Edith and William likely met when William was working as a milk peddler in Hornellsville, Edith's hometown.[30] The couple adopted a daughter named Ruby and established a home together in a "modest little cottage on D. C. Cook's farm, on the Chapinville road," near the outskirts of Canandaigua, New York.[31]

Howard remained a visible character within the rural community, and yet despite this visibility, no one suspected that he had been assigned female at birth. The *Ontario Repository-Messenger* later reported that he "was well known by the merchants here where she habitually traded." However, this close contact did not raise any suspicion that he was not male—or if there was any suspicion, it did not infringe on his ability to carry out his life publicly as a man, as he enjoyed all the privileges that came along with masculinity. For example, he was allowed to enjoy a right that all women in the early twentieth century were denied: the right to vote. The *Repository-Messenger* reported that Howard "was a voter and regularly supported the republican candidates."[32]

The *Repository-Messenger* was not the only local paper to publish accounts that indicated Howard's masculinity had never been questioned by members of his community. The *Ontario County Journal* reported, "Working upon the farm among the men in summer, splitting wood and caring for the cattle in winter, many a night . . . in her action at home and among people, everywhere, she was a man. She voted and drove to town to trade."[33] As such, it appears that the rural outskirts of Canandaigua provided Howard and his wife, Edith, with an ideal environment in which to live their queer lives. Judging from appearances, the Howards were a happy family; the *Ontario County Journal* referred to William and Edith's marriage as unfolding "with almost uninterrupted happiness."[34] Similarly, the Syracuse *Telegram* reported that "those who know the Howard family best declare they lived not only happily, but that there was an unmistaken affection between husband and wife."[35]

However, their happiness was brought to an end in March 1902, when William suddenly died three hours after ingesting tablets for a cough. Given that he had previously been healthy, the circumstances surrounding Howard's death prompted his wife to ask for an autopsy. However, the autopsy revealed more than the official cause of death (which, it turned out, was a cardiac event, unrelated to the ingested tablets).[36] Coroner O. J. Hallenbeck also discovered Howard's "true sex," noting in his report that Howard's genitalia was that of a "normal woman or adult female human being."[37] However, the coroner's report is fascinatingly contradictory, as it includes a sworn statement from Howard's widow, who refers to Howard as her "husband" and utilizes male pronouns throughout.[38] In this way, the coroner's report reflects the local coverage of the story: newspapers acknowledged the discovery of Howard's "true sex" yet continued to depict his life as that of a "good man."

As newspapers throughout western New York covered the story, they generally published ambivalent accounts of Howard's life and marriage. Howard's case was discussed as being unique, while at the same time his behavior as a man was cast in entirely normative terms. Rochester's *Democrat Chronicle*, for example, reported of Howard's half brothers (who, significantly, were described as "members of respectable families") that "though the family had known of the strange predilection of [the] deceased for many years, they had been unable to induce her to array herself in the proper garb for a member of her sex."[39] In these quotations, Howard's behavior, although out of the ordinary, is nonetheless described according to the scripts of normative male heterosexuality. Indeed, after assuming male attire "on her father's farm" to perform chores, Howard soon "escorted girls about to parties and dances, spent money freely on them, and finally, as is seen, she married a woman named

Dwyer."[40] As such, Howard's life as a man was narrated along the course of normative heterosexuality: his courtship of women was conducted chivalrously, and he quickly settled down into married life, without an extended, raucous bachelorhood. Not only did this narrative remember Howard's earlier life fondly, it also produced the women who had been involved with Howard in those years (and their families) as entirely normative.

As the story circulated away from the local context, however, newspapers were less likely to publish supportive accounts of Howard's story. For example, the most common iteration was a brief Associated Press wire that appeared in at least twelve newspapers nationwide. This version relayed only a few details about Howard's life and did not provide any details explaining the origin of his queer embodiment or the rationale behind his marriage:

> CANANDAIGUA, N.Y.—March 22—A person who was known here for five years as William C. Howard died suddenly Wednesday night, and an autopsy showed that the supposed man was a woman. Howard, who was about 50 years old, and who was employed as a farm hand, came here five years ago with a woman, who was known as Mrs. Howard. Two children were born to the supposed wife.
>
> The dead woman worked for farmers in the neighborhood, and those most intimately acquainted with the family never had the slightest suspicion that she was not a man. The cause of the woman's death is a mystery. On Wednesday night she took two tablets for throat affection, and died in fifteen minutes. The medicine was sent from Wellsville, this State, where relatives reside. The authorities are completely mystified as to all matters touching upon the woman's life. They do not know her right name. Two men, claiming to be half brothers, attended the funeral, but refused to divulge any information. An inquest is to be held, and some light may be thrown upon this strange case.[41]

In this account, both Howard's life and death are cast as mysterious, and very little context is given to readers to help them understand the story. Even though Howard and his wife had been lifelong residents of the region, they are here produced as relative strangers, without anyone to speak on their behalf, other than former employers of Howard's, whose only insights were that Howard's "true sex" had eluded them. Additionally, Howard's story is fashioned as a mystery because of the strange circumstances surrounding his death. Although precious few details about his death are revealed, those that are provided suggest that distant family members might have sent Howard poisoned tablets. Indeed, throughout the brief account, readers are encouraged to consider the story as one that is "strange" and "mysterious"—two of the most common words used in the headlines that accompanied the article (e.g., "A Strange Story" or "Mysterious Death Comes to a Mysterious Woman").

Another remarkable aspect of the national coverage of Howard's story is the (almost) complete lack of connection that journalists drew between his case and George Green's, despite the numerous similarities between the two. Both individuals passed as men for decades, lived with wives in rural areas, and died within days of each other, and yet national newspapers fell silent regarding these similarities. For example, the *Chicago Tribune* published an article discussing Green's "deathbed discovery" on March 22, 1902.[42] When the paper reported Howard's death *the very next day*, its coverage opened as follows: "History fails to record a stranger case of deceit in sex than that which came to light here today when it was proven beyond dispute that 'William C. Howard,' for years the 'husband' of Mrs. Dwyer Howard."[43] At no point in the article did the *Tribune* acknowledge that they had published a very similar story the day before, nor was there any discussion of the similarities between the two cases. Similarly, the *Washington Post* opened their coverage of George Green's story as follows: "One of the most remarkable cases that has ever been known in this section is alleged to have come to light in Ettrick, Chesterfield County to-day." Yet the following day, when the paper reported on William Howard's story, no reference was made to the similarities.[44] The *Chicago Tribune* and *Washington Post* were two of at least ten newspapers nationwide that reported the stories of both Green and Howard, and, like the *Tribune* and *Post*, most of these newspapers made no connection between the two cases.[45]

What can be made of this lack of connection, of this seemingly willful refusal to link these two cases? Perhaps it reveals the reality of the fast-paced newsroom of the early twentieth century, where editors were not allowed the time to step back and think about the day's news (especially

news that appeared as a simple reproduction of an AP newswire) in relation to what they had printed just days before. However, the stories
were so similar that it seems like perhaps the lack of connection was
deliberate.

By characterizing the stories of both Green and Howard each as
"one of the most remarkable cases that has ever been known," newspaper editors of metropolitan newspapers were able to present the rural
countryside as the bastion of wholesome "American" value, untainted
by the corrupting influence of the city. As such, they maintained the
constructed binary of rural/urban, whereby rural spaces were pure, and
urban areas were potentially corrupting of innocence. This binary—
which became even more visible during the 2016 presidential election,
with constant discussions of coastal cities constituting "bubbles" out of
touch with "real America"—was also an effective structuring device in
the early twentieth century. At the time, U.S. cities were changing rapidly
in both economic terms (e.g., industrialization and the increased inequi-
ties of wealth it brought with it) and demographic terms (e.g., fast-paced
immigration). In the context of such swift change, it is perhaps unsurprising that newspaper editors sought to utilize the symbol of the "rural"
to represent the nation's past, as the space wherein "American" values
remained unchanged by the tides that were reshaping the nation's urban
centers.[46] Further, with anxiety surrounding the "New Women" and the
woman's suffrage movement, perhaps it is unsurprising that newspaper
editors might want to imagine gender transgressions as a phenomenon
isolated to urban centers.

However, the local coverage of George Green and William Howard
reminds us, once again, that binaries are often constructed and incomplete representations of reality. In Howard's case, the newspaper accounts published in the local context provide us with clear evidence that
the rural communities of western New York afforded William, Edith,
and their children a supportive environment, both during William's life
and after his death. In fact, the *Ontario County Journal* even reported
that Howard's gender expression was respected after his passing, as the
paper stated that his body was buried in male clothing.[47] Thus, just as
George Green's community found it acceptable for his funeral to be held
at the Catholic church and his body to be laid to rest in the adjacent
Catholic cemetery, William Howard's community was willing to tolerate

the queer choices of their community member, even in death. These cases both suggest that rural communities had more elastic understandings of masculinity and the relationship between sex and gender than have previously been understood. For both the people of Ettrick, Virginia, and Canandaigua, New York, the behavior of Green and Howard mattered more than their genitalia.

Of course, some might dismiss these two examples as evidence of a tendency to not to want to speak ill of the dead, or a reflection of a respect for one's elders (both George Green and William Howard being older than fifty). No doubt, the fact that both men were dead rendered them less of a threat to their community, and their age likely allowed their actions (particular with regard to sexual encounters) to be seen as harmless. Nevertheless, the fact remains that both George Green and William Howard *chose* to live their lives in rural communities, and those choices must be taken seriously. Both men moved several times throughout their adult life, and neither one chose to relocate to an urban area.[48] These deliberate choices, I argue, reveal to us a side of queer history that has been obscured by an over-emphasis on metropolitan areas and urban enclaves. In order to prove this point a bit more forcefully, the following case study provides an opportunity to explore the aftermath of a "true sex" revelation on an individual who was still living. Indeed, the case of Willie Ray provides an opportunity to assess the level of acceptance afforded to individuals who transgressed gender expectations in the early twentieth century.

Willie Ray

Willie Ray first emerges in the public record on the 1900 federal census, which lists Ray as a twenty-five year-old white male born in Tennessee. At the time the census was taken, he was living as a boarder and working as a farm laborer in Booneville, Mississippi, a town of about one thousand people in the northwest corner of Mississippi in the predominantly rural Prentiss County.[49] There are no known records of Willie Ray's life prior to 1900; it is likely that he moved to the Prentiss County area between 1890 and 1900, and perhaps it was during this time that he began living as a man (although it is more certain that it was in this period that he began living under the name Willie Ray). The facts surrounding Willie Ray's life in Mississippi become a bit clearer in 1903, when he was part of a lawsuit that received attention in newspapers across the nation.

In July 1903, Willie Ray filed charges against a man named James Gatlin, who allegedly "got after Ray with a horsewhip."[50] According to the newspaper reports of the trial, Gatlin was upset with Ray for being "too attentive to Mrs. Gatlin." Thus the stage was set for a classic love triangle that certainly would have attracted attention in at least the local papers, which frequently covered such interpersonal dramas. However, a startling revelation that emerged in Willie Ray's cross-examination ensured that the story would be covered in newspapers across the South.

During the trial, Willie Ray was placed on the stand and cross-examined by the defense lawyer. The lawyer asked Ray to comment on the accusation that he had maintained an improper relationship with Mr. Gatlin's wife. In response, Ray revealed to the courtroom that he was biologically female. Now, why would Willie Ray choose this moment to reveal his "true sex"? The *Jackson Evening News* reported that Ray revealed his "true sex" "when it was necessary . . . to deny an allegation."[51] This account suggests that once the Prentiss County court realized that Ray was biologically female, the idea that he was flirting with Mrs. Gatlin would be debunked because same-sex desire between two biological women was inconceivable. However, this logic relies on the idea that people in Prentiss County were ignorant of the possibility of same-sex desire, and that they were completely isolated from the nascent discourse of sexology or popular representations of gender and sexual transgressions that appeared in the national press.[52] While it is probable that some people in Prentiss County were unaware of sexology, to suggest that they had never conceived of affection between two members of the same sex is to discredit the savviness of individuals in rural communities.

Instead, it is more likely that Willie Ray chose to reveal his "true sex" on the stand as a way of incriminating Mr. Gatlin and avoiding punishment for having an improper relationship with his wife. Indeed, whereas Gatlin's behavior (whipping Ray with a horsewhip) may have seemed justified to the court when it was done to protect his wife from an unscrupulous man, Ray was likely aware that the court would view the same action very differently if the victim of his attack were a woman.

This calculation proved to be accurate; once Ray disclosed his "true sex," Jackson's *Daily Clarion-Ledger* reported that Gatlin was "was bound over to the circuit court under a bond of $250, which he was unable to give, and was sent to jail."[53] For his part, Ray was also arrested and held for a brief period of time—not for improper sexual conduct, but for masquerading in male attire. However, in 1903, there was no law in Booneville (or anywhere in Mississippi, for that matter) that prohibited wearing the clothes of the opposite sex, and Ray was quickly released from custody.[54] Thus assured of the legality of his queer body, Willie Ray apparently continued to live in Booneville and dress in male attire.[55]

As Willie Ray's story circulated away from the local context and onto the pages of national newspapers, the narrative remained strikingly similar to the one that appeared in the Mississippi press. The most common iteration, which appeared in newspapers such as the *St. Louis Republic*, *Atlanta Constitution*, and *New York World*, read:

> The people of Prentiss county, Miss., are wondering how Miss Willie Ray managed to palm herself off upon them as a man for nearly eight years without her sex being suspected even by her most intimate friends and neighbors.
>
> Miss Ray has lived in Prentiss county since 1895, and during the first five or six years worked for various farmers for wages. She dressed as an ordinary farm hand and made regular trips to Booneville, the county seat, each Saturday afternoon, riding horseback, to all appearances a neat-looking boy of quiet habits, although a steady chewer and smoker of tobacco.
>
> Willie was known all over the country as a first-class field hand, a hard-worker and good for his debts. Last year the girl in masquerade decided to start out as an independent farmer and rented a small farm, bought a small store and began to run into debt, as all small farmers are expected to do.
>
> Her sex was discovered last week at the court house in Booneville, where she was a party to a lawsuit, and since then Willie has had to wear skirts.
>
> She came from Tennessee, is about twenty-five years of age, and when asked her reasons for posing as a man said that she did it in order to go out and do a man's labor for a living.[56]

Just as in the national coverage of George Green and William Howard, Willie Ray's story is depicted as an incredible and unusual tale. His case is cast as remarkable because of the success with which he passed as a man, and because of his ability to fulfill the demanding (masculine) tasks of farming for so many years without detection. Perhaps Ray's story appealed to newspaper editors nationwide because it presented a narrative that appeared incredible—how could a woman pass as a man so successfully? In such iterations, the story was not "woman dresses as man and pursues women," but rather "town was fooled for several years by woman masquerading in male clothes."

The national coverage of Willie Ray's story illustrates a clear investment, on the part of newspaper editors, in portraying the rural community of Prentiss County as entirely ignorant of the potential of same-sex desire, and intolerant of gender transgression moving forward. Ray's alleged relationship with Mrs. Gatlin generally did not appear in the national press; when it did, the accounts made clear that Ray revealed his "true sex" in order to "disprove an allegation that had been lodged."[57] As explained above, this logic depends an understanding of rural spaces as ignorant of same-sex desire. While Prentiss County was portrayed in the national press as lacking all knowledge of nonnormative sexuality, one attribute the area *did* supposedly have was a legal regime to regulate gender expression.

Indeed, the most common iteration of Ray's story included one significant alteration of the truth: it suggested that Ray was forced by law to "wear skirts" and abandon his "masquerade" as a man. Although national newspapers discussed how incredible it was that Ray had been able to pass successfully as a man in rural Mississippi, these narratives also made clear that his queer choices were untenable moving forward. Revealed to be a young, single woman, journalists depicted Ray as being in need of an authority figure, and since he was outside the bounds of his nuclear family, the state is imagined to have stepped in to enforce proper gendered behavior. In this way, journalists credited the state as rectifying the unique episode, thus bringing an end to what national papers portrayed as a temporary gender transgression, and restoring rural Prentiss County to its "natural" state of normative gender expression. However, it is worth remembering that Mississippi *did not* have any municipal laws on cross-dressing in 1903, nor did it create any in the wake of Willie Ray's case. In fact, as of 1903, only five cities in the South had laws against cross-dressing (Charleston, Houston, Nashville, Dallas, and Memphis).[58] As newspapers across the nation imagined that Willie Ray was forced to give up his masquerade in male attire, the reality in Mississippi was much different.

Contrary to the perception of the South (and rural spaces more broadly) as uniformly unfriendly toward queers, Willie Ray was not forced to wear female clothes after his "true sex" was revealed, nor was he run out of town. Just as William Howard's family abided by his choices and allowed him to be buried in men's clothing, the local response to Willie Ray reveals how communities can (and did) produce gender in ways that were occasionally at odds with legal and medical discourses. Booneville continued to be a supportive place for Ray to live, even after his 1903 trial. In fact, Willie Ray continued to live in Booneville for at least seven years after his trial. Perhaps most surprising of all, on the 1910 census Willie Ray is listed as living with none other than Fannie Gatlin herself (the woman with whom Ray had allegedly been flirting in 1903), as well as her two children. Although Fannie Gatlin reported to the census that she was widowed, it appears that this was untrue, as Mr. James Gatlin also appears on the 1910 census, very much alive, and also still living in Prentiss County with his sister (his entry indicates he was divorced, although no divorce records exist).[59]

Thus the Booneville in which Willie Ray lived was far queerer than the national press imagined in 1903—and far queerer than historians have imagined over one hundred years later. It is telling that Willie Ray chose to stay in Booneville after his neighbors learned of his "true sex." This choice seems to provide clear evidence of what Colin Johnson has written extensively about in his work *Just Queer Folks*: "that there were, and may very well still be, certain strategic benefits for gender and sexual nonconformers inherent to the kind of familiarity that typically governs everyday life in rural areas and small towns, including the complicating degree of personalism that such familiarity introduces into the process of policing unconventional behavior."[60] Given that structures of familiarity regulate and police behavior in rural communities like Booneville, Willie Ray was able to express his gender without retribution. It is likely that Ray's reputation for being an honest man and hard worker had built up enough goodwill from the Booneville community that they were willing to allow his cross-dressing to continue. Rachel Hope Cleves refers to this phenomenon as the "open closet" in her work *Charity and Sylvia: A Same-Sex Marriage in Early America*. She argues, "The open closet is an especially critical strategy in small towns, where every person serves a role, and which would cease to function if all moral transgressors were ostracized."[61] Just like the women in Cleves's study, Willie Ray's queerness was unexceptional because he was accepted as a valued member of Booneville. However, Ray also benefited from the value placed on masculinity in his farming community; his gender transgression resulted in having another hardworking male farmhand to assist in the manual labor required for daily community subsistence. Because he was seen as being a "good man"—that is, a productive member of the community—his gender transgressions were allowed to continue unabated. Thus, like George Green and William Howard before him, Willie Ray was able to create a livable life for himself in rural America.

Joe Monahan

Peter Boag's *Re-dressing America's Frontier Past*, published in 2011, remains the most thorough treatment of gender transgression in rural areas. In this important work, Boag suggests that cross-dressers were not only ubiquitous in the frontier in the late nineteenth century, but were also "very much a part of daily life on the frontier and in the West."[62] One of the individuals Boag mentions in his work is Joe Monahan, who may be the most well-known cross-dresser from the period (Monahan was even the subject of a motion picture).[63] Joseph Monahan was reportedly born as Johanna or Josephine Monaghan in Buffalo, New York, around 1850.[64] By 1870 he was living as a man in Silver City, Idaho, and working as a miner.[65] For the next thirty-four years, Monahan lived in and around Owyhee County, Idaho, making a living performing various jobs within the rural economy, including mining, farming, and raising cattle. After his death, local papers reported that although he generally lived a solitary existence, Monahan had been well liked by all who knew him, and that his skills with a revolver were highly regarded in the community.[66] Monahan's death in January 1904 drew a great deal of commentary because it was only while preparing his body for burial that neighbors discovered his "true sex."[67]

On the local level, newspapers discussed the revelation of Monahan's "true sex" in a remarkably un-sensational way. Silver City's *Owyhee Avalanche*, for example, was rather elusive in its description of the revelation, referring to Monahan's decades in male clothing as a "peculiar case of mistaken identity." The paper continued:

> Joe came to this city in 1867 and worked at different things for several years . . . he (or rather she) toiled on for awhile and then took up a homestead about ten miles from Rockville, where he lived in seclusion, and accumulated a nice little herd of horses. Joe dressed in men's clothing and no one ever thought of the husky young fellow's disguise until preparation for burial revealed her identity. She was 56 years old at the time of her death and had lived in a dugout ranch for 25 years, had served on juries, voted at all elections and was a good shot with revolver or Winchester.[68]

Positioned on the "local" page, between announcements such as "No charges for engraving initials on silver ware bought at Rowetts" and "John Oliver has a fresh supply of candies," it appears as though the *Owyhee Avalanche*'s editor perceived the revelation of Monahan's "true sex" to be rather mundane; in fact, he or she did not even highlight the story with a headline.[69]

The revelation of Monahan's "true sex" may well have been unremarkable to those in the immediate community, as it appears that many had suspected Monahan was not exactly the person he presented himself to be. For example, Silver City's other weekly newspaper, the *Silver City Nugget*, described Monahan as having "small hands and feet, small stature and effeminate voice and want of beard," characteristics that had "caused many to remark that she might be a woman, or at least not a developed man."[70] Marginal notes written in the 1880 federal census support this description; next to Joseph Monahan's entry (wherein he is recorded as "male"), the enumerator penned in "Doubtful Sex."[71] This notation is telling, as Peter Boag has observed in his study of Monahan, because the census enumerator, Ezra Mills, was not a stranger to Monahan, but rather a neighbor. Boag writes, "Both Mills and Monahan resided in this very census tract; in fact, Mills counted his family's dwelling house as the 221st and 'Joseph' Monahan's as the 218th, suggesting that they lived in close proximity and were more than casual acquaintances."[72] However, despite the suspicions that some in the community clearly had about Monahan's identity, there is no record that would indicate he was ever confronted about his "true sex."

In fact, a letter published in the *Buffalo Evening News* on January 11, 1904, claims that suspicions about Monahan's "true sex" did not affect the way others in the community viewed him, even when he lived among cowboys. The letter, attributed to W. F. Schnabel of Coldwell, Idaho, was reportedly sent to the superintendent of police in Buffalo, New York, in an attempt to find Monahan's next of kin. Schnabel recalled, "While I was a cowboy years ago he often gave me letters to mail and all were addressed to a Mrs ___ in Buffalo, NY. Now I have entirely forgotten her name."[73] Noting that Monahan had "quite a bit of property in cattle and a few horses," Schnabel stated that he hoped to locate Monahan's sister because he "want[ed] Joe's relatives to get her property and not strangers or the county." Most interesting to our purposes here, however, are the ways Schnabel described Monahan's standing in the community. He wrote, "It was always surmised that Joe was a woman, but no one could ever vouch for the truth of it." Regardless of that fact, "the cowboys treated him with the greatest respect, and he was always welcome to eat and sleep at their camps."[74] Thus, combined with the evidence in the *Silver City Nugget* and the 1880 federal census—both of which indicate that several people in the community suspected Monahan's "true sex"—Schnabel's letter suggests that the rural Idaho communities within which Monahan lived tolerated his queerly gendered body.

Boag discusses Monahan as an example of a cross-dressing individual who was able to find acceptance in Idaho due to the unruly nature of frontier communities. However, the acceptance (or at least tolerance) that Monahan was able to find in Owyhee County, Idaho, may have had less to do with the community's specific geographic location than it did with the nature of rural communities more generally. Indeed, like Willie Ray in Mississippi, Joe Monahan's gender transgressions were embraced as a personal eccentricity—one that was permissible because Monahan's community knew him to be a harmless hermit at worst, and a hardworking member of the community at best. His gender transgression—like the transgressions of George Green, William Howard, and Willie Ray—was tolerated by his rural neighbors. Thus, while some queers in this period found solace in the anonymity of the city, others found comfort and protection through the structures of familiarity that regulate social life in small towns.

Conclusion

As this chapter has illustrated, not all trans men chose to live in urban spaces at the turn of the twentieth century; rural spaces could provide refuge for queer individuals in ways that urban spaces could not. This finding puts pressure on the historiographic assumption that queer history is, and always has been, urban history. It also should push scholars to reevaluate the role "community" has played in historiography as well.

Thus far, most LGBT history has utilized the optic of community as one of its main organizing structures. Indeed, as Miranda Joseph has noted, "community is almost always invoked as an unequivocal good, an indicator of a high quality of life, a life of human understanding, caring, selflessness, belonging."[75] In the historiography of LGBT history, the formation of a LGBT community has been heralded as a positive good—a necessary stage toward both personal fulfillment, on the one hand, and political equality on the other. Aside from Joseph, very few scholars have critically engaged with the assumptions around the notion of "community" and its place in LGBT history. All too often, the assumption is made that LGBT individuals have sought community with others like them, and that LGBT history is, therefore, by definition, a community history. What, then, do we make of individuals like George Green, William Howard, Willie Ray, and Joe Monahan, who were seemingly content living far removed from other queer individuals (with the possible exception of their wives)? What do we make of people, like these individuals, who chose to live in rural communities, among people who were unaware of their "true sex" (or were simply too polite to ask)?

The lives of Green, Howard, Ray, and Monahan reveal the need for two major revisions to the ways LGBT history has thus far been conceived. Their lives suggest that historians must develop new ways of conceptualizing the past and rely less heavily on the notion of an LGBT community. Indeed, in recent years, the focus on "identity" has fallen out of favor, but the rubric of community has been more difficult to break. Historians and queer studies scholars are now increasingly hesitant to uncritically assign an identity category to our antecedents, and yet there remains the assumption that our subjects desired to find others "like them." This is likely because LGBT historians have not been trained to think about the significance of individual lives, particularly individual lives lived in spaces that are often depicted as outside the purview of LGBT history. However, the lives of Green, Howard, Ray, and Monahan suggest that perhaps an overreliance on the optic of "community" has rendered a great deal of LGBT history illegible.

Additionally, the lives of Green, Howard, Ray, and Monahan also suggest the need for rethinking the ways LGBT history has been conceptualized. Indeed, as an umbrella term, "LGBT history" has all too often been used to refer to gay and lesbian history, with much less attention paid to the "B" and "T." Gays and lesbians formed urban subcultures at the turn of the twentieth century, yet we still know relatively little about the role that trans men played in those communities, or even if trans men imagined themselves as being part of those communities. However, the lives of Green, Howard, Ray, and Monahan suggest that trans men could, and did, lead full lives outside the boundaries of urban gay and lesbian subcultures. Their life stories are reminders to us that a singular focus on urban communities limits our understanding of gender and identity at the turn of the century in America, as well as today. As such, this chapter serves as an example of what it might mean to abandon the notion of LGBT community in favor of other modes of belonging and social membership within LGBT history.

3

"The Trouble That Clothes Make"

Whiteness and Acceptability

The previous chapter discussed the ways some trans men were able to find the support needed to lead livable lives in rural areas in the late nineteenth and early twentieth centuries. George Green, William Howard, Willie Ray, and Joe Monahan were able to find acceptance (or at least tolerance) in their rural communities because the structures of familiarity that regulate life in small communities afforded them forgiveness of their gender transgressions.[1] They were tolerated as eccentrics and allowed to live their queer lives relatively unimpeded. However, it is worth noting that one of the main factors that likely allowed for Green, Howard, Ray, and Monahan to be accepted as merely "eccentric" was that they were all white. Rural spaces likely would not have been as tolerant of the gender transgressions of individuals of color. For that matter, given the prevalence of lynching in the South in the early twentieth century, if Willie Ray had been black, the accusation that he had become too friendly with a white man's wife could have cost him his life.[2] The whiteness of Ray, Green, Howard, and Monahan afforded them all privileges that trans men of color could not easily access in the late nineteenth and early twentieth centuries. Their whiteness ensured they could travel without harassment, find employment, and seek romance with impunity. This chapter will dig deeper into the implications of whiteness on the tolerance that some trans men were able to gain at the turn of the twentieth century. In so doing, this chapter will add to our understanding of the ways whiteness afforded privileges to all individuals perceived as white—even queer ones.

Stories of trans men and other gender-transgressive figures (including cross-dressers and women posing as men) appeared with great frequency in the popular press during the first decades of the twentieth century. Such stories had wide appeal, as they spoke to many of the central anxieties of the day. Rising tides of immigration, the women's rights movement, as well as increasing industrialization and urbanization transformed the ways Americans lived, worked, and engaged with those around them. To many, these changes seemed to threaten the stability of the nation because they challenged two of the most fundamental power structures of U.S. society: male dominance and white supremacy.[3] In a world where previous claims to authority and power seemed tenuous at best, stories of individuals remaking themselves and inventing new identities had great allure. However, such narratives had the potential to create great anxiety as well. Thus newspapers around the nation (as institutions invested in maintaining the status quo) had to develop narrative conventions through which to articulate stories of gender transgressors that would neutralize their radical potential. Stories about young women posing as men to travel alongside their sweetheart or commit a crime were relatively easy for newspapers to delegitimize; narratives often focused on how poorly they imitated men, or how their girlish foolishness rendered them easily identifiable as female.[4] Stories of trans men, however, were more difficult to contain. How would newspapers explain how an individual assigned female at birth could pass successfully as a man for years, even decades? Journalists at national newspapers responded by developing a surprising narrative strategy.

The most widely circulating stories in this period did not pathologize trans men, but instead celebrated their successful performance of masculinity. Indeed, such stories provided a means for newspapers to explore the normative values associated with masculinity and community membership. The most positive stories were focused on individuals who excelled at embodying not simply masculinity but a particular type of masculine identity: that of the white, economically independent citizen. As such, stories of white trans men became a means through which national newspapers could extol the virtues of normative citizenship—to celebrate the importance of hard work, economic productivity, independence, and service to the community. In a context where much was changing, newspaper editors mobilized stories of trans men to assure readers that patriarchy, citizenship, and white supremacy still regulated who had access to the power of self-determination.

This chapter will draw on the scholarship of whiteness and ethnic studies to understand the historical power that whiteness has played in shaping the perception and reception of trans men in the early twentieth century. When I use the term "whiteness," I am referring not simply to the perceived racial status of an individual but to something that "could be owned as an asset and as an identity."[5] Legal scholar Cheryl Harris describes "whiteness as property," calling attention to the various ways whiteness has served as a "valuable asset—one that whites sought to protect and those who passed sought to attain, by fraud if necessary. Whites have come to expect and rely on these benefits, and over time these expectations have been affirmed, legitimated, and protected by the law."[6] White individuals, as the political philosopher Hannah Arendt has argued, are granted "the right to have rights," whereas people of color and undocumented immigrants are seen, in Lisa Caucho's words, as "ineligible for personhood."[7] As the historian Khalil Muhammad has illustrated, in the early twentieth century blackness was "refashioned through crime statistics. It became more a more stable racial category in opposition to whiteness through racial criminalization. Consequently, white criminality gradually lost its fearsomeness."[8] Thus, as blackness was becoming increasingly associated with criminality, whiteness was being increasingly associated with innocence.

I am interested in exploring the historical power that whiteness has placed on the bodies of white trans men, manifested within the newspaper stories produced around the moment of the revelation of their "true sex." Newspaper stories do not merely report facts but "perform beyond the function of information," as Isabel Molina-Guzmán has noted.[9] Additionally, as Ruby C. Tapia has observed, newspaper stories pass on social values, "immortaliz[ing] ideologies of patriarchal capitalism and white supremacy."[10] Indeed, whiteness (in terms of racial identity and American nationality) was a vital component to the most popular stories of trans men in the first decades of the twentieth century. One of the privileges afforded to white individuals is that their stories are allowed to be stories of individuals. Their successes are the result of individual hard work, and journalists often ignore the structures through which white privilege operates and/or sustains individual achievement. Similarly, the failings of white individuals are seen as the result of individual honest mistakes, not moral failings or the "natural" ineptitudes of their race or nationality.[11] As such, whiteness operated in two ways in stories of white trans men in the first decades of the twentieth century. Newspapers framed their stories as singular, unbelievable events. This framing celebrated the achievement of the individual passing, while also assuring readers that they need not worry about a growing trend of gender transgressions. Just as newspapers after 1890 moved away from common labels such as "female husbands," white trans men were most often discussed as discrete cases, unconnected to any similar stories reported in the past. Second, whiteness provided a vehicle for white trans men to be understood as potentially valuable citizens. Coupled with their successful performance of masculinity, the whiteness of the trans men discussed in this chapter served to insulate them from the damning charge of sexual deviance.

This chapter will focus on the trans men who received widespread attention in the nation's newspapers in the first decade of the twentieth century—all of whom were white. Their stories circulated far wider than did those of George Green or William C. Howard (discussed in the previous chapter). Prior scholars have credited sexologists with having substantial explanatory power in the early twentieth century; however, even at the level of national newspapers, popular representations of trans men during this period remained loosely connected to sexological theories on gender and/or sexual deviance. As I will argue in this chapter and the next, proper gender embodiment was defined in the press through its constitutive interconnections with sexual, racial, ethnic, class, and national concerns; a queer body might raise public concern because of its gender nonconformity, but the precise nature of the threat it posed was dictated by its adherence to or violation of the characteristics of normative citizenship (defined by whiteness, heterosexuality, marriage, and productivity—sexual and economic). In short, race and other normative categories had far more influence on public response to queer bodies than did sexology, even into the 1910s.[12] Furthermore, newspaper stories of white trans men served as a venue to celebrate normative characteristics.

"Whiskers for Tammany Men"

The most widely circulating story of a trans man in the early twentieth century was that of Murray Hall, who successfully passed as a man in New York City for decades until his death in 1901. Indeed, it was not until his death that his "true sex" was revealed, much to the surprise of everyone around him. Hall's case was reported in newspapers from coast to coast (and small towns and cities in-between). The case attracted wide attention because it seemed so remarkable to contemporaries; Hall had led a very public life and was successful in arenas thought to be the exclusive provenance of men; he was a Tammany Hall politician, married two different women, and ran a thriving business. Although Hall's case came to the nation's attention at a time when there was vigorous debate about women's capacity for politics, newspapers reported Hall's case in a remarkably positive fashion; they expressed surprise and shock but rarely condemnation.

Murray Hall was born in Scotland around 1840 and immigrated to the United States as a child. Very few records remain that shed light on Hall's early years, but it is apparent that by the 1870s he was living as man in New York City. It would later be reported that he married twice, though his only recorded marriage occurred on Christmas Eve, 1872, to Celia Frances Lowe of Maine.[13] Together the pair raised an adopted daughter, Minnie, until Celia's death in 1898.[14] Celia was an attractive woman, though taller than average (reportedly six feet). She and Hall must have been quite a pair, as Hall was much shorter (just under five feet). Nonetheless, they seemingly worked well together, partners in life and business. Celia ran an employment agency and Hall was a bail bondsman in addition to having an active career in politics. It is unclear what the nature of Celia and Hall's marriage was, but Hall did have a reputation in the neighborhood for staying out late at the pubs, drinking his share of whiskey, and flirting with women other than his wife.

By all accounts, no one suspected Murray Hall of being anything other than a cisgender man. He was afforded all the privileges that accompanied being a white, economically independent, married man in New York City in the late nineteenth and early twentieth centuries. Hall was active in the political arena, a long-standing member of the Iroquois Club, and on the General Committee of the famed Tammany Hall, one of the major political machines in New York City. Hall was well respected within the organization and effective at soliciting votes for his candidates and the Democratic ticket. He voted in every election and served on at least one jury—both of which would have been impossible for him to do had he been viewed as a woman.[15]

One of the great passions of Hall's life was collecting rare books. He was interested in a wide range of topics, and thus no one found it strange when, in the last months of his life, he took an increased interest in medicine, tracking down treatises on human anatomy and maladies. As it turned out, Hall was suffering from breast cancer and sought to treat the disease himself instead of seeing a doctor, which would have required that he reveal his "true sex." Determined to take his secret to his grave, he suffered alone while attempting to heal himself. With Celia three years gone, no one alive knew of Hall's secret, not even his daughter, Minnie.[16]

He succumbed to the cancer at his home on Sixth Avenue on January 16, 1901. He was taken to the coroner's office, where his anatomy was at last revealed. Hall's death meant that he could no longer control the information about his personal life, and news of the revelation of his "true sex" spread quickly through the nation's newspapers. The news was a shock to everyone who knew him, as apparently his performance of masculinity was so complete that even his small frame, smooth whiskerless face, and "boyish" voice did not raise suspicion. By the time coroner Antonio Zucca filed Hall's death certificate with the New York City Department of Health, the news had been leaked and newspapers across the city (and the nation) had reported the remarkable story.

Newspapers coast to coast reported the story with dramatic flair and highlighted the conundrum posed by Hall's death: how could someone who had excelled at all things masculine have been, in fact, a female? The *San Francisco Chronicle* reported, "For thirty years she consorted with men as one of them; for thirty years she voted the Democratic ticket in this city . . . for the last six years she was a member of the Iroquois Club at 4 West Thirteenth Street, the leading Tammany organization of the Fifth district. She took part in political parades, carried torches and banners, went to saloons and cigar stores, and treated when it was her turn, but not once did anyone suspect her sex."[17] Anticipating its readers' curiosity about Hall's physical appearance, the *Chronicle* offered a detailed description of his body: "Murray H. Hall was four feet seven inches in height and weighed 115 pounds. She was smooth-faced and deep-voiced. Her attire was the usual clothing of men. She wore her hair clipped close. Her features were prominent and not softened by feminine grace. She was a fighter, too. She once tried to thrash two stalwart policemen and gave them a tussle before they subdued her. The woman conducted an employment agency on Sixth avenue and accumulated $40,000. She leaves this to an adopted daughter."[18] Here and elsewhere in national coverage of Hall's story it's almost as if the writer wished to assure readers that normative gender boundaries are still in place—the list of masculine behaviors is meant to imply that these *are* masculine behaviors and that Hall was a very good *mimic* of them—rather than to question the meaning of masculinity and how we define or measure it. Indeed, Hall's behavior here is described as completely masculine; how else could he have passed successfully for three decades?

One of the dominant themes in both local and national press coverage was that Hall's life was remarkable and surprising but not deviant or pathological. Journalists tracked down and interviewed anyone they could in order to shed light on Hall's case, and rarely did those individuals have anything negative to say about him. For example, Joseph Silk, an owner of a bookstore in Murray Hall's neighborhood and a longtime acquaintance of Hall, reported, "Hall's actions and habits did not suggest effeminacy in the least. Hall spat like a man, drank like a man and swore like a man. Hall's voice was slightly nasal, though not deep, and 'his' walk did not suggest a woman."[19] Similarly, the *New York World* described Hall's performance of masculinity as entirely convincing, despite the fact that he "was about 4 feet 8 inches in height, and did not weigh more than 100 pounds," and his "voice resembled a boy's more than that of either a man or woman . . . Still nobody ever suspected that she was not a man, because she worked and voted for the Tammany ticket, stayed out nights with the politicians, could drink as much whiskey as any man in the district, and especially because of the exceeding warmth and volume of her profanity. Strongest of all the reasons for the belief that Hall was a man was the fact that two women had called her husband."[20] Newspapers such as the *New York World* did not conjecture about the nature of Hall's marriages—a silence that preserved the respectability of all those involved, and also protected Hall from the suggestion of sexual deviance. His marriages are presented as merely another element of his masquerade: a fiction, nothing more.

The silence around Hall's sexuality is no accident; it was a product of his identity as a white, middle-class, middle-aged man. Even though his gender transgressions marked him as exceptional, the press never treated him as a "freak." As journalists pieced together the elements of his life story, their investigations were restrained by a sense of decorum. Furthermore, although Hall married twice, nowhere is he referred to as a "female husband," as Frank Dubois had been in the 1880s. Hall's life as a man was framed in entirely normative terms, and even when his corpse was discussed, it was described using respectful language, even in newspapers far removed from New York City. *Daily Review* of Decatur, Illinois, for example, reported the coroner's jury verdict, which found "that the deceased came to her death from natural causes, and that she was a lady."[21] The word "lady" registers a surprising level of respect; instead of simply indicating biological sex (as does the word "female"), "lady" has class and moral connotations. Not all "women" are "ladies," as it is a distinction, not a standard classification.[22]

Another remarkable component of the newspaper coverage of Hall's story is the fact that the specter of woman suffrage only rarely came to the fore. In 1901 there was great debate, waged loudly in New York State, about whether women deserved a place in politics.[23] Suffragettes were often demonized in the press as being masculine (and potentially sexual inverts) because of their political engagement.[24] Given this context, it is remarkable that journalists did not draw on this established narrative as a means of pathologizing Hall. There were a few references to the suffrage movement but no allusions to the purportedly masculine nature of suffragists.

One paper that offered a surprisingly positive reference to the suffrage movement was the *New York Herald*. This publication had a spotty record when it came to support for the woman suffrage movement. In fact, in 1850, the *Herald* published a front-page headline that read, "Woman's Rights Convention: Awful Combination of Socialism, Abolitionism, and Infidelity . . . Bible and Constitution Repudiated."[25] The paper's nationally syndicated coverage of Murray Hall was much less sensational. For example, an article titled "Murray Hall's Life" opened with the following words: "At last woman has proven her equality with man. At last Susan B. Anthony is vindicated. The astounding career of Murray Hamilton Hall, a woman, known all her life as a man, demonstrates Miss Anthony's claim that women can hold their own with men in all departments of life—in business, in politics, and in public affairs."[26] Hall's actions were taken as evidence of the veracity of suffragist claims of equality, not of a shared pathology among biological women who desired political participation. Furthermore, both Hall's actions and the claims of suffragists were portrayed positively, and in fact Hall's life as a man was seen as an endorsement of claims of female equality made by women like Susan B. Anthony.

A few people in New York did not respond as positively to the example of women's capacity for political service that Murray Hall's case seemed to suggest. In an article titled "Whiskers for Tammany Men," fellow political mover and shaker Abraham Gruber told the *New York Times* that a bill should be passed that established facial hair as a prerequisite for political activity. Gruber explained, "We want a law providing that Captains in Tammany Hall politics must wear whiskers."[27] While such sentiments belie a certain anxiety, the *Times* and other papers assured readers—through their repeated discussions of how "remarkable" and singular Hall's case was—that there was no *real* threat of other women donning male attire to acquire political rights. Hall was produced as an exceptional individual whose accomplishments were unparalleled; this narrative element helped to counter any anxiety that Hall might inspire others to act similarly.

Indeed, not one of the papers used Hall's case to suggest that *all* women should have the right to vote or should be allowed in politics. In fact, undergirding the descriptions of Hall's career as a man as "wonderful" was the understanding that he was capable of things most women were not. Undergirding the press representations of Hall was the assumption of male superiority: the notion that the majority of women were simply too weak or otherwise untalented to successfully carry out a "masquerade" such as Hall's. Throughout the newspaper coverage of the Hall case, journalists discussed Hall as a singular individual. He was exceptionally, uniquely capable of mastering the art of masculinity and of "passing" as male for decades.

For example, Murray Hall's story was the subject of a full-sheet, front-page spread in the Sunday supplement to the *New York World* in the days following the revelation of his "true sex." Notably, in this coverage (which was syndicated in smaller newspapers nationwide) Hall was not pathologized, but rather his case was described as "amazing" and "wonderful." This narrative—that Hall was unique, wonderful, and exceptional—should be understood as a privilege of both masculinity and whiteness. However, beyond highlighting the privileges that masculinity and whiteness have historically afforded certain queer individuals, it's worth pausing to first unpack how marginal sexological theories of gender and sexuality were in popular representations of Hall.

The coverage of Murray Hall's case contained occasional references to sexology, but sexologists were never cited as the foremost authority on the Hall story. For example, in the *New York World* Sunday supplement spread, an article titled "Famous Cases in the Past Where Women Have Lived as Men, Reviewed by Cyrus Edson, M.D." began with a brief discussion of sexology and referenced the theory of sexual inversion, though not by name. Dr. Cyrus Edson explained to the *World*, "There is a very large class of these cases which are due to a diseased brain or perhaps a defective brain. I refer to the cases of women who are born with a masculine mind, a mind that endows its possessor with all the masculine tastes and desires . . . it has been estimated by those who have studied the subject very carefully that one woman in 720 is thus affected. She has the mind of a man . . . her tastes are all masculine. This frequently leads to grave mental disease."[28] However, the *World* made a distinction between these medical cases of "mental disease" and cases such as Murray Hall's, describing the latter category as "cases that have been carried out to their successful termination, wherein the motive was of the highest, have been examples of the noblest heroism possible for human beings to reach." The paper characterized such cases in the most positive light possible, explaining "the splendid acting, the unspeakable hardships overcome, all indicate a determination that seems superhuman."[29] This characterization—which was found throughout the *World* spread—depicted Hall not as a freak, a sexual invert, or someone with a "grave mental disease." Instead, he was a hero, someone whose actions should be celebrated because they were performed with conviction and completeness.

The *World* feature went on to describe around twenty other cases of individuals assigned female at birth who lived as men. This is a notable break with the general trend within Hall coverage; whereas most newspapers lingered on the uniqueness of Hall's case, the *World* placed Hall in conversation with previous similar cases. However, rather than citing sexology as providing the precedent or a lens through which to understand Hall's seemingly strange choices, the *World* discussed other "superhuman" individuals, including many cases of individuals who posed as men in order to serve in the military, such as Civil War veterans Charles Fuller of Company D of the Forty-Sixth Pennsylvania Infantry Regiment, and Franklin Thompson of Company F of the Second Michigan Infantry Regiment.[30] The paper moves breezily from case to case, with very little discussion or narrative framing:

> One other disguised woman has successfully carried out her scheme among the Pennsylvania miners.
>
> Her name was Mrs. Julia Forest. She was distinguished from many other subjects of these interesting experiments in being of good birth, the daughter of an Episcopalian clergyman, well-educated, attractive in person and manners. At 16 Julia eloped with a miner, who afterward became injured and was unable to work.
>
> Shortly it was known in the mine that John Forest, a cousin of Julia, had taken her husband's place in the mines. For a long time she had practiced this innocent deception and earned the money to support her sick husband and children.
>
> For 20 years Mrs. Jane Westover was the town barber of Marlborough Conn. The best class of citizens would be shaved by no one else than this gentle expert with the razor, who had come to town one day in a man's coat, trousers and derby hat, and who never changed her style of dress.[31]

The article continues in this way, citing case after case of remarkable individuals who accomplished tremendous feats. Like the individuals mentioned above, the majority of those cited by the *World* were exceptional in some way—whether because they were able to gain reputation among the "best class of citizens" in town (as was Jane Westover), or because they were of noble birth (such as Christina, queen of Sweden; or the Austrian countess Carolina Vay). The cumulative weight of these cases illustrated to readers that Murray Hall was not a freak, but rather a person who ranked among a rarified class of individuals who were "examples of the noblest heroism possible for human beings to reach." These individuals were so patriotic and hardworking that their personal drive was incompatible with the secondary status of womanhood. They felt called to serve their communities and/or their nation as men, and as such should be celebrated.

Thus, in order to make sense of Hall's life, journalists occasionally discussed other cases of trans men and cross-dressing women. However, the archive of stories they drew on was not that of sexological literature, which, by this point, had become an established field of study in the United States as well as Europe. The stories that were mentioned centered on other "exceptional" individuals whose time in men's clothing was purportedly motivated by the purest of desires—most commonly, patriotism. For example, the *Boston Journal* reported, "Miss Hall's female predecessors in men's garb have often distinguished themselves as soldiers, duelists and in other ways, indicating a bold spirit . . . Several women served as soldiers in the Civil War—one, Mrs. Williams Lindley, fighting by her husband's side. That this is not a freak of the 'new woman' merely is shown by the valor of Deborah Sampson, who fought and was wounded in the Continental uniform to the Revolution."[32] An important distinction is drawn between the "new women" of the early twentieth century, who fought for expanded public roles for women, and patriotic cross-dressers. White trans men, such as Murray Hall, were portrayed by the *Boston Journal* as acting purely in their own interest, motivated by individual (noble) passions, such as the desire to serve one's country.

Herein lies one of the most important distinctions in the ways the mass-circulation press discussed gender variance in white individuals in the early twentieth century. Whereas in an earlier period, newspapers mobilized a singular terminology to describe trans men and gender-transgressive women (such as "female husbands"), the discourse in the mass-circulation press had shifted by 1901. Instead of using a common term to describe trans men and/or gender-transgressive women, the mass-circulation press increasingly centered its analysis on the singularity of the individuals described. Just as Murray Hall and his exceptional mastery of masculinity was described in the mass circulation press as "amazing" and "remarkable," so were his predecessors—each unique and remarkable, rather than being members of a cohesive, identifiable group. This categorization was enabled by the whiteness of each of the individuals described; their success at mastering masculinity was celebrated as an individual triumph (or perhaps excused as an individual eccentricity), a narrative production that would have been inconceivable had the individual been a person of color.

"The Trouble That Clothes Make"

In 1908, newspapers across the country once again bore witness to a trans man whose "true sex" was revealed after many years of being understood as male. This time, however, it was not upon the individual's death that his body was revealed; immigration officials at Ellis Island uncovered longtime U.S. resident Frank Woodhull's anatomy when he returned to the United States after a visit to Europe.[33] Woodhull was held at Ellis Island for a short time before being evaluated by the Board of Special Inquiry, which ultimately determined that, despite cross-dressing and falsifying his sex and name on the ship's manifest, he was nonetheless eligible for entry into the United States. This decision was based largely on the basis that he was not liable to become a public charge. On October 5, 1908, Frank Woodhull was allowed to leave Ellis Island—still dressed in the suit that he had arrived in.[34] At a moment in which national newspapers were frequently articulating anxiety about the rising tides of immigration, newspapers coast to coast discussed the Woodhull case, but they did so without condemnation. Instead, newspaper coverage of Woodhull's case was remarkably positive—a phenomenon that again attests to the power of whiteness in rendering queer individuals as potential citizens rather than "foreign" outsiders or deviant threats to the nation.

Frank Woodhull's story received widespread attention in the national press, appearing in at least twenty-five newspapers, including the *Los Angeles Times, San Francisco Call, New York World, New York Sun*, and *Fort Worth Star-Telegram*. While Murray Hall's death precluded him from appearing in the press as a speaking subject, Woodhull's voice (and firsthand explanation of his queer embodiment) was a prominent feature of the newspaper coverage. What is more, newspaper editors consistently produced Woodhull as an ideal citizen: hardworking, self-sacrificing, and law-abiding. Thus, representations of Woodhull were reliably positive, even as the story circulated into newspapers across the nation. Newspapers celebrated Woodhull's admission into the country as a reasonable solution to an innocent problem.

The dominant narrative that emerged within newspapers nationwide explained that Woodhull decided to live as a man out of necessity, rather than free choice. According to newspaper reports, dressing as a man was the only way that Woodhull could support himself financially. For example, the first story the *Los Angeles Times* ran on the Woodhull case opened as follows: "This is the history of an honest, industrious woman, and enlisted soldier in the army of labor, who found herself almost hopelessly handicapped by lack of female attractiveness and encumbered with a man's mustache, fighting for fifteen years a losing battle. Then, as her only alternative, she dons male attire, smoothing pleasantly and profitably the rough road ahead of her."[35] Similarly, the *New York Tribune* reported, "Nature had blighted her with a thick black mustache and an unusually low toned voice, and it was in accordance with these unwelcome handicaps that she was forced to disguise herself as a man, associate with men and earn her living in occupations usually followed by the male sex."[36] In such accounts, Woodhull's body was handicapped in ways that forced him to assume the dress of a man in order to earn an honest living. Indeed, the *Tribune*'s use of the term "unwelcome handicaps" is significant because it drives home the point that Woodhull had not embraced the life of a man willingly: it was forced on him by the "natural" limitations of his body.

According to the national press, it was not only Woodhull's lack of feminine attractiveness that rendered him handicapped, but also a serious case of rheumatism. The *New York World* quoted Woodhull as explaining, "Until I was thirty-six . . . I worked mostly as a drudge doing housework. Then Rheumatism attacked me so fiercely that I could not continue the work. The little down on my upper lip gave me a masculine appearance so I determined to bury my identity in male attire. . . . I chose canvassing as the easiest means of earning a livelihood and started out selling toilet articles and have held to the vocation ever since."[37] In passages such as this, newspapers throughout the nation produced Woodhull's queer body not as an indication of sexual deviance but as evidence of the lengths he was willing to go to remain economically productive. Indeed, newspapers highlighted the fact that Woodhull's queer embodiment enabled him to be self-sufficient. The *New York Sun* quoted Woodhull as saying, "By adopting man's dress I have been able to live a clean, respectable and independent life, asking favors of nobody, man or woman."[38] In this way, Woodhull articulated his queer body as evidence of his dedication to economic independence, not sexual deviance.

This rationale likely appealed to Progressive Era readers who were accustomed to the association between poverty and moral degeneracy. Economic independence was a vital component in Progressive Era constructions of citizenship, and those in poverty were often cast as lacking personal fortitude rather than being the victims of structural inequalities. Notions of poverty in this period built on earlier constructions of the "pauper," a figure that, according to Nancy Fraser and Linda Gordon, "was like a bad double of the upstanding workingman, threatening the latter should he lag. The image of the pauper was elaborated largely in an emerging new register of dependency discourse—that of morality and psychology. Paupers were not simply poor but degraded, their characters corrupted and their will sapped through reliance on charity."[39] Thus, Woodhull's queer body was produced as evidence of the lengths to which he was willing to go to prevent becoming dependent on the state—a dedication that suggested his strong moral fiber.

Additionally, the newspaper narratives produced Woodhull's queer body as emblematic of his triumph over another problem on which U.S. society was fixated in the early twentieth century: disability. In the late nineteenth and early twentieth centuries, cities across the nation became increasingly concerned with regulating potentially problematic populations, and one result was the passage of numerous "ugly laws," which sought to control the public visibility of "unsightly beggars." For example, in 1881, Chicago passed an ordinance that read, "Any person who is diseased, maimed, mutilated, or in any way deformed, so as to be an unsightly or disgusting object, or an improper person to be allowed in or on the streets, highways, thoroughfares, or public places in this city, shall not therein or thereon expose himself to public view, under the penalty of a fine of $1 for each offense."[40] Such laws were passed with the explicit purpose of limiting the public visibility of disabled beggars. In this way, economic status determined which bodies would be deemed "ugly" and therefore in violation of public space. As Clare Sears has argued, ugly laws and regulations regarding cross-dressing, both of which were passed in cities throughout the nation at the end of the nineteenth and early twentieth centuries, marked the beginning of a "new municipal regulatory trend" wherein a dense legal matrix was formed to dictate "the kinds of bodies that could move freely through city space—and the type of bodies that could not."[41] Public concern over "deformity" was also deeply imbricated in concern over immigration. As Susan Schweik has argued, "A tensely conjoined mixture of ableism, biologized racism, and nativism emerged in American culture, an equation of the unsightly with the alien and the alien with the beggar."[42]

Although cross-dressing, disability, and immigration were each being increasingly policed by municipal and federal laws in 1908, the acceptability of these forms of embodiment was also influenced by other factors, particularly race and class. As such, the fact that Woodhull was allowed entry into the United States in this context attests to the power that whiteness and economic productivity exerted in creating the presumption of corporeal acceptability. Of course, Woodhull's whiteness and middle-class status did not automatically confer acceptability, but newspapers produced this quality narratively by relying on tropes of normative citizenship in which independence was particularly valued, and disability and poverty were associated with moral degeneracy. Woodhull's purported ugliness as a woman was cast as a disability overcome by the donning of male attire, and therefore his queer body was displayed as evidence of his hardworking and independent nature.

At a time when disability disenfranchised individuals from citizenship, newspapers produced Woodhull's queer embodiment similarly to the figure disability studies scholars have recently defined as the "supercrip." The supercrip model, according to Eli Clare, "frames disability as a challenge to overcome and disabled people as superheroes just for living our daily lives."[43] The trope of the "supercrip" celebrates individual achievement and is often dependent on the subjugation of any discussion of the material realities and/or the discrimination that people with disabilities face on a daily basis. The supercrip trope is particularly useful in the present context of neoliberalism, as it frames disability as an issue that can be overcome by individuals rather than an issue that merits structural changes. However, the trope also had appeal in the Progressive Era, when personal responsibility and independence were particularly celebrated qualities. By highlighting Woodhull's personal accomplishments in overcoming his disability, newspapers detracted attention from Woodhull's rather trenchant critiques of sexism and ageism. Indeed, in articulating the necessity of his queer embodiment, Woodhull told the *New York Sun*, "At my age . . . there is nothing that I can do in women's clothes. Employers want young and good looking girls or women nowadays."[44] Thus, while Woodhull's story could have easily been narrated as a tragic story of the realities of sexism and ageism in the United States, the national press instead framed it as a triumphant one, starring a plucky individual (or "supercrip") who was willing to stop at nothing in order to avoid dependency and lead a productive life.

Woodhull's economic independence was a vital component of his acceptability to the Ellis Island Board of Special Inquiry, because the most common exclusionary provision used by the Immigration Bureau in the early twentieth century was the "likely to become a public charge" clause, which allowed officials to exclude any immigrant who appeared unable to support him- or herself.[45] In addition to federal restrictions regarding nation of origin, this clause provided immigration officials with another means for policing the border against "undesirable" immigrants. As Margaret Gardner and Donna Gabaccia have illustrated, this clause proved to be particularly useful in limiting the entry of single women. Indeed, because dependency was thought to be women's natural status at the turn of the century, women were vulnerable to exclusion under this clause.[46] Even married poor and working-class women were frequently denied entry based on the "likely to become a public charge" clause, in fear that they might one day give birth in publicly funded hospitals.[47] Thus, the fact that newspapers described Woodhull's queer body as enabling him to avoid dependency was vital to his acceptance as a "desirable immigrant."

Indeed, newspapers nationwide frequently connected Woodhull's purportedly moral character with his economic independence. For example, the *Syracuse Herald* reported that it was only because Woodhull dressed as a man that he was able to "earn a regular income as a book agent and maintain her respectability."[48] The maintenance of respectability was intimately tied to the ability to support oneself financially, a logic that appeared throughout the national coverage of Woodhull's story. The *New York Tribune*, for example, wrote that Woodhull "has more than enough money with her to entitle her to escape the 'public charge' clause of the immigration law. The officials consider her a thoroughly moral person."[49] In the same article, the *Tribune* also described Woodhull with the characteristics of middle-class respectability, writing that "her manner and conversation show refinement and some culture."[50] Such associations were common throughout the coverage of

Woodhull's case; in fact, the *Chicago Daily Tribune* and *Hutchinson News* of Hutchinson, Kansas, both characterized Woodhull's life dressed in male clothes as "blameless," thereby alleviating him of any suggestion of moral degeneracy.[51]

Similarly, the *New York Sun* highlighted the fact that Woodhull was a law-abiding individual and unaware that dressing as a man was against the law. This dedication to abiding by the laws of the United States was further illustrated by Woodhull's reported unwillingness to forge his identity in naturalization papers. The *New York Sun* explained, "She had been urged to become a citizen by some of her male acquaintances, who never suspected her sex, and she had refused because she did not want to break the law."[52] This statement not only produced Woodhull as a law-abiding individual, it also provided an explanation for his alien status—this status was not representative of Woodhull's lack of desire for U.S. citizenship, but, on the contrary, was emblematic of his respect for the laws of the United States. For these reasons, newspapers asserted Woodhull's fitness for entry into the United States. The *New York Times*, for example, characterized Woodhull as "a desirable immigrant" who "should be allowed to win her livelihood as she saw fit."[53] Similarly, the *New York Tribune* reported, "She is an alien, but not an undesirable one, and had it not been for the clothes she might have been admitted to the country."[54] Thus Woodhull's body was produced in the press as being representative of his identity as an ideal potential citizen—one who was hardworking, economically independent, and law-abiding.

Woodhull's queer embodiment was never articulated as signifying his deviant sexuality, nor was his morality ever questioned. Sexological theories are nowhere evident. As one widely circulating story reported, "Just what this desire to masquerade in clothes of the opposite sex means no one has ever been able to explain."[55] Despite the fact that sexologists had been publishing theories on gender and sexual deviance in the United States for several decades by 1908, the national press was, just as it had in the instance of Murray Hall, unwilling to cite sexological theories as offering a plausible explanation for female cross-dressing. Instead, the syndicated *New York World* article "The Trouble That Clothes Make" contextualizes Woodhull's story in relation to other instances of cross-dressing, at times normalizing the desire to experience the world from a different perspective. The author muses:

History is forever repeating itself on this line. . . . . "If I were a man," sighs the young woman bent on a career, "it would be so much easier." And then she dons her brother's clothes, takes them off, and sighs again.

"If I were a girl—well, wouldn't I make it lively for some of these fellows!" murmurs the smooth-faced college chap, and then he dons a décolleté gown, takes the leading role in a college play and, with thanksgiving welling up in his heart, resumes masculine attire.

At the girls' boarding school or college the masculine roles in the annual plays are eagerly sought.[56]

This framing places Woodhull's action in the context of an innocent, youthful, and oft-repeated human desire to explore, rendering his behavior innocuous. The article goes on to discuss other examples of individuals who had been assigned female at birth but lived as men, many of whom chose to don men's clothing in order to remain with their husbands. The author explains, "Sometimes man and wife, driven to desperation by a fruitless search for work, will decide that the latter must don male attire in order to remain at her husband's side on his dreary way," including instances of women posing as men to ride the rails, work in mines, and swing axes as lumberjacks.[57] This framing— cross-dressing as means to maintaining heterosexual unions—assured readers that sexual deviance was not a motivating factor behind the women's sartorial choices. And, lest there be any doubt of the nature of the marriages, the author mentions that in the case of Frances Arnold, the lumberjack, she toiled alongside her husband "until the stork visited their home and she exchanged the axe for the cradle."[58] These details are significant in that they, unlike sexological writing of the day, produce queer embodiment as something that is commonly occurring, innocuous, and compatible with normative social relations, including heterosexual marriages and procreation.

Of course, Woodhull's whiteness was an incredibly valuable asset in securing both the positive framing in the press and his entry into the United States.[59] As Eithne Luibhéid has argued, immigration officials have, since the late nineteenth century, treated various "officially designated identities," including gendered, racial, ethnic, and class-based ones, as evidence of the likelihood of sexual impropriety when evaluating prospective immigrants. Working-class Chinese women, for example, had a very difficult time gaining entry into the United States in this era "because their intersecting gender, class, ethnic, and racial identities led to suspicion that they were likely to engage in prostitution."[60]

Additionally, the practices that immigration officials across the country developed varied, depending on the demographics. For example, in 1908 (the year Frank Woodhull returned to the United States), the common practice at Ellis Island was that all noncitizens were forced to go through the processing center and undergo a medical examination prior to entering the country. The standard medical examination at Ellis Island was rather cursory (nicknamed the "six-second physical"), and required no undressing or intimate contact.[61] The methods deployed in such medical examinations were heavily influenced by racialized notions of disease, and differed greatly from those mandated by public health officials at Angel Island, where the passengers seeking entry were largely Chinese and Japanese. Beginning in the 1890s, the medical inspections at Angel Island became more intensive, due in large part to concerns of epidemic disease (particularly the bubonic plague and cholera), which many believed to be entering the United States from East Asia. With Asian immigrants produced as potential "contagions," the intrusive medical examinations at Angel Island appeared justified. As Nayan Shah describes, "Upon arrival at Angel Island, Chinese men and women were led to sex-segregated barracks . . . unlike at Ellis Island, men and women were examined separately at Angel Island because of the intrusive nature of the physical examination. In the examination of Chinese men, a PHS officer would command the detainees to line up and strip to the waist."[62] Thus, had Woodhull not been detained for appearing sickly, he would have likely passed through Ellis Island without his "true sex" being detected, a feat that would have been much more challenging had he been an East Asian immigrant. Indeed, newspaper and immigration records indicate that this feat was not impossible, as trans man and Irish immigrant Michael Minch passed successfully through Ellis Island several times, at least twice in the 1890s and once in 1908.[63]

Of course, it is not only race or nationality that shape perceptions of criminality; class plays a vital role as well. As Margot Canaday argues, the "likely to become a public charge" clause was the provision most often cited in the exclusion of immigrants suspected of sexual perversion in this time period, in large part because the state had yet to formulate a method for otherwise excluding suspected sexual deviants.[64] However, because both the press and the members of the Ellis Island Board of Special Inquiry saw Woodhull as thoroughly hardworking and thereby economically independent, his gender deviance was not considered to be a sign of sexual deviance, and he was allowed entry into the United States. In this way, Woodhull's example illustrates that notions of proper gender embodiment were not defined in isolation or solely in reference to proper sexuality, but rather formed constitutively with race, class, and nationality.

Figure 3.1. Eugene De Forest, 1915. Image from the *Los Angeles Evening Herald*.

Throughout this book I have been arguing that queer bodies could be rendered acceptable through an invocation of the positive values associated with normative U.S. citizenship, a line of reasoning that is illustrated quite literally in the case of Frank Woodhull. At a time when national newspapers frequently articulated the dangers immigrants posed to the nation because of their deviant sexuality and/or improper gender formations, newspaper narratives surrounding Woodhull's detention at Ellis Island never once cast his queer body as emblematic of personal deviance or immorality. The fact that Woodhull was not only allowed entry into the United States, but that newspapers around the nation celebrated this decision by immigration officials, illustrates that the acceptability of a queer body was regulated—both legally and culturally— by racialized, gendered, and classed definitions of proper citizenship. Despite his queer embodiment, newspaper editors did not produce Woodhull as danger to the nation, and his story circulated nationally as an allegory about personal responsibility. In a way, Woodhull was cast as the nation's most desirable immigrant.

"Pleads to Wear Male Attire"

Seven years later, in 1915, another white trans man captured the attention of newspapers nationwide, and as with Woodhull and Hall before him, his story was narrated positively. Eugene De Forest was born Mary Bradley in Newtown, Connecticut, in 1849. Bradley grew up in an affluent family with two older brothers, and in 1867 he left home to attend Vassar College.[65] Ten years later Bradley married Rev. John M. Hart in Newtown.[66] The marriage was short-lived; by 1880 Bradley, who was thirty years old at the time, had relocated to San Francisco and found employment as a teacher of elocution.[67] By 1891 Bradley had assumed a new name (Eugenie De Forest) and was gaining a reputation in San Francisco as both an elocution teacher and a stage actor with a particular knack for male impersonations.[68] Sometime between 1893 and 1897, Bradley assumed a new name and new identity: no longer the female Eugenie De Forest, but the male Eugene De Forest. He remained in San Francisco and retained his occupation as an elocution teacher. It is perhaps a testament to the open community of 1890s San Francisco that De Forest made this transition without leaving the city; in fact, he continued to work as a voice teacher on the very same block in the Union Square neighborhood where he had set up shop in 1891.[69] He remained in San Francisco until at least 1909, and by 1915 he had relocated to Los Angeles, where he continued to work as a drama teacher.[70] Though it is possible that in San Francisco De Forest's community understood him to be (and accepted him as) a trans man, it appears that in Los Angeles he was understood to be a cisgender male.

Thus it came as quite a surprise to many when, in September 1915, De Forest was arrested and his anatomy was made public knowledge. "Drama Prof. Proves to Be Woman" screamed a *Los Angeles Evening Herald* headline.[71] This heading, like many others that appeared in newspapers in the subsequent weeks, called attention to the seemingly strange details of the case (the *Herald* initially referred to the case as "the most unusual legal fight ever waged in this city"), but as the story played out on the pages of local and national papers De Forest was characterized less as a "freak" and more as an unfortunate soul who was handicapped by his constitution. As the story unfolded, newspapers treated De Forest as a subject worthy of being heard and understood, rather than as an object of scrutiny worthy of derision. Just as with Murray Hall and Frank Woodhull before him, this treatment by the press (and the Los Angeles Police Department) was deeply influenced by De Forest's status as a white, middle-class, middle-aged individual. As such, Eugene De Forest's story is another example of the power of whiteness in rendering gender deviance acceptable in the early twentieth century. Thus, even though each man may have been guilty of crimes, their bodies were not automatically perceived as criminal because their race and gender presentation rendered them unrecognizable as criminal. Lisa Caucho has written extensively about this phenomenon in her book *Social Death*, where she observes that "criminal activity was *unrecognizable* without a black body."[72] In the context of the early twentieth century, because the female "sexual invert" was not yet a recognizable social figure, the gender variance of Hall, Woodhull, and De Forest was not enough to condemn them—due to their whiteness and their class status, their gender deviance was unrecognizable as deviance.

Throughout the early coverage of de Forest's case, newspapers across the country defined him as someone who had attained status and respect in his community. The *Los Angeles Times* referred to him as a "well-known teacher of dramatic arts" at LA's Blanchard Hall, and also mentioned that he was a Vassar graduate.[73] This status was repeatedly mentioned, and De Forest was mostly commonly referred to as "Professor De Forest" as the story circulated into papers nationwide.[74] Papers also discussed De Forest's successful stage career. The *Los Angeles Times* wrote that "in 1885 and 1886 she played opposite Mme. Janauschek, one of the foremost actresses of her time, who is said to have appeared more often before the crowned heads of Europe than any other tragedienne. Later the professor often appeared in the role of Hamlet."[75] Even the woman to whom De Forest was engaged at the time of his arrest was apparently wealthy and respected. The *Los Angeles Evening Herald* described her as being a "girl of class" who lived in a "big mansion"; when interviewed by *Herald* reporters she was "dressed in a stylish blue gown and wore a considerable amount of jewelry."[76] These descriptions, bolstered by De Forest's race and class status, helped to produce him as a valuable member of society. As such, he was allowed by the police to explain and defend his actions, and the press afforded him the space to tell his story in his own words. Although he was defined as a gender deviant, his other identity category afforded him the privilege of being able to tell his story in his own words, and having those words respected, rather than contradicted, in the press.

Immediately upon his arrest, De Forest began providing explanations for his queer embodiment, which appeared in the local and national press. And, just as with Woodhull and Hall before him, sexological discourse was nowhere evident. De Forest, as an educated and well-read individual, perhaps had read the theories of sexual inversion himself, but he did not explicitly reference them in his explanations. Instead, he cited "pre-natal influence" as shaping his gender identity—an explanation that shifted the responsibility for his gender expression away from himself and onto his mother. In the *Washington Post*, for example, De Forest stated:

A year before I was born my little brother died . . . my mother's heart was broken when he passed away and when she realized she was going to be blessed with another child she prayed constantly for a boy, one to take the place of my little brother. Every day she went into the bedroom he had occupied and upon bended knees begged God to give her a baby boy just

like brother. . . . when baby came it was a girl and I am the girl. It is not
strange to me that the influence of my mother over me prior to my birth
gave me the instincts of a boy.[77]

This explanation was purportedly supported by medical officials. The
New York World reported that "Prof. De Forest declares she holds cer-
tifications from physicians and city officials of San Francisco and San
Jose authorizing her to dress as a man and warning the public not to
interfere with her action."[78] Significantly, the *World* allowed De Forest's
statements to stand without cross-examination; the paper did not ask for
verification of such documents, nor did it attempt to contact said doctors or city officials in order to validate De Forest's claims. De Forest is
allowed the last word in this regard, an allowance that substantiates the
presumption of innocence on the part of the press—a presumption no
doubt connected to his race and class status.

Newspapers made clear that De Forest displayed no evidence of
"mental derangement."[79] The *Washington Post* and *Los Angeles Times*
both reported, "Drs. F. F. Byington and E. H. Wiley have visited the professor, and both declare she possesses all the characteristics of a woman.
They declared medical history recites a number of instances similar to
this case, and that it is not unusual for a physical woman to have the instincts of the opposite sex. . . . They declared she is mentally normal."[80]
These "expert opinions" regarding De Forest's normality are extremely
significant components of the newspaper narratives of his queer embodiment; they not only verify De Forest's own explanations but also
serve to render De Forest's body acceptable. Additionally, they help to
normalize De Forest's seemingly strange embodiment by explaining that
"it is not unusual for a physical woman to have the instincts of the opposite sex." Whereas sexologists at the time were exceedingly interested
in producing "sexual inverts" as a deviant group whose inverted sexual
instincts were evidence of a pathological disorder, the implications of De
Forest's embodiment here appear wholly distinct (and innocent). This
clarification that sexological theories of gender deviance did not apply
to the De Forest case also had the effect of producing De Forest as an individual whose personal testimony could be trusted. This was important
in the context of the burgeoning field of sexology because sexologists
often attributed sexual inversion to mental disorder. All told, the fact

that newspapers allowed De Forest the space to explain the rationale behind his embodiment is evidence that De Forest was not presumed guilty by the press (or the police). Additionally, the respectful way the press treated De Forest illustrates how journalists saw his queer embodiment as disconnected from the possibility of sexual deviance. This distance was vital to the construction of De Forest's acceptability because newspapers revealed that he had previously been married to one woman and, at the time of his arrest, was engaged to a second one.

Throughout the press coverage of the story, journalists provided De Forest with opportunities to explain his relationships with women, and he used this space to make clear that these relationships were nonsexual. For example, he purportedly married a woman named Margaret Barton Hawley around 1911, though no official records of the marriage exist. He told the *Los Angeles Examiner* that although when he met Hawley there was an immediate mutual attraction, he initially kept his distance because he felt "there could be no marriage."[81] The *Washington Post* similarly reported that "De Forest explained 'he' notified her in advance that there were obstacles in the way which would prevent them from living as husband and wife, but if she desired to live in the ideal, in companionship based on higher planes, 'he' was willing, and she consented, but soon tired and separation followed."[82] While many newspapers reported that De Forest's marriage to Hawley did not last long, the explanation they consistently provided for the divorce was that Hawley grew dissatisfied with the arrangement, which, De Forest reiterated, was based on "companionship, nothing more."[83] In this way, De Forest was vindicated of any suggestion of sexual deviance, as it was made clear that he was the one who pursued marriage; De Forest did not seduce the innocent girl into doing anything she did not want to do. Additionally, the press made frequent references to how their relationship was one of marriage in its purest and highest form—companionship—and therefore was scrubbed of any suggestion of sexual immorality.

Eugene De Forest's treatment in the press paralleled in many ways the treatment he received from legal authorities in Los Angeles. Just as he was allowed the opportunity to explain himself in the press, he was allowed to negotiate with the police in determining what should happen after his arrest. For example, in an article titled "Pleads to Wear Men's Attire," the *Los Angeles Examiner* quoted him as saying to the authorities, "I would become ill and die if I should be compelled to wear women's clothes. I cannot help that feeling. I have prayed and struggled, I have asked God to give me strength to accept conventions, but there is something within me that makes my present role in life. It is my personality. Do not, please, oblige me to become a woman. If you should I would not want to live and I know that death would come very soon."[84] Similar statements were published in newspapers nationwide, including the *Washington Post*, San Jose's *Evening News*, the *Oakland Tribune*, and the *New York World*, as well as the other major local papers, including the *Los Angeles Evening Herald* and the *Los Angeles Times*.[85] Apparently convinced by De Forest's plea and the consultation of doctors and De Forest's attorney, the Los Angeles Police Department elected to release De Forest without penalty and allowed him to continue wearing male clothing.

What is significant about this decision by the Los Angeles Police Department is not simply that it allowed De Forest to continue to live as a man, but the way the press framed it. Newspapers articulated the verdict as necessary because any other decision would have resulted in De Forest's death. For example, the *Evening News* of San Jose reported, " 'Professor Eugene De Forest' . . . who described herself as 'a woman with the soul of a man' when detained by Los Angeles police Tuesday night, was granted permission by the police department to continue wearing the garb of a man as she has done during the past 25 years. . . . Permissions to appear as a man was granted when Professor De Forest insisted that even the touch of feminine garments would kill her."[86] In this way, newspapers produced De Forest's life as one that was worth living, and one that should be protected by the police and respected by the community. Indeed, most national newspapers that covered De Forest's case reported not only his arrest but also his release from police custody, thereby framing his queer body as one with the right to life.

"Ellis Glenn Just Can't Be Good"

In the summer of 1899, a handsome sewing machine salesman appeared in the small town of Butler, Illinois, where he quickly became one of the most desirable men in town. The *Quincy Daily Whig* reported that Ellis Glenn "was a great favorite with the ladies" and "easily moved in the best society."[87] Glenn wooed and won Ella Dukes, the daughter of one of

Butler's most respectable families, and the pair began to plan a wedding for that October. Several weeks in advance of the wedding, Glenn was arrested, accused of forging a $4,000 check. As Glenn was apparently well liked by all the Duke family, Ella's father supplied Glenn's bond and he was released from jail. A few days afterward, Glenn traveled to St. Louis, ostensibly to purchase wedding clothes. When the train from St. Louis arrived in Butler that evening, it did not contain Glenn, but rather a letter written by a T. H. Terry, reporting that Glenn had "fallen off a wharfboat [sic] and drowned in the Mississippi while bathing."[88] This turn of events raised questions in the minds of local law officials, who suspected that the story was merely an attempt by Glenn to avoid his pending court trial. After a brief search, Glenn was located in Paducah, Kentucky, where he was staying in a boarding house under the alias T. H. Terry. The state attorney brought him back to Illinois, where he pled guilty to charges of fraud at the county courthouse in Hillsboro.[89] However, when Glenn was admitted into the Chester penitentiary in late November that year, wardens discovered that his body lacked the anatomical components generally associated with masculinity. When asked to clarify this turn of events, Glenn explained that he was not actually Ellis Glenn but his twin sister, and that the pair had switched places in Paducah. According to the story, a deep sisterly devotion motivated her to take the fall for her persecuted brother.[90]

This revelation created quite a stir in southern Illinois and was discussed widely in the nation's newspapers. The widespread coverage gained the attention of law officials in Parkersburg, West Virginia, where an Elbert or E. B. Glenn—an individual who bore a striking physical resemblance to Butler's Ellis Glenn—had allegedly committed several forgeries in 1897. Thus reasonably sure the individuals were one and the same, officials in Illinois decided to annul Glenn's initial sentence and transfer the prisoner to West Virginia for an entirely new trial. This new trial, however, was not simply about determining his guilt or innocence in regard to the alleged forgery. It was centered wholly on determining Glenn's "true" identity as either, as the *Chicago Tribune* described, "a latter day martyr or . . . an adventuress so exceptional as to lack a class."[91] In other words, the prosecution was charged with proving that the Glenn who committed the forgeries—the Glenn previously known as a man—had in actuality been a woman posing as a man.

Likely due in large part to the scandalous nature of Glenn's story, the case was covered extensively in the nation's dailies.[92] In fact, Glenn's trial received such extensive coverage that the New York Times reported, "It is believed much difficulty will be found in securing a jury, owing to the widespread interest which has been taken in the case."[93] Widely circulating dailies such as Pulitzer's St. Louis Post-Dispatch and the Chicago Tribune sent correspondents to Hillsboro and later Parkersburg to cover the story. Dailies and weeklies published in small cities and towns also covered the story with great interest throughout its lengthy proceedings, relaying information gleaned from wire services.[94] In fact, when Glenn's trial finally began in the summer of 1901, it constituted one of the most widely reported stories in newspapers across the nation.[95]

By late July, it appeared clear to many that Glenn's acquittal was imminent. On July 21, 1901, the St. Louis Post-Dispatch reported, "That she will never be convicted is regarded as a certainty. Public sentiment is conspicuously in her favor. Even those who believe her guiltily share in the general desire for her acquittal if for no other reason than she has so successfully precluded the possibility of establishing her identity."[96] Significantly, because the St. Louis Post-Dispatch had a correspondent in Parkersburg to cover the trial, it is safe to assume that its account reflected the public sentiment of the locals who had witnessed the trial up close. Thus, despite the general acceptance of the fact that Glenn had posed as a man for several years and maintained relationships with several women, the people of Parkersburg hoped for his acquittal.

As it turned out, the Post-Dispatch was correct in its prediction, and on the last day of July 1901 newspapers across the country reported Glenn's acquittal—a verdict arrived at because the jury could not come to a unanimous decision regarding his "true" identity.[97] The case was not entirely closed, however. The prosecution appealed the decision, and in 1903, a Supreme Court ruling remanded the case for retrial.[98] Ultimately, in the summer of 1905, four years after Glenn's initial trial, the prosecution decided to not retry him on the belief that they could not prove without a reasonable doubt that Ellis and E. B. Glenn were the same person.[99]

Less than three months after the case was finally dropped, Glenn reappeared in the news. Papers across the country reported that he was once again in legal trouble, this time in Lapeer, Michigan. It was reported that Glenn, "masquerading in male attire as a real estate agent," swindled money in a land deal in Clare County, Michigan.[100] The *Detroit Free Press* described Glenn as "the smoothest person ever arrested" in Lapeer, and news of the arrest quickly made its way into newspapers nationwide, including the *New York World*, the *Chicago Daily Tribune*, and the *Baltimore Sun*. In these accounts, Glenn's gender deviance was produced as intimately connected to his legal infractions. The *Chicago Daily Tribune*, for example, referred to Glenn as "the notorious woman-man, sewing machine agent, barber, waiter, real estate broker, paper hanger, forger, 'good fellow.'"[101] Newspapers that had covered Glenn's initial arrest with deep interest and a sympathetic tone, such as the *St. Louis Post-Dispatch*, also got in on the act and published articles that portrayed him as irreconcilably deviant. For example, in an article titled "Ellis Glenn Just Can't Be Good," the *Paducah Sun* described Glenn as a cold and calculated criminal by focusing largely on his deceit of Ella Duke during his stay in Butler, Illinois, several years earlier. Whereas Duke had mainly disappeared from the narrative by the conclusion of Glenn's trial in 1901, here she reappeared front and center and provided an excellent foil against which to dramatize the gravity of Glenn's past deception.[102]

Other newspapers, such as the *Baltimore Sun*, highlighted Glenn's criminality by referencing the past beliefs held by law enforcement officials who had grappled with the case. The paper reported, "As on the two other occasions when she was arrested, she was in male attire when caught . . . the police never had a doubt that she was a criminal, but they were never able to prove it to the satisfaction of juries or judges, and after two of her greatest crimes she was able to leave the courtroom a free woman. This last arrest seems to settle the question."[103] As the *Sun* correctly predicted, "Ellen" Glenn was convicted of the charges in November 1905 and sentenced to one to ten years in the Detroit House of Correction.[104]

While Ellis Glenn's whiteness initially secured him protection and legal recourse that would have been unimaginable for people of color at the time (the 1890s and early 1900s being the height of lynchings for African Americans), once his criminality was proven beyond a doubt in 1905 the ways the press depicted him changed drastically. Whereas previously his successful mastery of masculinity was celebrated as a tremendous accomplishment, after his 1905 arrest Glenn's time in men's clothing was rendered as a pathological attempt to merely access privileges (including access to white women) that were not rightfully his. The fact that he was arrested "masquerading" in male attire illustrated with finality that Ellen and Ellis Glenn were one and the same, and thus he was guilty on numerous accounts: not only had he swindled money and broken hearts, but he had lied to the police and to the jury during his 1901 trial. As such, the press depicted him as a hardened criminal with no hope for rehabilitation. Not even his whiteness could redeem him now—in fact, he was seen as a particular disappointment because he had been granted, over the course of several years, the respect and interest generally only provided for white men.

Significantly, when the preeminent sexologist Havelock Ellis wrote about Ellis Glenn in the third edition of his landmark text *Studies in the Psychology of Sex: Sexual Inversion*, he referenced only the newspaper coverage of Glenn's 1905 arrest. In a passage where Ellis recounts a series of brief stories of "female inverts," he writes, "Ellen Glenn, *alias* Ellis Glenn, a notorious swindler, who came prominently before the public in Chicago during 1905, was another 'man-woman,' of large and masculine type. She preferred to dress as a man and had many love escapades with women."[105] In this succinct account, Glenn fits within Ellis's understanding of sexual inversion in that Glenn's physicality ("large and masculine") signified his inversion, hence his romantic and/or sexual relationships with women.[106] Additionally, described as a "notorious swindler," Glenn similarly fits within Ellis's notion that homosexuality and criminality were closely linked in women.[107] Thus it is perhaps no surprise that it was only coverage of Glenn's 1905 arrest that caught Ellis's eye; as discussed above, it was this coverage that most clearly linked same-sex desire, criminality, and queer embodiment.

Conclusion

Havelock Ellis's selective reading of the newspaper coverage of Ellis Glenn's story is illustrative of an important distinction in the ways gender variance was understood at the turn of the twentieth century. For sexologists like Ellis, the body of a "sexual invert" was a deviant body.[108] However, to the mass-circulation press and, likely, U.S. society more broadly, the category was not yet as salient. As this chapter has shown, the categories of whiteness and masculinity were extremely powerful in regulating which bodies were afforded respect, understanding, and sympathy. Instead of being run out of town (or lynched) when he was arrested for forging a large sum of money, Ellis Glenn's father-in-law assumed his innocence and provided his bail. Later, he was afforded his day in court while the nation breathlessly followed the case. Similarly, the cases of Murray Hall, Frank Woodhull, and Eugene De Forest were covered widely in the press, and in each case journalists assumed the individual's innocence. While their stories began with the accusation of wrongdoing (assuming a false identity), newspapers nationwide provided these individuals with the opportunity to explain their actions. Their guilt was never assumed, and their deviance was not thought to be integral to their identity.

The press in the early twentieth century frequently acknowledged that the boundaries between femininity and masculinity were porous and contested. However, not all bodies were allowed to test the boundaries. Gender normativity was (and is) deeply imbricated in other social categories, and thus white, middle-class, able-bodied, and economically productive bodies were granted more leeway. The cases discussed in this chapter shared many similarities—each of the men were middle-aged, white, and successful in business, to some degree. They fulfilled the social expectations of white masculinity and were accordingly provided the respect and sympathy only afforded to white men in U.S. society. Hall, Woodhull, De Forest, and Glenn (initially) were each granted the status of subjects in the press and by legal officials in their communities. Although Hall was not alive to witness the ways his life as a man was memorialized, he perhaps would have been gratified to see the press (both local and national) celebrate how he had so successfully performed his masculine role. Frank Woodhull and Eugene De Forest, however, were able to reap the rewards of normative white masculinity, in that they escaped their encounters with state officials unscathed, and their communities allowed them to continue living as male. Their white and male bodies ensured that the press and the state did not automatically perceive them as criminal, even if their bodies lacked the anatomy generally associated with masculinity. But there were limits to the actions that whiteness could render acceptable, as the case of Ellis Glenn illustrates.

However, even Glenn's case highlights the power of whiteness in rendering gender variance acceptable; Glenn was granted the presumption of innocence or, to quote Hannah Ardent again, "the right to have rights," something that would have been unimaginable had Glenn exhibited the same behavior while African American or a nonwhite immigrant. The distinct ways Havelock Ellis discussed the Glenn case highlights that for sexologists, sexual/gender variance had the effect of stripping his body of white privilege.[109] However, as the other examples in this chapter illustrate, the popular press was not as willing to disregard one's white racial privilege. As the next chapter will explore, the national mass-circulation press was deeply committed to collapsing gender and sexual deviance as the exclusive provenance of the nonwhite and noncitizen. Indeed, ascribing value to white trans men was dependent on the devaluing of nonwhite gender/sexual deviants.

4

Gender Transgressions in the Age of U.S. Empire

Much of this book thus far has focused on the local responses of communities to their queer neighbors. I have argued that trans men in rural areas and small towns were tolerated by their communities due to the structures of familiarity that regulate small-town life. However, the ways neighbors interpreted the queer bodies in their midst were dependent on not only local circumstances but also global phenomena. The late nineteenth and early twentieth centuries witnessed the rapid growth of the U.S. empire. In these years, U.S. interventions in Hawaii, the Philippines, Cuba, Puerto Rico, Guam, Panama, the Dominican Republic, and Haiti introduced Americans to new ways of imagining their role in the world, while debates over the statehood of New Mexico and Arizona forced conversations about what it meant to be an "American." Central to these debates were discussions of proper sexual and gender definitions, and aberrant gender formations were deployed to justify imperialism and regulate which populations were eligible for inclusion in the body politic.[1] In previous chapters, I have shown that sexological discourse played a limited role in defining local responses to trans men, and that even when the stories circulated on a national scale journalists rarely referenced sexological theories of sexual inversion. As this chapter will argue, in an era of expanding U.S. empire, notions of "foreignness" provided a ready means for national newspapers to pathologize queer bodies, and this narrative was used far more frequently than the medical discourse of sexual inversion, even into the 1920s. This chapter will look at moments where we can see the interplay between global and local forces, moments where international geopolitical events affected the lives of trans men, shaping the ways their bodies were interpolated by local authorities, journalists, and national newspapers.

"Bright-Faced Girl-Boy"

Elvira Virginia Mugarrieta was born in 1869 in San Francisco to a Mexican father and Anglo mother.[2] His mother was Eliza Garland Mugarrieta, the daughter of Louisiana congressman Rice Garland. His father, José Marcos Mugarrieta, worked as Mexican consul in San Francisco. Prior to his marriage to Eliza Garland, Mugarrieta served fourteen years in the Mexican army, fighting against U.S. forces during the Mexican-American War. He remained a strong supporter of Mexican nationalism until his death in 1886, directing Mexican patriotic society activities and working as a Spanish instructor in San Francisco.[3] Raised in this context, Elvira no doubt understood from an early age the importance of negotiating between cultures. Indeed, Elvira was born just two decades after the Mexican-American War, a time when Mexicans were widely regarded as an inferior people unfit for the privileges of U.S. citizenship.[4]

It is impossible to know how Elvira identified racially or nationally. It is clear, however, that when he began living as a man in adulthood, he never publicly claimed a Spanish name or provided details about his family of origin, perhaps as a means of distancing himself from any association with Mexican Americans. For example, as an adult, Mugarrieta first appears on the historical record in 1897 in Stockton, California, where he was dressing as a man and living under the rather fanciful moniker "Babe Bean." The *Stockton Daily Record* introduced Bean to the city by writing, "Babe Bean is the name the bright-faced girl-boy goes by, but what her real name is she alone knows, and is not liable to divulge it, as she claimed to come from one of the best families in the land."[5] This choice of name was one of the first ways he began to define himself to the public; significantly, he chose a race-neutral appellation. Whereas his birth name would have conveyed his Spanish (and potentially Mexican) heritage, the whimsical designation "Babe Bean" helped him to appear nonthreatening—an important characteristic for a stranger entering into a new community. Furthermore, Bean's claim that he came "from one of the best families of the land" had racial connotations, as many in Stockton would have likely assumed that "best" meant "Anglo."

It appears that Bean vigorously defended his race-neutral (or Anglo) appearance. When Bean got wind that the *Stockton Daily Record* published a report from a reader in nearby Farmington that suggested he

was actually a woman named "Clara Garcia," he was very quick to deny
the report. Several days later, the same paper reported that, "when she
was taken by the man from Farmington for Clara Garcia, her indignation knew no bounds."[6] Significantly, Bean did not have the same reaction when, two weeks earlier, "a Charles Engles from Montana" wrote to
the paper stating that he thought Bean was his long-lost sister.[7] The racial implications for the two claims of identity are clearly very different,
and thus Bean's forceful response to the suggestion that he was "Clara
Garcia" is likely an indication that he was invested in distancing himself
from any indication he was Spanish or Mexican American. Indeed,

BABE BEAN.
[From a Photograph Taken for the Mail.]

Figure 4.1. "Babe Bean" / Jack Garland, 1897. Image from the *Stockton Evening Mail*.

he was possibly aware of the state's emergent penchant for conflating foreignness with sexual and/or gender deviance, and assumed that presenting himself (or allowing others to read him) as an Anglo would provide him with some protection against suggestions of deviance.[8]

Bean's deliberate choice regarding his name was just one of many tactics he deployed as a means of avoiding persecution in Stockton.[9] These efforts were effective, and he was described in the *Stockton Daily Record* as a "pretty, dark-haired, dark-eyed girl who is masquerading as a boy and whose life history would give the novelist a plot for one of the most readable books of the age."[10] The Stockton public was so taken with Babe Bean that he served as a guest correspondent for the *Stockton Evening Mail*.[11] Furthermore, drawings of Bean that appeared in Stockton papers depicted him as a well-dressed, boyish-looking adolescent white girl, and his portrayal was devoid of the cartoonish images used in the Stockton press to depict nonwhites or sexual/gender deviants.

Although the construction of the identity "Babe Bean" enabled Mugarrieta to lead a livable life in Stockton for a short while, it was likely not a satisfactory life since it was predicated on a disavowal of his masculinity. Indeed, when probed, he claimed to be a woman who wore men's clothing for its ease and comfort while traveling alone. When Mugarrieta more fully articulated a male identity in late 1899, he used the then-dominant discourse of militarism and manifested his masculinity by pledging his allegiance to imperial projects such as the Philippine-American War. Perhaps Mugarrieta had become swept up in the discourse surrounding the war, which celebrated the conflict as a means to regenerate white American manhood, or perhaps he simply recognized the war as an opportunity to claim a male identity. Regardless of the reason, what is clear is that in October 1899, Mugarrieta, dressed as a man, stowed aboard the Manila-bound military ship, the *City of Para*.[12]

One reason Mugarrieta may have been motivated to participate in the Philippine-American War was to lay claim to masculinity—or more precisely, militarized white masculinity. As Paul Kramer has argued, "On the United States' side, the promotion of the ends of imperial war led to two interrelated processes of racialization. In the first, American imperialists racialized themselves as 'Anglo-Saxons' in order to legitimate the controversial U.S. war as racially and historically inevitable: Americans were inheritors of Anglo-Saxon virtues, foremost among them the capacity for empire-building."[13] Participating in the military conflict enabled Mugarrieta to join a project that was clearly articulated in racial terms.

However, if Mugarrieta was hoping to pass as male both on board the *City of Para* and once in Manila, he was unsuccessful. During the journey to Honolulu (the ship's first stop) Mugarrieta's "true sex" was discovered after he fainted upon receiving a small pox vaccination. According to James G. Hutcheson, a member of the U.S. Army and fellow *City of Para* passenger, Mugarrieta was not ostracized after the revelation; in fact, the crew rallied around their unconventional passenger. Hutcheson told the *San Francisco Chronicle* that, despite the captain's orders, the men on the ship helped conceal Mugarrieta's presence after they left port in Honolulu, and their stowaway was thus allowed to arrive at his intended destination: Manila. Mugarrieta continued to enjoy the support of his fellow men while in the Philippines. As Hutcheson explained, "She remained in Manila or its vicinity for some months doing freelance newspaper work, and most every day visited one or more of the companies of our regiment. As all of our regiment knew, she was a woman, she was called Bebe or Babe by most of our men. She much preferred to be called Jack and when her work took her to regiments where she was not known, she passed as Jack Bean."[14] This report is seemingly verified by an article in the *Manila Freedom* (an American military newspaper published in Manila during war), which referred to Mugarrieta as "Miss Beebe Beam (better known as 'Jack')." The article went on to characterize Jack as being very well liked, stating that "'Jack' has made friends wherever she has gone and is a particular favorite with many regiments both regular and volunteer who are ever extending her a hearty welcome and do everything possible for her interests and comforts, especially the Twenty-ninth U.S.V. who have proved themselves very devoted to their Jack ever since she joined them on the Para."[15] While these articles suggest that Mugarrieta was very popular in Manila, they provide precious little information about what precisely he did there. Indeed, though he was often referred to in press accounts as a "freelance journalist," the only article published under any of his pseudonyms appeared only after his return to the United States.

This article, titled "My Life as a Soldier" and attributed to "Miss Beebe Beam," was published in October 1900 in the Sunday magazine section of all of William Randolph Hearst's newspapers. Mugarrieta opened the article with the statement, "As a newspaper woman and the daughter of

Figure 4.2. "My Life as a Soldier" feature, starring "Beebe Beam" (Jack Garland), 1900. Image from San Francisco's *Sunday Morning Examiner*.

an army officer, all my ambition and interest and inclination naturally gave me the fever to go to Manila when things were at their liveliest there."[16] In this quote, he is clearly manipulating the racial expectations of the reader: although the statement on the surface places Mugarrieta in a line of patriotic (Anglo-Saxon) servicemen who valiantly battled on behalf of the United States, his father actually fought *against* the United States during the Mexican-American War.[17] By omitting this detail, Mugarrieta was able to narratively pass as Anglo. Regardless of whether he identified as Anglo, he no doubt understood the racial implications of obscuring the detail that his father had been a Mexican general.

While it is impossible for us to know whether Mugarrieta had fully bought into the war rhetoric, or whether he was simply using this rhetoric to render his queer embodiment acceptable, what is important to note here is that throughout "My Life as a Soldier," Mugarrieta illustrates a keen awareness of the connections between race, gender, imperialism, and citizenship. Furthermore, it appears that expressing his allegiance to the imperial project did have some tangible benefits; for example, in the preface to "My Life as a Solider," Mugarrieta was introduced to the reader as an "adventurous writer" who only wears male attire "for convenience and protection." The article's introduction further celebrates Mugarrieta's willingness to "defy conventionality and try to live down public prejudice against [his masculine clothing]."[18] Thus, because Mugarrieta had articulated his support for the imperial project and explained that he was driven by patriotic duty to document the Philippine-American War, his queer embodiment was not pathologized, nor was its legality questioned. Rather, the Hearst feature celebrated Mugarrieta's queer embodiment as emblematic of his patriotism and courage.[19]

Despite the fact that "My Life as a Solider" normalized Mugarrieta as a woman, it appears that upon his return from Manila in 1900 he began to live full-time as a man, taking the name Jack Garland. Read with Jack's case in mind, the following claim from Kristin Hoganson's *Fighting for American Manhood* rings particularly true: "As the nation celebrated its victory, some observers concluded that American men had done more than prove their manhood in war—they had improved it. Manhood, they opined, was the greatest legacy of war."[20] Indeed, after his return to the United States, Garland got a tattoo on his left arm to memorialize his experience in the Philippines. Above a large American flag, Garland had the words "Manila 1899" etched. Underneath the flag were several numbers—including twenty-nine, the infantry unit with which he traveled with on the *City of Para*—along with two crossed guns, with the word "Jack" at the bottom.[21] In this way, Garland rendered himself intelligible as a normative white male by invoking imperialism and militarism, and articulating his allegiance to the state. By physically marking himself on the American side of the Philippine-American War, Garland made his whiteness and masculinity manifest in opposition to abject Asian-ness—a strategy that was likely of particular importance given that he spent much of the rest of his life in San Francisco, a city with a very large (and, at the time, much maligned) Asian American population.

Additionally, the name that Garland selected for himself upon his return from Manila is very significant in terms of his construction of a new identity. In transitioning to live full-time as a man (rather than claiming the identity of a woman dressing in men's clothing), he eschewed the rather quirky names "Babe Bean" and "Beebe Beam," and opted for the more serious sounding "Jack Garland." Garland was not a randomly chosen surname; rather living under his father's family name, Mugarrieta, he chose to use his (Anglo) mother's maiden name, Garland. This decision is in line with Spanish surname practices, wherein children are commonly given both paternal and maternal family names and may choose to go by both or either. Although Garland was *not* given his mother's surname at birth, he no doubt was aware of these naming practices, as well as how a Spanish surname might be interpreted in California. His choice to eschew Mugarrieta for the Anglo name Garland may have been a strategic choice to ensure that he was perceived as white—a perception that likely also made it easier for him to pass as male.

Thus Garland's example serves as an important reminder that the boundaries of proper gender and sexuality emerging at the turn of the twentieth century were defined not simply in the local or national context, but were inextricably linked to global imperial processes. Moreover, it reminds us that under the right circumstances, queer embodiment could be produced as emblematic of patriotic citizenship. However, as whiteness studies scholars have reminded us for decades, the acquisition of whiteness is a precarious process, and changes in the global political context can strip racial privilege in an instant. For example, on the eve of U.S. entrance into World War I, German Americans who had previously been enfolded into the comforts of whiteness were suddenly viewed with suspicion and cast as dangerous outsiders by politicians and the press. Perhaps, then, it should not be surprising that the next time Garland appeared in the national mass-circulation press after "My Life as a Solider" was in December 1917, when he was arrested on the suspicion that he was "a woman German spy . . . operating under the guise of a man."[22]

Initial reports of Garland's arrest caused alarm because the figure of a female cross-dressing spy seemed to hold a dagger at the heart of the nation-state—a body held together by patriotism, white supremacy, and heteronormativity. Perhaps aware of this, Garland mobilized the same strategies he had used to explain his queer embodiment in "My Life as a Soldier"; he legitimized his queer body (while simultaneously seeking to narratively articulate whiteness) by using tropes of nationalism. For example, the Los Angeles Times reported, "When asked why she wore male attire, Beebe Bean[23] said: 'I fought in the China Boxer war with Gen. Woolaston, and consequently I find them [male clothing] more convenient.'"[24] Although there is no record of Garland's participation in the Boxer Rebellion, this explanation produced his queer embodiment as emblematic of his identity as a patriotic and self-sacrificing citizen, similarly to how his participation in the Philippine-American War had been mobilized in the press seventeen years earlier. Precisely why Garland chose to cite his (likely fallacious) participation in the Boxer Rebellion instead of mentioning his verifiable participation in the Philippine-American War is unclear. However, it seems likely that this decision was a strategic one, made to capitalize on the ways that images of the Boxer Rebellion circulated in the U.S. imaginary, where the Boxers were figured as anti-Western forces who targeted Christian missionaries.[25]

Just as he had seventeen years earlier, here Garland produced his queer embodiment as representative of his support of state projects, thereby articulating his cross-dressing as emblematic of his status as a productive (and patriotic) citizen. Not only did this tactic clarify Garland's patriotism by distancing him from the traitorous activity of spying, it also addressed the fact that his whiteness was called into question by his alleged German-ness. In addition to aligning himself with the West by setting himself in opposition to the Boxers (or the Chinese more broadly), Garland also reverted to the pseudonym Babe Bean (or Beebe Bean, as the Los Angeles Times referred to him). As I discussed above, this moniker had the dual effect of portraying Garland as innocuous and childlike, and hiding any nonwhite racial identifiers to help him pass as white. In each of these ways, Garland dealt with his arrest through methods that reassured the police (and the people of Los Angeles) that he was not a threat to the community. As such, readers were likely not surprised when the *Los Angeles Times* reported Garland's release from prison after the charges proved to be false.[26]

Significantly, the narrative of Garland's arrest played out much differently in newspapers outside of Los Angeles. Both the *Washington Post* and *Chicago Daily Tribune* reported Garland's arrest, but each characterized his queer body as being much more dangerous than the *Los Angeles Times* did. The *Post*, for example, described Garland as "a frail girl, masquerading as a man, whose career since under detective surveillance has excited mystery and suspicion."[27] Additionally, both the *Washington Post* and *Chicago Daily Tribune* took the information regarding Garland's alleged participation in the Boxer Rebellion out of context, reporting only that "she was in China during the Boxer uprising and admits to having traveled extensively abroad."[28] Garland's allegiance is completely ambiguous. Not only is Garland's voice removed, but this narrative framing also makes it unclear why he was in China at all. Given the charges under which he was arrested, the suggestion is that Garland may have been part of a nefarious covert operation overseas. Additionally, at a time when the United States was engaged in a world war, the line "she . . . admits to having traveled extensively abroad" likely raised suspicion of anti-American activities. Significantly, neither the *Washington Post* nor the *Chicago Daily Tribune* followed up on Garland's arrest to report that the charges brought against him were proven false. Thus, it appears that while the national press was eager to publish stories that associated queer embodiment with anti-Americanism and foreign nationals, few papers were interested in casting queer individuals as innocent victims of overzealous policing—particularly individuals who were thought to be German or otherwise "foreign."

In this way, perhaps there is striking similarity between Garland's coverage in the Los Angeles press and the local narratives of rural trans men discussed in chapter 2. As I argued there, some trans men were able to find tolerance in rural communities because the structures of familiarity provided acceptance in ways that urban areas could not. Although

Los Angeles was an urban space in 1917, the editors of the *Los Angeles Times* likely understood that when they discussed the story of Jack Garland, they were narrating the story of someone's friend or neighbor. Furthermore, the editors' perception of Garland as a patriotic white citizen no doubt shaped their representation of his story; accepted as a valued community member (despite his queer embodiment), he was allowed to tell his own story. However, once Garland's story left the local context, his subjecthood mattered less. Separated from any semblance of familiarity, Garland no longer appeared as a speaking subject. Newspaper editors on the national scale represented him simply as a gender deviant who threatened national security. In this way, coverage of Garland's 1917 arrest is a useful reminder of the precariousness with which trans men lived in the early twentieth century. They could develop calculated embodiment strategies to pass as white and cisgender, but a great deal was always out of their control, as their bodies were constantly read in relation to changing global forces.

"He Was a Government Spy and a Nihilist"

The eagerness with which the national press connected foreignness with gender and sexual deviance in the early twentieth century can also be clearly seen in the case of Nicolai De Raylan. De Raylan was born in Russia in 1874 and immigrated to the United States in the early 1890s. The reason for his migration is unclear; several theories were later presented in the press, including that he was "smuggled out of the country because of a terrible secret he learned concerning his father," and that he was a spy for the Russian government. What is clear is that by 1893 De Raylan was living in Chicago and working for the Russian consulate.[29] He married twice. His first marriage ended in divorce in June 1903; two months later he married a "chorus girl" named Anna Armstrong.[30] By late 1906, De Raylan had fallen ill with tuberculosis and traveled to Phoenix in hopes that the desert air would improve his health. Unfortunately this was not the case, and he passed away on December 18, 1906.[31]

However, De Raylan's story was far from over. His death set off a firestorm of newspaper coverage that lasted well over six months, for when the coroner disrobed the body he discovered that De Raylan was anatomically female. This discovery elicited several questions in the minds of journalists across the country: How could De Raylan have passed successfully as a man for at least a decade? How was De Raylan able to marry not one but *two* women, and why would they both strenuously object to the suggestion that he was anatomically female? Furthermore, when it was noted that De Raylan left behind a sizeable estate, questions emerged about how someone purportedly working as a secretary was able to amass a fortune. Journalists attempted to answer these and other questions in the hundreds of articles published about De Raylan and his wives in the period between winter 1906 and spring 1907. Throughout this proliferous coverage, the fact of De Raylan's nationality—and purported connections to nefarious revolutionary activities and/or political subterfuge—took center stage. Indeed, De Raylan's foreignness provided a ready means through which national newspapers could (and did) naturalize his gender and sexual deviance, and cast him as a deviant outsider.

De Raylan's story first appeared in the *Chicago Tribune* on December 19, 1906, and quickly spread to newspapers nationwide.[32] As the story circulated to the pages of the *Washington Post, San Francisco Call, Boston Journal,* and *Dallas Morning News,* wild speculation continued about De Raylan's "true" identity, which included not only his "true sex" but also the reason he immigrated to the United States and his occupation while in Chicago. For example, the *Pittsburgh Press* reported, "Near the close of her 18th year came the mysterious crisis in her life, which drove her from Russia and caused her to disguise her sex to the end of her life. What this crisis was no one in America seems to have been able to learn. It has been said by Russians in Chicago that there is reason to belief [*sic*] that De Raylan became connected with the revolutionists in a plot against the government, was detected and forced to flee into exile to escape death or Siberia."[33] Such accounts portrayed De Raylan as a dangerous and volatile individual, suspect not only because of his queer embodiment but also because of his connection to radical and subversive politics. Newspaper articles frequently made associations between De Raylan's subversion of his "true sex" and his involvement in political subterfuge. For example, in a widely circulated interview, a woman who had worked as a domestic servant in the De Raylan home suggested, "I was always suspicious that he was connected with the Russian secret service, and I think it probable that his work in that direction was one of the reasons for the concealment of the fact that he was woman. I also have reason to believe that several prominent Russians in Chicago knew the secret."³⁴ In this way, De Raylan's queer embodiment was connected to his nefarious political connections, highlighting his foreignness.

Speculation abounded in the early coverage of the De Raylan case about the precise nature of his activities in Chicago. An AP wire reproduced nationwide reported, "De Raylan's connection with the revolutionary party is seen in her presence at meetings of the West Side 'bund' and the secret conferences with fellow countrymen and the numerous dispatches sent to Russia."³⁵ Elsewhere it was reported that De Raylan "received constant communications from Russia, all of which he destroyed upon reading."³⁶ Articles published later in the spring of 1907 were more explicit about De Raylan's alleged political ties. For instance, the *Los Angeles Times* reported, "That 'he' was a Russian is not doubted, though guesses are evenly distributed between the contention that he was a government spy and a Nihilist."³⁷ Such accounts reiterated De Raylan's status as an outsider with nefarious political connections. Unlike many of the other trans men discussed in previous chapters, he was characterized as wholly outside the local and national community; he was a foreign contagion who was potentially very dangerous to the United States.

Discussions of De Raylan's romantic relationships with women also played a central role in newspaper narratives about him. It appeared that De Raylan had been quite a Lothario, having been married at least twice, and that he hadn't been faithful during either of his marriages. In the initial coverage of De Raylan's story, newspapers frequently mentioned De Raylan's first romance soon after revealing how he initially began living as man. For example, a widely reproduced AP wire reported that De Raylan began dressing as a man in Russia when "trouble with her parents over a revolutionary secret drove the De Raylan girl from her home in Elizabethgrad, Russia, when 18 years old. She went to the town of Kameyets, and there, as a man, won the love of a young girl, Jenya Vassilovitch."³⁸ The article went on to explain that the romance "clung to" De Raylan, and that the pair frequently exchanged letters. This anecdote helped to characterize De Raylan as an individual who had a romantic interest in women, and also suggested that he was irresponsible with the emotions of others. Indeed, the AP story revealed that Jenya (whom De Raylan reportedly referred to as his "angel girl") "wrote pitiful letters, begging to be brought to this country, saying that should would be good and true."[39] A slightly longer version of this story appeared in the *Chicago Daily Tribune*, where it was suggested that De Raylan "lost the love of 'Jenya' . . . through an affair with a girl of the Neva quarter in St. Petersburg."[40] De Raylan's libertine nature again is highlighted, as it is suggested that from the very beginning of his time as a man he was unfaithful to women. De Raylan was portrayed in the press as an untrustworthy individual whose life was predicated on deceiving those around him—even those he purportedly loved, like his "angel girl" Jenya.

Although the standards of decorum prevented newspapers from explicitly discussing Nicolai De Raylan's sexuality, they made clear through repeated references to his relationships with women that he was sexually deviant. What's more, the press frequently portrayed his sexual deviance as related to his foreign status and his participation in radical political activities. The *Bryan Morning Eagle*, of Bryan, Texas, reported, "The motive for De Raylan's masquerade . . . is mixed. Part of it dates back to her early affair with a girl in southern Russia at the first period of her assuming 'manhood,' and part of the explanation is found in her connection with revolutionary 'bunds' in this country and Russia."[41] Readers were likely familiar with the portrayal of foreigners and individuals who participated in radical politics as inherently sexually deviant, and thus what the *Bryan Morning Eagle* portrayed as a "mixed" motivation was likely interpreted as a single cause with two manifestations (same-sex desire and connections with revolutionary "bunds").[42] These components of De Raylan's story allowed the press to create a narrative about De Raylan that cast him as a deviant outsider whose values were completely antithetical to normative "American" values.

Unlike in the cases of the trans men discussed in previous chapters, the local and national press could find nothing redeeming in De Raylan's story. Whereas individuals like George Green, William C. Howard, and Willie Ray were seen as hardworking and valuable members of their communities, Nicolai De Raylan was a deviant outsider. Additionally, whereas the majority of the men discussed previously had relationships with women, those relationships rarely took center stage in newspaper narratives about their lives. Often, their connections with women were characterized as a means for them to pass more successfully as male, and any allusion to a sexual component of the relationship was elided. However, in De Raylan's case, his dalliances with women were central to the newspaper narratives about his life. What's more, De Raylan's life as a man was depicted as being in part *motivated by* his desire to pursue romantic relationships with women. Additionally, his marriages in the United States were rendered pathological in the press because both women were apparently shocked at the revelation of De Raylan's "true sex"—that is, not only was he involved in underground political networks and had fooled the public in Chicago that he was a man, he had also victimized both of his wives by concealing from them his true identity.

Indeed, both De Raylan's widow and his ex-wife (Anna De Raylan and Eugenie Bruchulis) figured prominently in the coverage of the case. The women's testimonies added to the salacious nature of the coverage. Anna De Raylan refused to accept the news, and suggested to the press that Nicolai was still alive or, if he was in fact dead, that "there is something mysterious in the whole affair."[43] On December 20, 1906, the *Kansas City Star* reported, "Mrs. De Raylan was almost hysterical with grief when seen at her home." She told the paper, "These stories of his not being a man are preposterous. He was a man and one of the finest fellows in the world."[44] In the *Chicago Tribune*, she hypothesized that the allegations against her husband were "the work of his enemies," and that "he was connected to the revolutionists."[45] The *Pawtucket Times* of Rhode Island also published quotes from Anna De Raylan, but in these she cited the specific knowledge that wives are granted concerning their husband's anatomy: "Mr. De Raylan was not a woman, but a good, kind man . . . I think I ought to know as much as the doctors about it, and I say he was a man."[46] The article also went on to quote De Raylan's first wife, who told the paper, "Certainly De Raylan was a man . . . he had all the weaknesses of men."[47] Immediately following this statement was a discussion of De Raylan's divorce from his first wife, which was apparently prompted by De Raylan's proclivity for carriage rides with women who were not his wife. Such quotes provided readers with the notion that De Raylan had victimized both women by being unfaithful as well as by concealing his "true" identity.

One remarkable aspect of the local as well as national coverage is that De Raylan's gender and sexual transgressions were often discussed as emblematic of his identity as a foreign spy and likely swindler. The vast majority of coverage discussed De Raylan's case as exceptional and one of a kind, but during the six-month period in which De Raylan was a frequent feature in the press at least four newspapers nationwide published articles that placed De Raylan in conversation with other women who had lived as men. However, sexological theories of gender and sexual deviance were nowhere present in these accounts, even as national newspapers gathered "similar" cases for analysis. For example, in an article titled "The Peculiar Mania Which Drives Some Women to Adopt the Clothes of Men," the *Washington Post* reported that women "masquerading" as men often had rather innocent origins, and that "perhaps the underlying sentiment with the majority of them is the desire to 'see how it seems' to look upon the world as nearly as possible from a man's standpoint."[48] While this interpretation cast cross-dressing as rather innocent (and arguably "natural"), the paper was quick to point out that not all Americans were as likely to experiment with gender expression. Under the subheading "Negroes Constant Offenders" the *Post* reported, "Negroes are frequent offenders, the police say, but owing to the peculiarities of the negro's physical construction the officers have difficulty in distinguishing a man from a woman when both are dressed alike, unless the opportunity is exceptionally good—another case of all colored peopled looking alike."[49] This crude logic exposes the ways that race and gender are co-constitutive, and highlights how normative expectations of gender are conceived relative to native-born, white, middle-class bodies. Furthermore, the *Post* quote illustrates the ways that people of color were imagined as being "constant offenders" in terms of gender and sexuality.

"Senor Ralphero E. Kerwineo"

Similar connections between gender transgressions, race, and foreignness can be seen in the national coverage surrounding the case of Ralph Kerwineo in 1914.[50] Born Cora Anderson in Kendallville, Indiana, in 1876 to an African American father and a mixed-race mother, Kerwineo attracted widespread attention when his arrest in Milwaukee in 1914 prompted the revelation of his "true sex."[51] Kerwineo had been living in Milwaukee since at least 1906 as husband to a woman named Mamie White.[52] Apparently, no one suspected that anything was unusual with the couple, and they lived happily as man and wife until early 1914, when Kerwineo strayed from the path of normative respectability. He began

RALPH KERWINEO.

Figure 4.3. Ralph Kerwineo, 1914. Image from the *Milwaukee Journal*.

staying out late at night, and eventually he left Mamie White for another woman, Dorothy Kleinowski, whom he legally married on March 24, 1914.[53] White was upset by this new arrangement and retaliated by reporting Kerwineo's "true sex" to the Milwaukee police—a revelation that resulted in Kerwineo's arrest and a maelstrom of newspaper attention from the local Milwaukee press as well as newspapers across the country. As with Nicolai De Raylan, national newspapers produced Kerwineo as a threat to the nation not by using the sexological discourses of sexual and gender deviance, but through his purported foreignness.

Throughout his time in Milwaukee, Kerwineo consistently represented himself as South American (often Bolivian) of Spanish ancestry, and occasionally stated that his first name was "Ralphero." These racial performances were seemingly conducted as a means of fitting in with the city's "new immigrants" and distancing himself from the much-maligned African American community. This strategy was perhaps possible in large part due to the unique racial makeup of Milwaukee. At the turn of the century the city had a very small black population, but it also had a large number of immigrants who were considered "not quite white." For these demographic reasons, Milwaukee provided a unique space for racial passing.[54] Kerwineo's strategy was apparently successful; whereas the 1880 and 1900 federal censuses marked Kerwineo (a.k.a. Cora Anderson) as black, "Ralph Kerwinies" (reportedly born in Spain) appears on the 1910 federal census as white.[55] Additionally, he was able to rent a home in the city's tenth ward, a neighborhood populated by mostly native whites, and secure a position as a clerk for the Cutler-Hammer company, whereas the majority of the city's black men worked as domestic servants.[56] However, once Kerwineo's "true sex" was uncovered, the identity of "Ralphero Kerwineo" was a liability in the national press, not the asset it had been in his years living in Milwaukee.

Significantly, Kerwineo's arrest occurred amid the Mexican Revolution and the six-month occupation of the port city of Vera Cruz by U.S. troops.[57] The front pages of newspapers nationwide were awash with headlines describing Mexican atrocities and the dangers that existed south of the U.S.-Mexico border, and the necessity to shore up the border was often articulated through the need to protect white women from dangerous Mexican men.[58] In this context, Kerwineo's carefully constructed identity of "Ralphero" had the potential not of helping him blend in, but of making him stand out as a dangerous deviant. Even Mamie White, Kerwineo's first wife, seemed cognizant of this shift. As she explained to the *Milwaukee Journal*, "The reason she [Kerwineo] pretended to be a South American was because the people of that country have soft ways and effeminate mannerisms, and she thought that was the best way to get along. Our dark skins helped that story."[59] In explaining Kerwineo's "masquerade" she mobilized tropes of racialized gender deviance, a move that illustrates how pervasive such narratives were in the early twentieth century. However, once the story circulated onto the national stage, journalists were no longer interested in clarifying Kerwineo's national identity, and instead pounced on the idea that

Figure 4.4. Ralph Kerwineo as depicted in the *Washington Post*, 1914.

he was a foreigner in order to highlight his alleged trespasses into U.S. citizenship rights, such as the right to marry.

For example, throughout the *Washington Post*'s coverage, and especially when discussing Kerwineo's relationships with women, the paper referred to him as "señor."[60] Given the context of the Mexican Revolution, it seems very likely that readers understood the *Post*'s use of term "señor" as a signifier of Kerwineo's status as a foreign contagion, an individual unqualified for citizenship rights such as marriage. Furthermore, given that non-Anglo bodies were frequently produced as dangerous due to their "naturally" deviant gender or sexuality in the early twentieth century, the term also served to naturalize the descriptions of Kerwineo's purported sexual deviance. Thus the *Post*'s repeated iteration of the term "señor" conveyed the message that Kerwineo's racial/national identity was implicated in his queer embodiment, sexual deviance, and adulterous behavior.

However, the paper's framing was not just narrative but also visual; three images accompanied the text of the article, each of which reminded the reader that Kerwineo was a dangerous, nonwhite individual who should not be trusted. Along the left-hand side of the page was a

Figure 4.5. Cartoon depicting Ralph Kerwineo behind bars, which appeared in the *Washington Post*, 1914.

photo of Kerwineo, dressed in a three-piece suit and bowler hat. The full-length shot allowed readers to see not only his full suit but also his relaxed stance with his hand in his pocket. Underneath the photo was a caption reading "'SENOR RALPHERO E. KERWINEO.' Cora Anderson, the Milwaukee girl who posed as a man, and whose 'marriage' to Dorothy Kleinowski aroused the jealousy of a third girl."[61] The danger posed by Kerwineo's figure was dramatized by the use of the word "senor"—reminding the reader of Kerwineo's nonwhiteness—and through references to Kerwineo's queer embodiment and likely sexual deviance. These dangers were brought home to the reader by a second image: opposite Kerwineo was a closely framed photo of Dorothy Kleinowski, whose dejected gaze directly confronted the reader. Unlike Kerwineo, whose stance was relaxed and nonchalant, Kleinowski's face glances pleadingly at the reader, soliciting sympathy for the pain Kerwineo caused her. For his part, Kerwineo stands opposite, unflinching. This positioning was no doubt deliberate; it suggests that Kerwineo was dangerous not only because of his nonwhiteness and his gender deviance, but also, more seriously, because of the threat he posed to white women.

The *Post* did not stop there. At the bottom of the page was a two-panel cartoon that depicted Kerwineo behind bars at the Milwaukee Police Station. These images are crucial to understanding the intent behind the *Washington Post*'s portrayal of Kerwineo. Commissioning an artist to draw Kerwineo afforded the paper's editors with the freedom to depict him however they saw fit, and also without reference to the reality unfolding in Milwaukee. The fact that the paper chose to depict Kerwineo behind bars must be seen as a deliberate move to signify his deviance, as by the time the images were published Kerwineo had already gone on trial and been released without charge. Rather than include those details, however, the *Post* suspended its narrative at the moment of Kerwineo's arrest, thus casting him as naturally deviant. Additionally, in the cartoon, the *Post* depicted Kerwineo still wearing the suit that lead to his arrest, and performing two activities closely associated with masculinity: smoking and shaving. Importantly, neither of these details is accurate: once Kerwineo was placed in police custody he was provided with "proper" clothes, and the *Evening Wisconsin* reported that he refused a box of cigarettes when they were offered as a means of wiling away the time, allegedly explaining, "Cigarettes went out of my life with my

masculine role . . . It is now chocolate and lady fingers for me."[62] However, depicting Kerwineo behind bars, relaxing with a cigarette while
lounging in his suit, suggested to readers that he was not only defiant
in his deviance (just as he appeared in the photograph above), but that
he was invested in keeping up his masculine appearance (through shaving) even when confined within a jail cell. Furthermore, it seems that
the activities of shaving and smoking are used to ridicule Kerwineo. In
the first image, the configuration of shaving cream gives him the appearance of a clown; in the second image, the way his cigarette smoke
refuses to be contained in his cell suggests that Kerwineo was intruding
on public space, even when confined in jail. The images also provide
the viewer with a similar experience to viewing an exhibition at a freak
show—a parallel which likely brought home to readers that Kerwineo
was not a sympathetic subject to whom they should relate, but rather a
spectacle at whom they should gawk.[63] In all these ways, Kerwineo was
cast as a disposable body, worthy of neglect. As Ruth Wilson Gilmore
has written, "Through forcefully twinned processes of articulation and
abstraction, lived narratives of difference become singularly dramatized
as modalities of antagonism, whose form of embodied appearance is the
overdetermined (racialized, gendered, nationalized, criminal) enemy."[64]
Through these processes, certain bodies are marked as always already
deviant, and in opposition to civil society. Thus the *Post* did not need to
cover Kerwineo's actual trial, as the verdict was already clear.

As the *Post*'s images highlighted, one of the biggest tragedies of Kerwineo's case was the victimization of a white woman. While she played a
relatively small role in local newspaper narratives, Dorothy Kleinowski
was central to national accounts. In fact, on the national scale, the most
frequently interviewed person was Kleinowski.[65] This trend is particularly evident in Idah McGlone Gibson's two-part series on Kerwineo,
which was syndicated by the Newspaper Enterprise Association and appeared in many newspapers nationwide. While Kleinowski's identity as
the daughter of Polish immigrants rendered her less "white" than her
Anglo-Saxon counterparts within early twentieth-century understandings of race, Gibson "whitened" Kleinowski's image by making no mention of her eastern European heritage, repeatedly referring to her with
phrases like "poor little Dorothy" or "the pretty little blonde girl," and
rarely mentioning her last name.[66] Racialized in this way, Kleinowski

could better play the role of the "normal" white woman who was most often cast in nationalizing narratives as the victim of sexual deviants.[67]

Whereas the few interviews Kleinowski provided to the Milwaukee press served to reassure readers that she was not broken up about the revelation of Kerwineo's biological sex, sensational accounts on the national scale portrayed her as thoroughly dejected. In the second article in the series, Gibson quoted Kleinowski as saying, " 'My heart was almost broken when I found out that Ralph was really a woman . . . *He was bigger to me than any man could be,' she went on through her tears, 'He did not ask anything of me only to be happy . . . I love him.' "*[68] In contrast to the brokenhearted Kleinowski, Gibson portrayed Kerwineo as a hardened criminal who had blatantly taken advantage of "poor little Dorothy." When asked if he was sorry that he dressed as a man for so many years, he answered, "Why should I be?" and explained that he married Kleinowski because his "vanity was touched" when he discovered that she had fallen in love with him.[69] In this way, Kerwineo was cast as deceptive predator, a categorization that was aided by the invocation of racialized tropes of the sexual danger posed by nonwhite bodies. Gibson wrote, "The profile of Miss Anderson is such as you see on old Egyptian and Roman coins, and her skin is of the copper tint, which shows the trace of Indian blood. Her hands and feet are small; her hair, as the little blond girl who was married to her put it, 'is black, blue black, a lovely color.' "[70] Significantly, in the midst of her description of Kerwineo's body, Gibson reminded the reader of Kleinowski's whiteness. However, Gibson did not merely insert a reference to Kleinowski's whiteness; she also asserted Kleinowski's attraction to Kerwineo's "blue black" hair, thereby linking his nonwhiteness to his ability to attract the affections of "normal" white women, implicating his racial identity with his sexual deviance, and positioning him as a threat to white men. Furthermore, in Gibson's account, Kerwineo's indigeneity was portrayed as a marker that indicated he was more closely connected to societies infamous for their licentiousness, such as ancient Egypt and Rome, rather than to the "modern" United States, thereby naturalizing his deviant sexuality by producing him as a "foreign" threat to "normal" white women like "poor little Dorothy."[71] Thus reliant on nationalizing narratives that connected nonwhiteness, homosexuality, and gender deviance, Kerwineo's guilt was never questioned in national newspapers.

However, the coverage of Kerwineo's story on the local level was far more forgiving, and local journalists were far less apt to interpret Kerwineo's body as inherently or definitively a foreign contagion. Indeed, for people in Milwaukee, Kerwineo was *not* a foreign contagion; he was a neighbor, coworker, or friend and was treated in the press as such. The same structures of familiarity that insulated Willie Ray from being ostracized after his "true sex" was revealed in a Booneville, Mississippi, courtroom in 1911 protected Ralph Kerwineo in 1914.

One of the ways Kerwineo was "domesticated" in the local press was through a clarification of his racial and national identity. Whereas the national press never questioned Kerwineo's foreignness (as evidenced by the *Washington Post*'s insistence on using the term "senor" to refer to him) or mobilized his racial ambiguity to associate him with ancient civilizations, the Milwaukee press allowed space for Kerwineo and his first wife, Mamie White, to explain their identities. Interestingly, just as the pair had utilized their racial ambiguity to blend into the milieu of new immigrants prior to the revelation of Kerwineo's "true sex," White continued to explain their identities. In the *Evening Wisconsin*, for example, White stated, "He is an Indian, of mixed Pottawatomie and Cherokee blood . . . I, too, am part Indian."[72] White provided a similar quote to the *Milwaukee Journal*, explaining that Kerwineo "is Potawatomie-Cherokee Indian, though only a half-breed."[73] Stating that Kerwineo was "only a half-breed" while she herself was "part Indian" provided an explanation for their dark skins. This explanation assured readers that they were not African Americans, Milwaukee's most maligned population, nor were they foreign, as "Ralphero" had occasionally stated previously.[74]

Of course, to understand the implications of this positioning, the context of settler colonialism is crucial. For much of U.S. history, the state has viewed Native people as queer because their kinship practices, residence patterns, and sex/gender systems often looked quite different from Western family structures, which have been based around ideologies of heterosexual binarism, private land/home ownership, and monogamous marriage.[75] It should be no surprise, then, that Native acceptance into the folds of U.S. citizenship has often been contingent on abandoning traditional forms of kinship, a process Mark Rifkin has called "the bribe of straightness."[76] By 1914, the bloody wars of conquest that had characterized much of the engagement between the United States and indigenous peoples in the eighteenth and nineteenth centuries were over, and therefore indigenous peoples represented a decreasing threat to the racial order of the nation (especially in contrast to African Americans, who were migrating to northern cities in record numbers, thereby posing an increasing threat). The characteristics that made Native people queer were seen as mutable (rather than inborn, like the inferiority of African Americans), and thereby subject to change through an investment in state-supported heteropatriarchy.[77] Thus, once Mamie White clarified that both she and Kerwineo were Native, the local press did not assume deviance, and instead called on state officials for an evaluation of their legitimacy as potential citizens—and thereby an assessment of their sexual normativity. Luckily for both Kerwineo and White, Milwaukee law officials were sympathetic to their story and cast them as respectable members of the community.

For example, the *Milwaukee Journal* interviewed Milwaukee Police Captain Sullivan, who characterized his interaction with White in wholly positive terms. He told the paper, "No woman ever came into my office who could use better English, or was apparently more refined than 'Mrs. Kerwineo,' and from my investigation, I believe that they are stating the truth when they say the only reason they set out upon this adventure was an economical one. They are not morally perverted in any way. I am convinced."[78] Sullivan cast White and Kerwineo as productive citizens (in contrast to "backward" Native peoples), a categorization that inherently denied the possibility of either party being sexually deviant. In this way, Sullivan's testimony published in the *Journal* operated as what queer theorist Sara Ahmed has referred to as a "straightening device," a production that brought their bodies in line with norms of heterosexuality and U.S. citizenship (or at least community belonging) more broadly.[79] It is likely that White was aware of the implications of her performance of respectability, just as Kerwineo was aware of the impact of his passing as the Spanish "Ralphero" during the years prior to his arrest. This racial positioning had the impact of both nullifying the suggestion of sexual deviance and carving out a nonwhite identity that was as unthreatening as possible.

These strategies had tangible benefits for Kerwineo and White, as both were depicted in the local press as "civilized" people of color. As such, their sexual deviance was not assumed by the local press or the citizens of Milwaukee more broadly; at no point in the local coverage did Kerwineo's gender deviance appear to be an indication of sexual deviance, and he was given multiple opportunities to explain his actions.[80] Importantly, Kerwineo's assertion that his marriage was completely conventional was supported in the local press by testimonials from members of the community. For example, on May 5, 1914, the *Evening Wisconsin* interviewed Joseph Traudt, one of Kerwineo's neighbors, who assured the paper that the couple was well respected in the neighborhood. As an example, Traudt told the paper, "After having seen the 'husband' help his 'wife' across a muddy street my mother said to me: 'How nice he is to his wife.'"[81] In this way, Kerwineo's living arrangements, which initially might have appeared unusual, were produced as understandable and perhaps even laudable. Additionally, he was depicted as a hard worker; his former boss at the Cutler-Hammer company told the *Evening Wisconsin* that Kerwineo was far more efficient than anyone he had previously hired in his position, justifying a raise from twenty-five to sixty dollars a month.[82]

When Kerwineo was ultimately put on trial for disorderly conduct, the local coverage of the trial made it clear that Kerwineo was innocent. The *Journal*, *Sentinel*, and *Evening Wisconsin* each published extensive testimony from Kerwineo himself and individuals speaking on his behalf. The *Sentinel* described Kerwineo's testimony as follows: "Answering questions put to her quietly and with the dignity of a refined, well-bred woman, the girl-man told the judge why she donned male attire. She said it was for the purpose of leading a clean life and to better herself financially."[83] Similarly, in describing Judge Page's decision to drop all charges against Kerwineo, the *Evening Wisconsin* stated that the judge was convinced that Kerwineo "adopted the disguise for moral and financial reasons and led an exemplary life while posing as a man, had never made overtures to others to do wrong and had innocently induced Miss Kleinowski into a mock marriage."[84] Judge Page's acceptance of the economic motivation behind Kerwineo's queer embodiment helped to produce Kerwineo's body as worthy of social membership, given the dominant connections between economic productivity and sexual normativity. As Margot Canaday has observed, immigration officials in the early twentieth century often relied on the "likely to become a public charge" clause in the immigration law as a way of excluding or deporting aliens suspected of sexual perversion, illustrative, in part, of "a Progressive-era association between poverty and immorality."[85]

Testimony in the local press from not just Kerwineo but also law officials and those who knew him as a man assured the Milwaukee public that Kerwineo's life in men's clothing was entirely normative and respectable—not queer. Indeed, if he had told the press that he was romantically interested in both women in his life, or that he could not imagine a life in women's clothing, the local press likely would have been less sympathetic, as his story would have violated the social norms in a profound way. Instead, Kerwineo took great pains to portray himself as an indigenous person who had wholly embraced the lessons of economic productivity and heteronormativity, and had gotten ensnared in gender deviance simply because of his overzealous desire to be a productive citizen. The local press was willing to accept this explanation and offer support for it.

However, the dissonance between local and national narratives surrounding Ralph Kerwineo illustrate that the structure of familiarity could not insulate trans men ad infinitum, nor could it inoculate trans men—particularly noncitizens or men of color—from being rendered pathological on the national scale. Specifically, journalists in national newspapers like the *New York World* or the *Washington Post* were not interested in publishing accounts of how well Kerwineo treated his wife or how hard a worker he was. Instead, they were more interested in publishing stories that fit within established plotlines that linked nonwhiteness/foreignness with sexual deviance and danger. Tellingly, these national narratives made no mention of sexology. Even in 1914, two decades after the figure of the "female invert" first emerged in the mass-circulation press, journalists utilized foreignness more readily than sexological theories to depict gender/sexual deviance. This trend continued well into the twentieth century, as illustrated by the case of Peter Stratford, another trans man whose death in 1929 prompted extended discussion in newspapers nationwide about non-Western religion and deviant sexuality.

"Masquerader Was Member of S.F. Cult"

Peter Stratford was born Deresley Morton in New Zealand around 1879. While the details of his early life are unclear, it is evident that by 1910 he had immigrated to the United States and was living in New York

City. At that point, he was still living as a woman and was sharing an apartment with another woman, Jenie Nawn.[86] At some point after 1910 he began living as Peter Stratford, and by 1918 he had moved in with Nawn's family in Hillsdale, New Jersey.[87] During World War I Stratford worked as a temporary clerk in a U.S. Army medical supply depot, where he oversaw shipments to the Panama Canal. Although he proved himself an exceedingly valuable employee, Stratford could not be hired permanently because he was not a U.S. citizen (and thereby ineligible to take the civil service exam); thus he was forced to resign this position in April 1919.[88]

At some point during the early 1920s Stratford began corresponding with a woman named Elizabeth Rowland from the Unity Metaphysical Center in Kansas City, Missouri. The center, which had been founded in 1881 as part of the New Thought Movement, offered a mail service to help those in need of spiritual healing.[89] Stratford, who was in poor health, may have initially written to the center to access the service, but once his correspondence with Rowland began he developed an emotional attachment to her. In 1925 he traveled to Kansas City to propose, and the couple was married in October of that year.[90] Stratford and Rowland eventually moved to California together, and by the late 1920s they were living in a hotel in the town of Niles. While the exact nature of their relationship is unknown, it was revealed after his death that Stratford maintained romantic correspondence with at least one other woman (Alma Thompson) during his marriage to Rowland.

While Ralph Kerwineo's story was discussed sympathetically on the local level because he was perceived to have lived as a "good man," the local press could find nothing redeeming in Peter Stratford's story. He was portrayed as an outsider—there were frequent references to the fact that he was living out of a trunk in a hotel room at the time of his death—with no connections to the local community, aside from a string of extramarital affairs and his "strange" religion. Indeed, at some point during Stratford's stay in California he became involved with Sufism, an Islamic form of mysticism that had gained a small following among artistic white elites in California in the 1920s.[91] The local and national press latched onto this aspect of Stratford's story and used it to cast him as a pathological individual who threatened the nation because his participation with "Oriental" religion was anti-American, and doubly so because he allegedly deployed the tenets of Sufism to woo innocent white women—particularly women who were not his wife.

Newspapers—both local and national—made much of the fact that investigators found over three hundred love letters to and from various women in Stratford's belongings. Several California papers, including the *Oakland Tribune*, the *San Francisco Chronicle*, the *San Francisco Examiner*, and the *Los Angeles Evening Herald*, published long excerpts of Stratford's love letters that served to highlight his infidelities and his participation in Sufism.[92] The *San Francisco Examiner* wrote, "A strange mixture of love, religion and Oriental philosophy was found yesterday in the letters of 'Peter Stratford.'"[93] Indeed, positioning Sufism as a cult, the paper went on to quote several of the letters from Stratford to his alleged mistress, Alma Thompson, wherein purportedly the "full philosophy of the cult" was explained: "'Peter' addresses Alma as 'Flower of God's love—dream of my soul since the world began.' And telling her: 'I recognize the Vast Immeasurable through you. It is because of our union. There is the vast circle in your consciousness, lacking one little segment to complete it. This tiny fragment is my soul, set in place to close the circle.'"[94] Such excerpts not only highlighted Stratford's "weird" religious beliefs but also served to suggest a connection between Stratford's religion and his deviant sexuality. Significantly, this linkage was wrought through "Oriental philosophy," and thus the threat posed by Stratford's sexual deviance was produced through racialized tropes. The frequent deployment of the term "Oriental" in the local (and national) newspaper coverage of Stratford's case helped to produce his story as a morality tale about the "yellow peril" that threatened the nation, its familial structures, and its racial purity.[95]

Local papers did not merely rely on the letters to speak for themselves; they also described the letters in their own words to make clear the connections between sexual deviance and "foreign" influence. In each of these instances, papers relied on Orientalist notions of the East as a space of sexual excess and deviance, and mobilized the notion of the "Orient" as a framework through which to understand Stratford's sexual deviance. The *San Francisco Chronicle*, for example, reported, "Mystic creeds imported from the exotic land of Buddha weave their nebulous tendrils about the life of the woman originally called Deresley Morton, when she came here from Australia many years ago. Divine healing and passionate declarations of love are found side by side in the records of many letters 'Peter' left behind when she was taken to the hospital from a room in the Belvoir Hotel, Niles."[96] In this account, Stratford's expressions of love are depicted as being inextricable from his devotion to Sufism; in fact, his body is portrayed as being physically within the hold of "mystic creeds imported from the exotic land of Buddha."

This connection was emphasized throughout the California coverage of Stratford's case. The *Los Angeles Times*, for example, characterized the letters written between Stratford and Alma Thompson as "mystically ardent, a mixture of oriental religious symbolism and poetically expressed affection."[97] Similarly, in an articled titled "Masquerader Was Member of S.F. Cult," the *San Francisco Examiner* reported that the letters revealed that Stratford's courtship of Rowland was "conducted . . . under the occult ritual of the sect that is ruled by 'Murschilda' here," while the *San Francisco Chronicle* and the *Modesto News-Herald* both reported that the pair's marriage was "performed according to the weird ritual of the cult."[98] The *San Francisco Examiner* brought things full circle when they reported that Stratford's death had led to the discovery of "a number of affectionate letters exchanged between [Alma Thompson], 'Stratford' and Mrs. Rowland."[99] In these narratives, Sufism was cast not only as a vehicle through which Stratford expressed his nonnormative sexuality, but also as the means through which Thompson and Rowland in turn expressed their desire for Stratford *and for each other*. The "Oriental" religion was the polluting influence that threatened the sexual purity of the nation.

This narrative can most clearly be seen in articles published in newspapers owned by William Randolph Hearst—a trend that illustrates the impact of the consolidation of the nation's newspaper industry in the 1920s. This narrative appeared in Hearst newspapers nationwide and was disseminated through Hearst's wire agency, Universal Service. For example, in an article titled "Belief in Oriental Cult Led Woman to Pose as Husband," the *New York American* reported that "judging from the sheaf of letters found today, 'he' carried on a voluminous correspondence with other women—members of disciples of Sufism, mystics and dabblers in cultism."[100]

Indeed, within the Hearst newspaper chain, Stratford morphed from a mere follower of Sufism to a leader of a "mystic" cult whose devoted included not only Rowland and Thompson but many other women. In an article titled "6 Women Face Hoax Inquiry," the *San Francisco Examiner* reported, "The relations of half a dozen or more women with 'Stratford' and the strange cult she apparently headed while posing as a man were being checked tonight." Unfortunately for the reporting journalists, the women had apparently gone into hiding and could not be located to provide further comment.[101] While it seems likely that the real reason the other women could not be found was that there were no other women, their alleged disappearance aided the Hearst papers' attempt to cast Stratford's "cult" as a secretive and underground organization. According to this narrative, members of the cult were willing to do whatever it took to protect the organization's "secrets." For example, on May 5, 1929, the *Los Angeles Examiner* reported that Rowland fled to San Diego, allegedly exclaiming, "I must protect the cult!"[102]

Whereas other papers ended their coverage of Stratford's case with his burial, the Hearst papers remained vigilant, moving on to suggest that Stratford's death had uncovered a vast international conspiracy to promote gender deviance. In an article titled "Masquerader Cult Hunted" the *Los Angeles Examiner* stated, "With 'Peter Stratford,' strange man-woman and dual personality, resting in a pauper's grave at Oakland, authorities yesterday were preparing a possible investigation into reports that an international cult sponsored such personalities."[103] The *San Francisco Examiner* similarly suggested that Stratford's death had revealed "startling disclosures" that "might lead to Nationwide investigation of strange cults with which she is said to have been identified—cults that sponsored 'dual personalities.'"[104] Thus relying on Orientalist notions of sexual deviance, the Hearst newspapers in California used Stratford's story to suggest a real and present danger that could not be buried with Stratford's body.

Importantly, this characterization falls in line with a trend evident in many Hearst newspapers in the early twentieth century. The era witnessed increased interest in alternative religions in the United States, particularly in California, and these "cults," as they were often referred to, provided the Hearst newspaper chain with tremendous fodder for scandal. As the Stratford case illustrates, fears about cults were often dramatized through discussions of deviant sexuality and racialized conceptions of danger. As Philip Jenkins has written, "In the first quarter of the century, religious cults were one of the very few areas of life in which whites, especially white women, would regularly defer to the authority of Asian leaders. Racist concerns about this authority were expressed in sexual terms. American women were said to be particularly vulnerable to the exotic enticements of Asian mysticism. Gullible women were thus reopening the gates of paganism."[105] Thus discussions of the Stratford case in the Hearst newspapers (particularly the *San Francisco Examiner*, *Los Angeles Examiner*, and *New York American*) are emblematic of an increasingly common narrative that dramatized the danger of cults by focusing on their purported (sexual) allure to otherwise "normal" white women.

As the story traveled out of California and onto the pages of newspapers nationwide, journalists and editors remained interested in using Sufism as a means to pathologize Stratford, but they also placed their own spin on the story. Both the Associated Press and United Press wire services released accounts that focused on Elizabeth Rowland. Unlike local narratives—which had produced Rowland as an individual who had embraced the teachings of Stratford's strange "cult" and was therefore an equally dangerous threat to the nation—newspapers outside California most frequently described Rowland as an innocent victim of Stratford's malicious and pathological actions. This strategy—focusing on the white women who purportedly were the "victims" of trans men's deception—should sound very familiar, as it was the same one used by the national press in their discussions of Nicolai De Raylan and Ralph Kerwineo.

In order for Rowland to appear blameless, however, newspapers first had to address the questions surrounding her involvement in the case. Whereas local newspapers depicted Rowland as a "mysterious figure in the movie colony," on the national scale Rowland was most often produced as a "normal" white, heterosexual, middle-class woman— precisely the type of woman that could symbolize the nation.[106] The *Chicago Tribune*, for example, explained that Rowland "has a son in college in Kansas City," which it then describes as the place "where she was married to Stratford in 1925."[107] By thus alluding to Rowland's previous marriage to a man, and her status as a mother of a son who was in college, the *Tribune* articulated her life course in line with reproductive futurity, a narrative device vital to her portrayal as the innocent victim. Additionally, the *Tribune* made it clear that Rowland was gainfully employed, and described her as "a personable woman with clear features, hazel eyes and above medium height."[108] Establishing Rowland's identity as a "normal," white, middle-class woman, newspapers such as the *Chicago Tribune* created a sympathetic figure to whom readers could relate, and with whose victimization they would sympathize, just as national newspapers had done with Dorothy Kleinowski when recounting Ralph Kerwineo's story.

In national accounts, Rowland emerged as the primary speaking subject. In contrast to Stratford, whose death not only revealed his "true sex" but also rendered him unable to speak for himself, Rowland's statements appeared frequently in Associated Press coverage. In papers such as Wisconsin's *Appleton Post-Crescent*, Texas's *Galveston Daily News*, and Maryland's *Cumberland Evening Times*, Rowland offered explanations that clarified her involvement in the case and highlighted her good nature and sexual propriety. She explained that she was introduced to Stratford while working at the Unity School in Kansas City, where she "found a letter asking prayer [*sic*] for a man by the name of Peter Stratford who lived at Hillsdale, N.J." The two corresponded for some time, and although she stated that she was initially quite impressed by Stratford's literary capacity, Rowland admitted that she felt pressured to maintain correspondence, explaining, "My letters to 'him' also seemed to be the very breath of life and often became a very great burden to me, because if I neglected to write, 'his' health was apparently affected." Rowland reported that after some time Stratford proposed marriage, and she felt obligated to say yes "because of 'his' pitiful condition." Thus Rowland clarified that she married Stratford solely because of her empathetic nature—not because of the allure of his "strange" religious beliefs or her sexual attraction to him. In fact, Rowland further clarified her sexual normality by explaining that, as a divorcée, she never intended to pursue a sexual relationship with another man—a stipulation she had made clear to Stratford prior to his proposal.[109] In these ways, Rowland characterized her initial contact with Stratford as completely innocent, and legitimized her marriage by stating that it was motivated by her caring nature, an explanation that was significant given that on the surface her marriage to Stratford may have seemed to indicate her sexual impropriety.

However, in the national press, Elizabeth Rowland was not the only innocent victim of Peter Stratford's dangerous behavior. While the California press cast Alma Thompson as the deviant mistress who shared Stratford's interest in "weird" religion, the national press more often cast Thompson as another innocent white victim of Stratford's deviant sexuality—a sexuality that manifested itself through Stratford's "strange" religious beliefs. Indeed, the *New York World* and *New York Times* both reported that "other letters to a woman in Los Angeles, addressed only as 'Alma,' revealed Peter's love for her as based on the tenets of the Sufi cult."[110] When Thompson explained her story in the *Billings Gazette*, she made it clear she did not share Stratford's affinity for Sufism; in fact, she claimed she was frightened by Stratford's mystical advances: "Peter wrote that he had seen me in his dreams and he knew exactly what I looked like . . . letters in this vein continued and I grew frightened, and falling into the strange language of his cults [I] told him I had received distinct orders to cease correspondence."[111] In this narrative Thompson casts herself not as a guilty mistress, but as another innocent victim of Stratford's deviant sexuality. Any suggestion of Thompson's sexual impropriety is cleared up by her explanation that she never met Stratford in person, and that she cut off communication once his letters took a "mystic" turn.

In the national narratives of Stratford's death, Sufism was invoked as a means to dramatize his danger to the nation. Indeed, the AP newswire reproduced in numerous papers nationwide described Stratford as a "personality deeply immersed in the lore of Sufism, a cult which centuries ago arose as the fundamentalist faction of Mohammedanism," and also highlighted Stratford's identity as an immigrant from New Zealand.[112] In this way, Stratford's whiteness was depicted as precarious, as he was both an immigrant and "deeply immersed in the lore of Sufism." Even more dangerous to the nation was the equivalence created between Stratford's sexual desire and his "cultish" religion practices, which highlights the correlation between the regulation of immigration and sexuality. As Lauren Berlant has argued, "Immigration discourse is a central technology for the reproduction of patriotic nationalism: not just because the immigrant is seen as without a nation or resources and thus as deserving of pity or contempt, but because the immigrant is defined as *someone who desires America*."[113] This desire can be productively used, but when immigrant bodies are perceived to convey nonnormative sexuality this desire is viewed by the general public and the U.S. government as pathological. Thus, in national narratives, Elizabeth Rowland and Alma Thompson, as middle-class, heterosexual, white women, represented the imagined national public, and their victimization highlighted the danger individuals such as Stratford posed to the nation.

One way local and national narratives of Stratford's death coincided was in their representation of Stratford's burial. Virtually all accounts (even those that published few other details on Stratford's life) provided an in-depth description of Stratford's desolate interment. The *Washington Post*, for example, portrayed the event as attended only by the "morbidly curious," who witnessed Stratford's burial in a "weed-grown, wind-swept potters' field with only a nameless, scrawny, wooden stake for a marker."[114] Newspapers nationwide used the fact that Stratford was buried in a potter's field to symbolize his deviance. Indeed, the term "potter's field" appeared again and again in descriptions of Stratford's burial. It is important to note that the term was not a reference to a specific burial ground but rather was deployed as a signifier of non-belonging. "Potter's field" is biblical in origin: in the New Testament, Hebrew priests used the silver offered by Judas upon repentance and "bought with them the potter's field, to bury strangers in."[115] Thus the use of "potter's field" exposes the coding that links morality, nationalism, and heterosexuality in opposition to immigrants, homosexuals, and other queer individuals.

Other accounts of Stratford's burial did not rely simply on the term "potter's field" to convey the image of desolation, and provided a more detailed description of the unkempt field wherein Stratford was laid to rest. The *San Francisco Examiner*, for example, described the "jumbled weeds" that were "torn aside" so that Stratford's "crude wooden casket" could be buried, while the *Oakland Tribune* made it clear that the only two witnesses to the burial were "Andy Anderson, a grave digger, and Joe Saul, an undertaker's assistant."[116] Similarly, an Associated Press article that appeared in at least a dozen papers nationwide opened as follows: "A grave in Potter's field yawned today for 'Peter Stratford,' a woman who for years masqueraded as a man, married another woman and worked at jobs varying all the way from heavy manual labor to writing critical essays. No one claimed the body."[117] Stratford was cast as a deceptive individual whose life was so unworthy of ceremony that even his grave was unimpressed by his remains.

Fundamental to this representation of Stratford as a queer outsider was his foreignness: he did not belong to any community (aside from his "cult"), and did not contribute in a positive manner to any community either. Indeed, it was not simply Stratford's queer embodiment that rendered him queer, but his supposed victimization of white women and his participation in "weird" religious practices. Stratford was figured similarly to the ways Lee Edelman has argued today's queers are figured in politics: "The queer comes to figure the bar to every realization of futurity, the resistance, internal to the social, to every social structure or form."[118] Indeed, newspapers highlighted the fact that Stratford's body had lain unclaimed for several days before its burial, and that attempts to locate his family in New Zealand had proved fruitless, in order to highlight his status as a queer individual who was unwelcome by his local community and his family abroad. Thus Stratford was buried apart not only from friends and family, but also from the boundaries of social membership, and it was this positioning that seemingly rendered Stratford's life (and death) particularly lonely.

Conclusion

As this chapter has shown, newspapers throughout the early twentieth century found that foreignness was a convenient means to pathologize nonnormative gender and sexual formations. Foreignness provided a framework for national newspapers to produce gender transgressions as wholly un-American. Queer embodiment in and of itself was not enough for newspapers to interpret one's presence as a threat. Rather, the threat was determined by the perceived combination of gender, race, nation, and sexuality—with race and nation playing a bigger role than gender and sexuality well into the twentieth century.

Perceptions of one's body were by no means stable, and were deeply dependent on the local and global sociopolitical context. For example, Jack Garland's queer body was produced in the national press as an asset to the nation while he pledged his allegiance to the imperial project of the Philippine-American War; however, he was seen as a potential threat to the nation in the midst of World War I, when his queer body elicited suspicion that he might be a German spy. This dramatic shift illustrates the precarious position in which trans men found themselves:

their gender variance rendered them susceptible to suspicion, and they had to constantly prove their trustworthiness to their communities. As the response to Jack Garland and Ralph Kerwineo illustrates, local communities were willing to be persuaded of their queer neighbors acceptability, provided those neighbors could prove their allegiance to the nation or show a history of respect for the institution of marriage and/or heteronormativity. However, once the stories circulated beyond the local context, both individuals were treated less as community members than as threats to the community. The structure of familiarity was stripped away, and both stories were distilled down to binaries that suggested the individuals in question were dangerous, deviant, and un-American. The distinction between the local and national narratives in these cases suggests how precarious the survival of trans men of color was in the early twentieth century—how easy it was for newspaper editors to erase their voices and replace their carefully constructed explanations with tropes of belonging that rendered them deviant outsiders because of their purported foreignness.

Of course, it was all the *more* possible for newspaper editors to erase the voices of trans men after their death: even the local papers cast Nicolai De Raylan and Peter Stratford as deviant outsiders. The stories of De Raylan, a Russian immigrant with purported connections to revolutionary activities in his home country, and Peter Stratford, a New Zealand immigrant with connections to the Islamic sect of Sufism, were distilled to stories in which their gender deviance was connected to their "foreign" identity. Their supposed "masquerade" as men was produced as the primary example of how they could not be trusted and could never be part of their communities because they were essentially, and at their core, outsiders. These stories are, therefore, powerful reminders of the power of whiteness and national belonging in rendering queerness unexceptional, another benefit in the long list of privileges white individuals enjoy but historians seldom acknowledge.

To Have and to Hold

Trans Husbands in the Early Twentieth Century

On August 16, 1882, an individual named Ethel Kimball was born on Martha's Vineyard. Kimball later moved with her family to Boston, and by the time she reached her twenties she began to run afoul of the law. Her first arrest is recorded in May 1904, for attempted forgery. She was later bailed out of jail by a member of the Wilson family (a family that, notably, she would marry into four years later). She was acquitted of all charges, though it would not be the last time Kimball would see the inside of a jail cell.

She married Frank A. Wilson in 1908, but married life did little to domesticate her. In 1911 she was again arrested, this time for "evading a motor fare amounting to $48."[1] According to the *Boston Daily Globe*, she had visited a Back Bay dealership and expressed interest in car. She requested that the salesman take her for a test drive, but "the result [was] that Mrs. Wilson and a party of women friends secured a ride to various outlaying sections of the city, the automobile finally winding up at an inn in Danvers."[2] Once at the inn, it was all too obvious that Kimball had no interest in the car—or, for that matter, for reimbursing the car salesman for his time or gas. As a result she was arrested and, perhaps because this was not her first offense, sentenced to two months in the Brighton House of Corrections.

Kimball reappears on the public record in 1921, and by this point he was no longer living as a woman but as a man: James William Hathaway. It appears that his transition occurred around 1919, while Hathaway remained in Boston. Around that time he began a relationship with Louise Margaret Aechtler, and the pair wed in November 1921 in the Union Congregational Church in Somerville.[3] Just as with his previous marriage to James Wilson, Hathaway's second nuptials did not end his penchant for criminal activity, and he was very quickly in police custody once again. In fact, just three weeks after his wedding he was arrested, this time on the charge of attempted auto theft.

Of course, this arrest was more eventful than his previous ones, as it resulted in the revelation of his "true sex." Once in police custody, officials discovered that Hathaway's body was not male in the conventional sense; the charges on which he was initially arrested were dropped, and he was "rearrested on the charge of falsifying a marriage record in Somerville."[4] The case went before the district court, wherein Hathaway's bride contended that she was unaware of her husband's "true sex" at the time of their marriage, or at any point prior to his arrest.[5] For Hathaway's part, he argued that the marriage was a "prank" and that Miss Aechtler was aware of his anatomy. Regardless of whose version of the story was true, after this arrest their marriage seems to have dissolved.[6] Hathaway was placed on probation and voluntarily entered the House of the Good Shepard.[7]

However, this stint did little to reform Hathaway's criminal impulses. Within eighteen months Hathaway was once again living as a man and back to his life of crime. He was arrested again in May 1922 and October 1923. Each time, he escaped lengthy sentences, though his 1922 arrest did prompt a psychiatric evaluation.[8] By 1924 he was involved with another woman: eighteen-year-old Pearl A. Davis. The pair met in Boston, where Davis understood Hathaway to be a woman "masquerading in male attire to close a real estate deal."[9] It is unclear whether the deal was successful, but what is evident is that the pair soon left Boston together and traveled around New England, with Hathaway still in men's clothing. In February 1924 they were arrested in Concord, Massachusetts, for registering in a hotel under false names (interestingly, at this point, Hathaway was posing as James Wilson—utilizing the surname of the man he married in 1908).[10] Undeterred, they traveled to Hartford, Connecticut, where they were married by Rev. George W. Hill on March 17, 1924. Less than a month later the pair was arrested again. They were both charged with perjury and sentenced to thirty days in jail.[11]

James Hathaway's story diverges in important ways from many of the other cases discussed in previous chapters. Whereas the driving force behind many of the individuals in previous chapters were normative logics (the desire to "settle down," be economically productive, be seen as a "good man," and become a contributing member of their community), Hathaway was an outlaw. Like Ellis Glenn in the 1890s, Hathaway maintained a pattern of wooing women, passing bad checks, and rarely making an honest living.[12] Perhaps this was because he felt his gender variance prevented him from reputable employment, or perhaps economic necessity required that his behavior stray from legal boundaries. Or perhaps he simply was an individual who sought to live outside of normative constraints, one of which happened to be gender. Whatever the motivation behind Hathaway's legal missteps, one way Hathaway *was* like many of the others discussed in this book is that he shared a desire to become a legal husband. Not once but *twice* did Hathaway present himself in front of legal and religious authorities in order to gain the status of husband. Even more remarkably, his second marriage was performed less than a month after he was arrested for forging his name at a hotel; having had numerous previous run-ins with the law, Hathaway no doubt knew that claiming a false name on a legal document carried much more risk than registering at a hotel under a pseudonym. However, he was undeterred and went through with the ceremony anyway.

Although the term "female husband" ceased to be used by the mainstream press in the 1890s, the *phenomenon* of trans men pursuing legal marriages to women did not disappear. In fact, Hathaway is one of dozens of recorded cases of trans men who placed their identities under state scrutiny in order to become legal husbands. Almost half of newspaper stories regarding trans men published in the United States between 1890 and 1930 mentioned the fact that the individual was legally married to, or was engaged to marry, a woman. The decision to marry is remarkable because it was one that imperiled one's carefully constructed male life by voluntarily placing oneself under state inspection, but it also was *itself* a criminal act.[13] Cross-dressing was not illegal in every city and state in the early twentieth century (though many municipalities were passing such legislation in this period), but falsifying one's identity on a marriage contract was. Thus, by entering into a legal marriage, trans men not only were making it more likely that they might be "discovered," they were making such discovery more punishable. Thus this chapter asks two related questions. First, what was it about the institution of marriage that motivated so many trans men to endure substantial risk in order to receive the legal recognition of their unions? Second, what was the response when trans men's marriages became public knowledge?

In answering these questions, this chapter will argue that many trans men saw legal marriage as a means of illustrating their status as "good men" to their communities. They understood that the best way to avoid scrutiny of their lives, and their gender, was to live according to the normative standards of their chosen communities, and being married was an integral part of that performance. Thus, while the act of getting married required that trans men put themselves at substantial risk of discovery, in the long term, marriage could serve as another tool to aid in passing. Indeed, marriage was a way of *becoming* a man. In an era where there was no access to hormone therapy, or no possibility of legally changing one's birth certificate or driver's license, attaining a marriage certificate as a man was perhaps the only way that trans men could inhabit masculinity in an official, state-sanctioned way. The marriage certificate was one of a precious few forms of documentation available to trans men that attested to their masculinity and validated their relationships with women. However, as this book has repeatedly shown, nothing, not even legal marriage, could offer complete protection for trans men in the early twentieth century. Thus the bulk of this chapter will trace how the public responded once the "true sex" of married trans men was discovered, and how that response changed by the late 1920s. This chapter will argue that while the phenomenon of trans men marrying women was discussed with increased sensationalism and negativity on the national scale by the late 1920s, local responses remained tepid—an insight that again highlights the need for scholars to look beyond the level of national discourse to understand the ways that local communities responded to their queer friends and neighbors.

Brief History of Marriage

Many scholars before me have studied and written about the institution of marriage at length, so I will not devote too much time here rehearsing established knowledge. However, it is worth noting a few central tenets. First, as Nancy Cott and Peggy Pascoe have argued, marriage as an institution has been one of the central ways through which the state has defined itself, regulating membership, racial belonging, and proper gendered behavior. According to Cott, "By incriminating some marriages and encouraging others, marital regulations have drawn lines among the citizenry and defined what kinds of sexual relations and which families will be legitimate."[14] Throughout the history of the United States, legal authorities and politicians have promoted a particular model of marriage for the populace, one that was marked by "lifelong, faithful monogamy, formed by the mutual consent of a man and a woman, bearing the impression of the Christian religion and the English common law in its expectations for the husband to be the family head and economic provider, his wife the dependent partner."[15]

Of course, ministers and legislatures did not always enforce these norms. For much of the nineteenth century in the United States, marriages based on mutual agreement rather than official ceremony were quite common, especially as the white population moved westward. Such informal or "self-marriages" were still regulated by the public—but in this case, it was the local community of friends, family, and neighbors that held the couple accountable. As Cott explains, "Without resort to the state apparatus, local informal policing by the community affirmed that marriage was a well-defined public institution as well as a contract made by consent. Carrying out the standard obligation of the marriage bargain—cohabitation, husband's support, wife's service—seems to have been more central to the approbation of local communities at this time than how or when the marriage took place, and whether one of the partners had been married elsewhere before."[16] Thus, as Cott and other marriage scholars have observed, marriage was regulated by religious and legal officials, as well as through informal means of community control. This insight highlights the importance of analyzing local responses to marriages (formal or informal) as well as the legal and religious codes that regulate access to the institution.

It is also worth noting that the white U.S. population was very mobile in the nineteenth century. In the context of Manifest Destiny, moving (especially westward) was often associated with new possibilities.[17] As such, many communities were growing quickly and therefore accustomed to the appearance of new transplants. In this milieu, what was important to community members when a new couple moved to town was not that they displayed their marriage license, but rather that they upheld the public expectations of marriage. Many of the trans men in this book seem to have taken advantage of this and embarked on a new life as a husband not by entering a church or courthouse with their beloved, but instead by simply moving to a new location and proclaiming themselves man and wife. This seems to be the case with George and Mary Green, who lived together as man and wife beginning in the 1860s in Pennsylvania, though no official marriage record is on file with the state. Even without legal documentation of their union, the pair were acknowledged as man and wife everywhere their peripatetic lives took them: they were Mr. and Mrs. Green in Swift Creek, North Carolina, where they lived in the 1880s, and in Ettrick, Virginia, where they were living when George died in 1902. No one was aware of the informal nature of their marriage, because all that mattered to their communities was that they *appeared* to uphold the standards of the institution: a monogamous, consensual partnership between a providing husband and a dependent wife. This tactic remained a viable one for trans men and their wives into the twentieth century. Indeed, Mamie White told the *Milwaukee Journal* that when she and Ralph Kerwineo decided in 1908 they wanted to live as man and wife, they simply moved to a new city. For over six years no one in Milwaukee was the wiser.[18]

As we move into the twentieth century, trans men continued to get married (legally and informally), but they did so against a changing backdrop of state regulations. As Michael Grossman has noted, the late nineteenth and early twentieth centuries witnessed a proliferation of new regulations on marriage. States began passing laws that regulated who could get married based on race, age, kin ties, and physical and mental health.[19] The expanded legal matrix did not deter trans men from entering the institution, but this new legal landscape did begin to shape public responses to their queer marriages if their "true sex" was revealed. This change was not immediate, however, and even in the 1910s, as states were passing laws that mandated eugenic blood tests prior to marriage and prohibited interracial marriage, trans men who were revealed to have married women faced limited, if any, legal punishments. This lack of punishment is due to the fact that the figure of the trans husband elicited limited public fear, because he was not yet an identifiable deviant social figure. Particularly on the local level, trans husbands were not viewed as dangerous in the same way that "lazy husbands" who abandoned their families were, nor were they viewed by community members as hazardous in the same way that the "feebleminded"—a population targeted by eugenic marriage legislation—were. Indeed, a further exploration of Ralph Kerwineo's story makes this point exceedingly clear.

"Eugenic Law Absurd"

One dynamic that was beginning to shape marriage legislation nation-wide by the 1910s was the growing eugenics movement. Increasing levels of immigration—particularly from eastern and southern Europe—and growing fears of miscegenation motivated a diverse group of politicians, scientists, doctors, and reformers to advocate a eugenic agenda focused on preserving the purity of the nation's racial stock through a variety of means.[20] And of course the rise of the eugenics movement was intimately tied to the growth of sexology, as the field had articulated homosexuality as being among the "propensities" that manifested itself as a result of compromised bloodlines since the late nineteenth century. Richard von Krafft-Ebing himself stated in his landmark *Psychopathia Sexualis* that "almost all cases where an examination of the physical and mental peculiarities of the ancestors and blood relations has been possible, neuroses, psychoses, degenerative signs, etc. have been found in the families."[21] At the behest of the eugenics movement, state legislatures addressed the problem of tainted bloodlines through sterilization statutes. As Nancy Ordover has observed, "Between 1907 and 1932, thirty states put such statutes in place . . . [that] established [medical panels] to grant or deny doctors the right to sterilize anyone with a real or imagined physical or developmental disability."[22] California, the third state to pass a compulsory sterilization law, was the first to include an explicit provision that the law could be used to sterilize "moral degenerates" and "sexual perverts showing hereditary degeneracy."[23] However, sterilization laws were only one way that states attempted to protect bloodlines within their future population. Another component of the eugenic agenda in the 1910s were marriage laws, designed to identify "problem" husbands and wives before they were allowed to marry and reproduce.

The state of Wisconsin was at the forefront of the crusade to implement new regulations on marriage. In late June 1913, the State Legislature passed the Medical Certification Law, or the "Eugenic Marriage Law" as it was popularly known. This law required all males seeking a marriage license to first undergo a medical examination for venereal diseases.[24]

While the law's passage created a great deal of debate, it wasn't the logic behind the marriage law that was questioned—in fact, an editorial published by the *Journal of American Medical Association* in the *Milwaukee Sentinel* suggested that "95 per cent of the medical profession of Wisconsin are in favor of the principle of the legal restriction of marriage to those who are physically fit to enter such a contract."[25] However, the wording of the legislation was vague, mandating only the "application of the recognized clinical and laboratory tests," but not mentioning any particular test by name or specifying which combination of tests were necessary to ensure that husbands were "physically fit to enter" the institution of marriage.[26] As a result, the bill drew sharp criticism from Wisconsin's doctors, who argued that the three-dollar fee mandated by the bill was not sufficient to cover the types of laboratory tests necessary to determine the presence of venereal diseases or genetic disorders. Doctors were quick to point out that the average fee charged for the Wassermann test for syphilis alone was well over three dollars.[27] Thus, when the bill went into effect on January 1, 1914, Wisconsin lawyers, doctors, and couples were ready to challenge its constitutionality, and the national press watched closely to learn the fate of the legislation.[28]

For many, Wisconsin's marriage law was the culmination of years of advocacy. In March 1912 the *New York Times* published an article titled "Eugenic Marriage Plan Praised Here," wherein Dr. J. W. Beveridge articulated the need for similar restrictions on marriage in order to prevent the continuance of inherited diseases in future generations. He told the *Times*, "As society and the State are founded upon the home as a unit, so the State has a right to bar disease that would enter the home through marriage just as it bars disease that would enter the country through the ports."[29] This article illustrates that in the early twentieth century, at a moment in which many elites were anxious about the incoming hordes of immigrants from eastern and southern Europe and Asia as well as changing gender roles, the rhetoric surrounding "eugenic marriages" articulated the regulation of marriage as vital means through which lawmakers could control the future of the nation. Indeed, the rhetoric promoting eugenic marriages was not simply about maintaining the physical health of future generations, but also about placing tighter restrictions on which bodies had access to the institution of marriage, an institution that Dr. Beveridge reminds us is at the heart of full and robust citizenship. Thus, advocating "eugenic marriage" legislation was one means through which lawmakers could prevent those whose class, race, or sexuality marked them as "undesirable" from attaining citizenship rights. As Cathy Cohen explains, "Many of the roots of heteronormativity are in white supremacist ideologies which sought (and continue) to use the state and its regulation of sexuality, in particular through the institution of heterosexual marriage, to designate which individuals were truly 'fit' for full rights and privileges of citizenship."[30]

This was the context in which Ralph Kerwineo's case emerged on the national stage in 1914. Recall that Ralph Kerwineo was the mixed-race Milwaukee resident, discussed in the previous chapter, who gained widespread attention after his first wife revealed to the Milwaukee police that her former husband had been assigned female at birth. Given the context of Wisconsin's then-new Eugenic Marriage Law, when it was revealed in the national press that Ralph Kerwineo had not only married a (white) woman, but that he had done so having passed Wisconsin's "eugenic marriage test," the stage was set for a scandal.

Although the local press covered Ralph Kerwineo's arrest and subsequent release with surprising sympathy, as soon as the story spread to papers outside the city limits, journalists cast Kerwineo as a dangerous deviant. What I did not mention in the previous chapter, however, was the fact that the national press mobilized Kerwineo's story as an argument for the need for more stringent marriage laws. Thus, not only did the historical context of the growing eugenics movement shape the ways Kerwineo's story was perceived by newspaper readers throughout the nation, but the movement provided a rhetorical strategy through which to pathologize Kerwineo and his purportedly deviant actions.

By focusing on the failure of Wisconsin's Eugenic Marriage Law, national newspapers such as Joseph Pulitzer's *New York World* articulated Kerwineo's story through nationalizing narratives of racial and sexual "otherness." The *World* published three articles on Kerwineo's story, each of which focused on Kerwineo's ability to secure a "eugenic marriage license."[31] For example, "Eugenic License to Girl as Man Ridicules Law," an article that, significantly, went on to be syndicated in several newspapers nationwide, reported that while the blood test showed that Kerwineo was free from blood disease, it "would not reveal the presence of another equally dangerous disease."[32] Given that homosexuality was often articulated in scientific and legal discourse as an issue of "tainted blood," it is likely that the paper was positioning homosexuality to be "equally dangerous" as maladies such as syphilis.[33] The following day, the *World* brought its coverage of Kerwineo's story to a close with an explicit appeal to extend the types of tests required by eugenic marriage laws: "The Eugenic law might work better for future generations if it were amended to give the police an opportunity to decide whether or not the groom is a 'he' or a 'she.' "[34]

Alongside this article, the *World* published two photographs: one of Ralph Kerwineo and one of Dorothy Kleinowski. Published under the headline " 'Husband' and Wife in Eugenic Marriage," these images reminded readers that the story was not simply about the victimization of one white woman; by connecting the images to the issue of "eugenic marriage," the *World* brought to the fore concerns about the future of the nation. In this way, the term "eugenic marriage" provided a convenient way for the national press to articulate Kerwineo's story through nationalizing narratives of racial and sexual "otherness." It helped to create a tidy morality tale that alerted readers to the need for increased vigilance concerning who had access to the institution of marriage and, thereby, full and robust citizenship.

The *Washington Post* published a similar account the day before. The headline "Eugenic Law Absurd" signals the centrality of the marriage law in national discussions of Kerwineo's story. Like the *World*, the *Post* ridiculed the Wisconsin law, arguing that the blood test was ineffective because it "revealed the absence of one disease, but did not show that the person was even of the masculine gender."[35] The article went on to include the same phrase that would appear in the *World* the following day, the expression of concern that the test "would not reveal the presence of another equally dangerous disease." Thus, by centering the narrative on Wisconsin's marriage law, national newspapers like the *Washington Post* and *New York World* highlighted Kerwineo's gender (and potentially sexual) deviance.[36]

Several things are important to take note of here. First, it is impossible to know with any certainty what audience interpretations of these articles were, or how many readers understood what the reference to "another equally dangerous disease" meant. For those readers who understood the reference to sexual inversion (or perhaps homosexuality), no doubt some remained unconvinced that the "condition" was "equally dangerous" to syphilis, or any other malady for that matter. If there had been unanimous, nationwide understanding that cross-dressing and marrying women was evidence of an inborn pathology, Ralph Kerwineo would have not, after all, been released from Milwaukee jail without charge, nor would so many of his coworkers and neighbors have been willing to speak up on his behalf after his "true sex" was revealed. However, the national coverage of Kerwineo's illustrates how sexological and eugenic lines of thought about homosexuality, sexual inversion, and pathology were beginning to penetrate into mainstream discourse. However, it is worth remembering that Ralph Kerwineo was discussed sympathetically in the Milwaukee press, and he was ultimately released from police custody without charge. Thus the response on the ground in Milwaukee shows that the increased presence of eugenic and sexological discourses in the national press were not yet determinative of local responses and courtroom decisions.

Similarly, the passage of Wisconsin's Eugenic Marriage Law did little to deter Ralph Kerwineo from pursuing a legal marriage to Dorothy Kleinowski. His decision to not only propose marriage to Kleinowski, but to take a blood test and take part in the official marriage ceremony, put Kerwineo and the male life he had carefully crafted for himself in grave danger. Why would he willingly put himself under such intense scrutiny, particularly when his first marriage was informal, without any official ceremony or legal documentation?[37] Perhaps it was because marriage allowed Kerwineo to legally claim his male identity. He explained to the *Milwaukee Sentinel*, "I had really become a man and imagined that the woman in me had perished with my years of change," and from this perspective perhaps Kerwineo felt the only "proper" thing to do when he realized that Dorothy Kleinowski was in love with him was to propose and legally marry.[38]

Additionally, the fact that the pair desired to stay in Milwaukee after their marriage may have played a role in Kerwineo's decision to legally marry Kleinowski. It appears as though the likelihood that a trans man would seek a legal, as opposed to informal, marriage corresponded to the decision to remain in the same city where the couple met or had familial ties. For example, in 1872 Murray Hall legally married Celia Low in New York, the city where they would spend their entire married life until Celia's death in 1898.[39] In 1882 Frank Dubois legally married Gertrude Fuller in

Waupun, Wisconsin, Fuller's hometown and the place where the pair set up house.[40] Ten years later, William C. Howard married Edith Dyer in Hornellsville, New York, Dyer's hometown.[41] In the 1890s Nicolai De Raylan married in his adopted hometown of Chicago; when that marriage ended in divorce in 1903 he quickly remarried, once again in Chicago.[42] Many other trans men were engaged at the time their "true sex" was revealed, thus stymieing their marriage plans. Such was the case with Milton Matson of San Francisco, who was arrested at the home of his fiancée in 1895.[43] Ellis Glenn was engaged to Ella Duke of Hillsboro, Illinois, when a series of events led to his arrest and revelation of his "true sex" in 1899.[44] Eugene De Forest was engaged to be married for a second time when he was arrested in 1911 in Los Angeles, the city where he had an established career.[45]

The cumulative weight of these examples suggests the importance that the legal institution of marriage played in the minds of many trans men in late nineteenth and early twentieth centuries, especially those who wanted to continue to enjoy the benefits of community membership within the place they had made their home. Given that marriage was closely associated with respectability in this period, trans men like Ralph Kerwineo were likely aware of the fact that if they desired to maintain long-term relationships with women while remaining in their community, then marriage was an important step. This step not only conferred trans men the respectability associated with the social role of "husband," it also affirmed their male identities. Indeed, while the *act* of getting married placed the identities of trans men under intense scrutiny—with Ralph Kerwineo even subjecting himself to a blood test—the state of *being* married helped to bolster their claims to masculinity, and perhaps provided the hope that their male identities would be taken for granted moving forward. Whatever the reason, it is clear that Kerwineo did not take the decision lightly, as he knew it was a risky move, and therefore he must have felt that the benefits of legal marriage outweighed the potential consequences.

"Wife Was Most Surprised of All"

Marriage laws have been one of the central ways states have regulated proper gender behavior and enforced normative gender expectations. One of the expectations of husbands has been that they provide financially for their families. The state has a vested interest in maintaining this formulation, lest women and children become a financial burden on public resources (dependence, of course, being women's "natural" state, according to the early twentieth-century logic). In 1913 the state of Washington passed a law to ensure that men fulfill their role as providers, popularly known as the "Lazy Husband Law." The edict was credited to Justice of the Peace Fred C. Brown, who in August 1913 published a nationally syndicated editorial about the law. He wrote, "The law means the passing of the old theory of criminal punishment—punishing the individual for the evil deeds committed—and in its place it provides for the criminal law of the future. It individualizes the offender so that the court can render judgment which will make the person charged with crime a better citizen and one that will provide for his family in the future."[46] Justice of the Peace Brown explains how he sees the role of the court as the arbiter of proper behavior within marriages, and furthermore, he makes a clear link between citizenship and husbandry. He went on to explain precisely how he imagined the law operating when neglected wives brought a case to the attention of the courts: "[The judge's] first duty should be to try to effect a reconciliation. He may allow the defendant his liberty with or without bond; if the defendant be found guilty, he may suspend judgment on condition that he support his family. Or the judge may send him to jail and order the county to place him at work on roads or other public improvements, and pay his family $1.50 a day."[47] In essence, the law provided judges with the option of sentencing "lazy husbands" to a term performing labor (often at a farm or, as Brown mentions here, on public improvements), during which time the neglected wife and family would receive daily remittances. Within weeks of the law's passage Washington courts received hundreds of petitions, and by the end of 1913 the state had paid out nearly $3,000 to wives and families whose husbands had been found to be "lazy."[48]

Of course, it is unlikely that Justice of the Peace Brown, or any other Washington lawmaker, anticipated that their law would be used to regulate the anatomical sex of Washington husbands—instead, they were hoping to police proper gendered behavior. However, in February 1916 a judge in Seattle faced precisely that situation. That winter, a Seattle charity noted the destitute conditions of Mrs. Margaret Gaffney and her three children, and learned that her husband, Robert, had abandoned the family some two months before. The charity filed a "lazy husband" charge against the husband, and a warrant went out for his arrest. Robert Gaffney was eventually brought before a judge; he was found guilty for failing to support his family and sentenced to a term in the prison stockade. However, after learning of his sentence, Robert appealed, and revealed to the court that he was not a cisgender man and therefore he could not be expected to fulfill the role of "husband."[49] Presented with this new information, the justice of the peace Otis Brinkler was forced to grapple with a set of unexpected issues. If Robert lacked the anatomical assets medically associated with maleness, was he still legally liable for spousal support of his wife? Furthermore, did his anatomy render his marriage any less legal?

Justice Brinkler apparently believed that Gaffney's anatomy voided his marriage, based on the logic that two women could not, by law, marry. If their marriage was no longer valid, then Gaffney could not be expected to fulfill the role of husband, nor be prosecuted under the Lazy Husband Law. However, what then should be Gaffney's fate? Gaffney did not deny that he had abandoned his wife, and his admission of his "true sex" also brought up the possibility of prosecution under perjury laws, as he had falsified information on his marriage license. Luckily for Robert, neither the state of Washington nor the city of Seattle had a law on the books that made cross-dressing illegal, and thus the judge did not have the option of prosecuting Robert for his queer embodiment. According to an AP wire, "The prosecuting attorney ruled that she could not be prosecuted for wearing men's clothing, and that as she is not in law the husband of the woman she married she could not be prosecuted for failure to support her supposed wife."[50] This report also suggested that when Robert was released from the county jail he "wore woman's attire and said she would not masquerade as a man again."[51]

The story was published in newspapers across the country, though it did not gain the same sort of widespread attention that many of the other cases discussed in this book did. Gaffney's story appeared almost exclusively in newspapers from Oregon, Washington, and Idaho—each states in which Gaffney had lived at some point. However, one widely circulating story appeared in newspapers throughout the nation, alongside a single-frame cartoon image of a courtroom. In the cartoon Robert was depicted with his back to the viewer, facing a very shocked Margaret.

Wife Was Most Surprised of All.

Figure 5.1. Cartoon depicting the courtroom scene of Robert and Margaret Gaffney, 1916. Image from Ironton, Missouri's *Iron County Record*.

The caption reads, "Wife Was Most Surprised of All." This image captures the central message of much of the national coverage of the case: that the most remarkable aspect of the story was that the wife had been fooled for so long, or that Robert's " 'wife' was the most surprised person of all."[52]

One effect the focus on Margaret Gaffney's "surprise" had was that it rendered the marriage sexually innocent. Journalists bolstered this representation by highlighting Robert Gaffney's explanations for the marriage, quoting him as saying that he "always had a good heart and wanted to give Margaret a home." This self-sacrificing nature was foreshadowed earlier in the article, wherein Robert told San Jose's *Daily News*, "I was ready to take off men's clothes three years ago . . . the only reason I did not was to save Margaret . . . from embarrassment."[53] It appears as though the journalists covering the case *also* wanted to protect Margaret from embarrassment, as records indicate that during the Gaffney's marriage she conceived and gave birth to a child, Mildred. More than likely this child was the result of an extramarital affair, and yet journalists chose to ignore the facts surrounding Mildred's conception.[54] With the exclusion of this detail they were able to portray Margaret as a completely innocent victim; not only had she been abandoned by her husband, but she was also misled in fundamental ways by that same husband.

Thus, in the national press, both Robert and Margaret were portrayed rather sympathetically; although the reason behind Robert's queer embodiment is not provided in the text, his laudable motivation behind his marriage is. Lest the reader interpret this article as an indication that women were fully capable of handling the hard work of men's labor, however, it also included the apocryphal detail that the reason Robert revealed his "true sex" was that he feared his sentence of hard labor. Papers reported, "When she was ordered to the stockades, she pleaded that she be given another form of punishment, declaring that the work would be too hard for her. It was then that she admitted she was a woman."[55] This rationale had the dual effect of neutralizing the threat posed by Gaffney (he couldn't *really* act like a man) and normalizing his gender deviance (he was physically weak, like all biological women).

However short Robert Gaffney's tenure in the public eye was, it nonetheless reveals a great deal about the state of marriage and perceptions of gender in the early twentieth century. In particular, Gaffney's story, and the stories of the other individuals involved in his life, shows that people's married lives were often messy and rarely lived up to the idealized image of the institution of marriage. Laws like Washington's "lazy husband" statute were deemed necessary because, all too often, marriages did not provide the stability they were purported to, nor did they discipline the behavior of those involved. Husbands abandoned their families, wives cheated on their husbands, and trans men married women, all despite the growing legal matrix evolving around them.

This was particularly true for individuals in the working class (like Gaffney's bride). Margaret Hart was born in Montana in 1886, the only child of immigrant parents. Her father, Nicholas Jonas, was born in France and her mother, Marianne Sykke, was born in Denmark. The pair married in Silver Bow, Montana, in October 1884, and two years later Margaret Christine was born. The trio did not stay together for long, as by 1900 Nicholas was living in Oregon, and two years after that Margaret (then just sixteen, with a fourth-grade education) was living as a married woman in Michigan.[56] She and her husband, Clem Hart, divorced four years later in 1906, but then both moved to Washington State.[57] The pair continued to be connected, despite their divorce, and in 1908 Margaret gave birth to a son, James Hart.[58] Margaret would have another son, Edward Hart, in 1910. Thus, when Robert Gaffney and Margaret met in 1910 or 1911 she may well have been pregnant with Edward.[59] Margaret and Robert legally married on September 25, 1911, and Margaret did, indeed have a third child during that marriage—a daughter, Mildred, born in 1915.[60] She was given the last name Hart, suggesting that she was the child of Margaret's first husband. Thus Margaret was a woman with a somewhat checkered romantic past, who met Robert Gaffney around the time she had been abandoned by her former husband while pregnant with their second child. This information provides important context for Gaffney's explanation that he married Margaret because he "wanted to give her a home" and that he hoped to "save her from embarrassment."[61]

Perhaps marrying Margaret and supporting her children was a means through which Robert could express his masculinity. Given that women's expected state was that of dependence in the early twentieth century, and men's expected state was that of a provider, supporting a family was one of the primary means through which men fulfilled social expectations for what it meant to be a "proper" man. Perhaps this is what motivated the marriage, or maybe he did (as he would later tell the *Tacoma Times*) truly take pity on Margaret and want to help her and her children. Of course, it is also possible that the two were involved in a romantic relationship that went sour. Indeed, if this is the case, then perhaps Margaret filed charged against Robert as a "lazy husband" to enact revenge, knowing full well that incarceration of her former husband would likely reveal his "true sex," thus shattering the life in Seattle he had created for himself.

It is unfortunately impossible to know the motivations behind the Gaffney's marriage, or to know precisely how much Margaret knew about Robert's identity and biology. What is recoverable, however, is the public reaction to the marriage and subsequent scandal. The response in the press (both local and national) reveals a great deal about public investments in the institution of marriage as well as normative investment in gender roles. Most notable, of course, is the fact that legally the charge of being a "lazy husband" was worse than falsifying an identity on a marriage license or assuming a false identity (in Robert's case, living as a man while inhabiting a body the state perceived as female). Indeed, Gaffney's case reveals how "lazy husbands" were seen as a threat to the social order in ways that trans husbands were not. While the actions of a "lazy husband" in failing to support his family were seen by the law in Washington as punishable by a sentence to the stockades or a term of labor at a farm, living as a man when one lacked the anatomy generally believed to be required for masculinity was not yet a crime. Perhaps this was because husbands abandoning their families and leaving their wives and children was an identifiable social problem, one that placed a visible burden on state government and/or local charities. The Washington press bemoaned both the failures of "lazy husbands" and the perception that the Lazy Husband Law was not being utilized by government officials as efficiently as it could with dramatic headlines like "Babies Starve Because Commission Doesn't Act."[62] On the other hand, officials in Washington had not yet encountered enough examples of trans men (or trans husbands) to perceive them as a threat to the social order, as evidenced by the lenient treatment Gaffney received after he revealed his "true sex."

This lack of anxiety around trans husbands is evident not only in the courtroom where Gaffney was released without charge, but it is also evident in the way Gaffney's story was told in newspapers throughout the nation. Unlike Ralph Kerwineo's story, which spread like wildfire because it spoke to anxieties around racial purity and eugenic marriages, Gaffney's story didn't hit the same nerve, in part because it didn't fit within established plotlines of deviant and threatening behavior. And, of course, he failed to fit the description of a threat to the public because his whiteness carried with it the presumption of innocence. As such, Gaffney's story appeared mostly in papers in the Pacific Northwest. When Gaffney's story did appear outside that tristate area, it did so as a mere blip on the radar, not a feature story set under a splashy, attention-grabbing headline. When the story appeared in the *New York Times*, for example, it did so on page 18. Even the most colorful coverage was still relatively tame, highlighting Margaret Gaffney's surprise at her husband's "true sex," but also providing a reasonable explanation for Robert's time in men's clothing.[63]

Perhaps the national coverage of Robert Gaffney's story was characterized as unremarkable because that's how Americans in 1916 viewed stories of trans men: unremarkable and relatively commonplace. While in the Pacific Northwest Gaffney's story attracted widespread attention because it was related to both local interest and the recently passed and much-discussed Lazy Husband Law, nationally the story lacked the same appeal. The story was both too mundane and too morally ambiguous to relate as a morality tale; Margaret Gaffney's identity as a previously married woman with three children made her claims that she didn't know her husband's "true sex" dubious, and the fact that she gave birth to a child during her five-year marriage to Gaffney carried with it the suggestion that she was not entirely innocent herself. Thus the story lacked a clear victim in the same way that Ralph Kerwineo's story had had, and so the national press rarely, if ever, made specific reference to Gaffney's wife.

"Ranch Tomboy in Legal Mess"

Of course, the press's response to trans men and their marriages was deeply dependent on historical context, and as time marched on into the 1920s things began to change. In fact, by 1929 the structure of the newspaper industry has transformed dramatically from the 1870s when Joseph Lobdell's story circulated. More specifically, increasing consolidation and standardization marked the newspaper industry of the 1920s. Newspaper magnates like E. W. Scripps and William Randolph Hearst created extensive chains of newspapers, and newspapers nationwide became increasingly dependent on syndicated news services.[64] In this climate, small, independently owned daily newspapers found it increasingly difficult to compete, and by 1936 the number of daily newspapers had fallen almost 17 percent from its peak in 1910—despite the fact that the U.S. population had grown dramatically in that time.[65] In this context, syndicated wire services became increasingly powerful and were providing newspapers with prepackaged news stories that left little room for local editors to shape the presentation.

In the early twentieth century, the two main wire services were the Associated Press and the United Press. The Scripps-McRae Press Association founded the UP in 1907, which by 1929 was the AP's main competitor, serving over 950 newspapers nationwide. Because the Associated Press operated as an exclusive wire franchise, the United Press had to offer more enticing items than its competitor, and thus UP wire dispatches tended to be a bit more "colorful" than those from the AP. Indeed, in 1912, the executive head of the United Press called for "brilliancy in the narration of the day's events . . . the interpolation in a news story of the individual point of view of the reporter."[66] The impact of these changes can clearly be seen in the newspaper coverage of trans men in the late 1920s.

One such example is the case of Kenneth Lisonbee, a trans man who was born Katherine Rowena Wing in Springville, Utah, in 1904. The grandchild of Mormon pioneer Joseph Smith Wing, his childhood was spent on his family's wheat ranch in central Utah.[67] By 1925 Kenneth was living as a man (going by the name of Kenneth Wing) in Los Angeles and training to be a barber.[68] Around this time Kenneth began dating a young woman named Eileen Garnett, and the pair married in 1927.[69] This marriage was short-lived, however, and Kenneth would later report that it was broken up when Garnett's family moved in with the newlyweds and discovered his "true sex."[70] After his marriage broke up, Kenneth began going by the name of Kenneth Lisonbee, perhaps to avoid legal persecution.[71] Sometime in mid-1928 Lisonbee returned to Utah

Figure 5.2. Kenneth Lisonbee and Stella Harper, 1929. Photo from author's personal collection.

for a visit, during which he became reacquainted with Stella Harper, a childhood friend. Harper accompanied Lisonbee when he returned to Los Angeles in October 1928, and the pair moved into an apartment at 203 West Garvey Avenue.[72] While this arrangement seemed to suit Lisonbee and Harper quite well, some in the neighborhood were suspicious of the couple, and on January 10, 1929, they were taken into police custody and Lisonbee's "true sex" was revealed.[73]

The revelation of Lisonbee's "true sex" was reported in newspapers nationwide—from Fresno, California, to Baltimore, Maryland—though this coverage was by no means uniform. Thus, even during a period wherein the press was consolidating dramatically, there were still multiple representations and interpretations of queer embodiment circulating in the nation's newspapers. However, one thing that remained consistent was that Lisonbee's acceptability or deviance was consistently defined against the characteristics of proper citizenship. Indeed, when Lisonbee's queer body was cast as acceptable, it was because his body was produced as emblematic of his identity as a proper citizen. On the other hand, in cases where it was cast as pathological, it was because his body was produced as emblematic of his identity as an individual who desired to live outside the boundaries of normative citizenship—particularly heterosexual,[74] monogamous marriage.

The Los Angeles in which Lisonbee lived was a dynamic and growing city, but it was much smaller than the sprawling metropolis we know today. The 1920s were a period of rapid growth for the city: its population more than doubled between 1920 and 1930 (reaching 1.2 million), and it moved up from being the tenth biggest city in the nation to the fifth.[75] And although this was a time of rapid consolidation within the newspaper industry, Los Angeles maintained a diverse field of local newspapers, including the *Los Angles Evening Herald*, the *Los Angeles Examiner* (both owned by William Randolph Hearst, and representing the most popular evening and morning papers, respectively), and Harry Chandler's *Los Angeles Times*.[76] Each of these dailies covered Lisonbee's story, but they did so in distinct ways. As will be discussed, the distinctions in the local coverage show that by 1929 the connection between queer embodiment and pathology that the national press had been articulating for decades was beginning to percolate down to the local level. However, the discourse of pathology was not yet hegemonic, and there still was room on the local scale for positive representations of non-binary gender expression—even if such stories involved marriage.

Hearst's *Examiner* was known for its splashy headlines and salacious stories of sex and betrayal, and thus it would seem as though Lisonbee's story would be particularly attractive to the *Examiner* editors. However, the paper published relatively scant coverage of the case, and the one article that did appear was hidden on page 5, without the banner headline customarily used to attract attention to the paper's more scandalous stories. The brief account focused on Lisonbee's arrest, and thereby highlighted his violation of the law. Although the precise reason for the police's initial interest in Lisonbee was unclear, the *Examiner* nonetheless produced his arrest as serving the social good because it led to the realization that he had an outstanding warrant for falsifying information on a 1927 marriage license. Thus it didn't actually matter *why* he was arrested because it was ultimately justified by the discovery that Lisonbee had previously committed perjury while attempting to marry Eileen Garnett.[77] This had the effect of both naturalizing Lisonbee's deviance and dramatizing his violation of the social order by focusing on his illegal 1927 marriage. In its description of Lisonbee's marriage to Garnett, the *Examiner* reported that Lisonbee had "vanished" once Garnett's parents discovered Lisonbee's "true sex," ostensibly leaving his bride heartbroken and initiating a two-year manhunt by Santa Ana authorities. Juxtaposed against the presumably heartbroken Garnett, it would seem that Lisonbee would be an easy figure to scandalize, and yet the tone of the *Examiner*'s coverage of Lisonbee's story was relatively tame compared to sensationalism generally associated with Hearst papers. The *Examiner*'s coverage ended there, and, reminiscent of the *Washington Post*'s depiction of Ralph Kerwineo discussed in the previous chapter, the paper published no follow-up interview with the police or Lisonbee himself, thus freezing its depiction of Lisonbee as a deceitful and pathological individual worthy of arrest.

The depiction of Lisonbee in the *Los Angeles Times*, on the other hand, could not have been more different. For example, the second *Times* article on Lisonbee had the innocent-sounding headline "Ranch Tomboy in Legal Mess," and it opened as follows: "She's just a tomboy ranch girl grown up and as soon as she can settle with the law about her escapade in impersonating a man and marrying another girl she is going straight back to her 200-acre wheat ranch at Springville, Utah, where the neighbors are used to seeing her in masculine attire and think nothing of it. No more adventuring about the world, but a railroad ticket straight home to dad, who always said she was the best boy he ever had."[78] In this excerpt, the *Times* produced Lisonbee's queer body through wholesome bucolic scenes and images of familial devotion, and thereby submerged any suggestion of same-sex desire by highlighting his contribution to the agricultural economy—thus underlining his identity as a productive citizen. The rural West serves the same legitimating function as it did in the stories surrounding Joseph Monahan discussed in chapter 2; Lisonbee had gotten off track as a result of city life, but he could redeem himself by returning to the hardworking ranching life of his youth in Utah.[79]

The *Times* also provided Lisonbee with multiple opportunities to explain his queer embodiment—opportunities Lisonbee utilized to narrate his seemingly strange choices through the logics of patriarchy and heteronormativity. For example, in explaining why he began dressing as a man, he told the paper, "I've always worn boy's clothes, helping my father on the ranch. My older sisters are all married. They were much older than I and so it was up to me to help my dad when the others left home. That's how I got the habit."[80] Lisonbee provides a logic for his queer embodiment that links it not only to the rapidly disappearing agrarian economy but to his familial devotion. In this story Lisonbee is as an unselfish family member who nobly stepped up to assist his father once his older siblings left the family home. While this story allowed Lisonbee to render his seemingly strange embodiment more relatable to the public, it was not entirely accurate: while Lisonbee did grow up on a wheat ranch in Springville, Utah, he had many siblings, including three brothers, one of whom was five years his junior.[81] However, if Lisonbee had admitted this to the *Los Angeles Times*, it would have perhaps seemed like more of a stretch for the paper to suggest that his father "always said she was the best boy he ever had." Thus Lisonbee likely utilized this deliberate omission to help produce his queer body as emblematic of his familial devotion and agrarian roots, which he likely expected would garner sympathy from law officials and the reading public. This explanation also established Lisonbee's respect for family, defined as a heterosexual couple and their children, which helped to establish a positive lens through which readers might understand his marriage to Eileen Garnett. In essence, he, with the aid of sympathetic journalists at the *Times*, established himself as a self-sacrificing family member, not a sexual deviant who represented a threat to the social order.

Indeed, Lisonbee went on to explain that his marriage to Eileen Garnett had been the result of a misunderstanding and emblematic of his caring nature. He told the *Times* that upon moving to Los Angeles he realized that male barbers could earn more money, and thus he began posing as a man in order to be more financially secure. Shortly thereafter he met Eileen Garnett; after a few months he discovered that she had fallen in love with him. At this point Lisonbee explained to the *Times*, "I told her at once that I was a girl, but she said I had broken her heart and that she would commit suicide . . . finally she told me that she only wanted to get away from her relatives and wanted me to marry her. I consented and we were married in Santa Ana by Justice of the Peace Morrison."[82] In this quote Lisonbee's marriage is cast as a noble deed, performed only to save the life of an innocent young girl. The sexual normativity of both parties is thus secured as Lisonbee did not intentionally set out to woo Garnett, and Garnett's desire to marry Lisonbee was attributed not to her emotional attachment to Lisonbee but rather to her desire to gain freedom from her family. Additionally, it is worth noting that Lisonbee went out of his way to mention the person who married the couple, and to identify his position as a justice of peace. This detail established that a secular authority, not a member of the clergy, conducted the marriage ceremony. Thus the couple was not guilty of deceiving church officials, an action that some readers might have taken offense at, even if the marriage was devoid of sexual immorality.

Throughout the *Los Angeles Times* coverage Lisonbee is portrayed as a sympathetic character whose actions were perfectly understandable and perhaps even laudable. Whereas the *Examiner* claimed that Lisonbee "vanished" once Garnett's family discovered his "true sex," Lisonbee provided an alternative narrative in the *Times*. Herein, it was reported that the revelation of Lisonbee's female body to Garnett's family resulted in a "general family row . . . in which it was agreed that Miss Wing should leave at once."[83] Thus Lisonbee did not "vanish" out of selfishness, nor did he abandon his heartbroken wife; rather he was forced to leave by Garnett's parents. Expelled from his martial home, Lisonbee returned to his family's home in Utah. There he became reacquainted with Stella Harper, a woman he had known since childhood. Harper "wanted to see a bit of the world," and so she accompanied Lisonbee when he returned to California. According to the *Los Angeles Times*, this decision required that the pair pose as man and wife: "Since Miss Wing had been wearing masculine attire continuously for four years, it was necessary that Miss Harper pose as her wife. Miss Wing took the name of Kenneth Lisonbee and practiced her barber profession to support herself and her girl friend."[84] In this quote the paper's support for Lisonbee's queer embodiment is laid bare; by articulating his queer embodiment through the tropes of productive citizenship, patriarchy, and heteronormativity, Lisonbee had so convinced the *Los Angeles Times* editors of his acceptability that they characterized his living arrangement with Harper as "necessary."

Whereas the *Los Angeles Examiner* froze its coverage of Lisonbee's story at the moment of his arrest, the *Los Angeles Times* and the *Evening Herald* both followed the story to its conclusion. On January 15, 1929, both papers published quotes from district attorney Z. B. West, the judicial official who ultimately decided the fate of Lisonbee's legal charges. Reminiscent of Judge Page's estimation of Ralph Kerwineo in his Milwaukee courtroom fifteen years earlier, West told both papers that Lisonbee "impressed me as sensible, serious, and sincere, and except for the one matrimonial slip, I cannot see that she has done anything particularly out of the way."[85] West's decision was based in part on his evaluation that Lisonbee "had no motive in donning masculine attire other than that she stated: to make a better success of the barber business." Had West suspected that Lisonbee's queer embodiment been motivated by same-sex desire, perhaps he would have not been so forgiving. However, because Lisonbee articulated his queer embodiment through the tropes of proper citizenship, West dubbed him as "sincere" and categorized his marriage to another woman as merely a "matrimonial slip," rather than a serious offense. Indeed, West depicted Lisonbee's marriage to Eileen Garnett in innocuous terms because he viewed it as innocent. He explained, "Although she committed *technical perjury* by misrepresenting the age of Eileen Garnett, 16, when she married her here, Miss Wing was not otherwise guilty of a criminal offense, the district attorney said. The statutes apply only where someone is damaged, he added, and nobody was harmed by Miss Wing when she donned male attire, married, and masqueraded as a man."[86] So, in the mind of District Attorney West, the offense the Lisonbee committed was not even related to his nonbinary gender expression; rather, it was related to the misrepresentation of Garnett's age on the marriage license. Lisonbee forging his name and sex was not perjury, according to West, and furthermore caused no harm or damage.

West's comments were expanded in the *Los Angeles Times*, where he explicitly addressed the politics of style. He explained, "I am of the same mind as the Los Angeles newspaper columnist who admitted that, with the way the Hollywood girls dress . . . there seems to be no standard attire for either men or women these days. No one now can say that there is such a thing as masculine attire or feminine dress."[87] Thus Lisonbee's queer body was produced as emblematic of American freedom and modernity, and thereby supported by District Attorney West as Lisonbee had proven himself to be "sensible, serious, and sincere."[88] In these ways, rather than being described as a body in need of reform, Lisonbee's queer body was portrayed as an expression of a uniquely American identity. Significantly, positive depictions of Lisonbee's queer body were not unique to the *Los Angeles Times*; indeed, they were a common element in the narratives produced by many newspapers nationwide.

Just as in the local press, national narratives of Lisonbee's story varied. However, unlike many of the cases discussed in previous chapters, it is possible to identify three distinct versions of Lisonbee's story that circulated nationally, each one served up by a different syndicated news service—a clear indication of the impact of the industry's consolidation. For example, one of the national narratives of Lisonbee's story can be attributed to the United Press wire service. In the case of Lisonbee, the United Press reporter interpreted his queer body as emblematic of his identity as an exceptional citizen and produced wire dispatches that established as much.

The UP account, which appeared in numerous newspapers nationwide, including New York's *Daily News* and Denver's *Rocky Mountain News*, characterized Lisonbee as "a suave, trouser-clad, white-aproned barber who discussed sports, politics and business with customers in a straight-forward masculine voice."[89] Here, Lisonbee's queer body was attributed to his drive to be economically productive; as had been in the case in the *Los Angeles Times*, his marriage to Eileen Garnett was only entered into because, upon learning Lisonbee's "true sex," Garnett insisted that he had "broken her heart and threatened to commit suicide."[90] Lisonbee's living arrangement with Stella Harper was similarly rendered harmless because it was cast as emanating from a lifelong friendship that had began "in the range country around Tintic, Utah," where the pair "rode the hills together in masculine astride cow points" on "her father's ranch."[91] No hint of sexual deviance was given, and Lisonbee's innocence was confirmed by the last line of the dispatch, which asserted that "authorities said they probably would take no action against the girls."[92]

While the narrative produced by the United Press was perhaps the most positive version that appeared on the national scale, it was by no means the most popular. Indeed, a much more common version was based on wire dispatches from the Associated Press, wherein Lisonbee's queer embodiment circulated as an indication of his desire to attain citizenship rights that were not rightfully his—specifically marriage. Newspapers such as the *Salt Lake Tribune*, the *Fresno Bee*, and the *Galveston Daily News* cast Lisonbee's queer embodiment as a danger to the institution of marriage because he had successfully wooed two women (Eileen Garnett and Stella Harper). This threat was dramatized by the revelation that Lisonbee had legally married Garnett and subsequently courted Harper, allegedly leading to an arrest on a Mann Act charge.[93]

Newspaper readers in 1929 likely would have understood the reference to the Mann Act as a suggestion of sexual impropriety. The Mann Act was in some ways the culmination of the efforts of Progressive reformers who sought to regulate extramarital sexual relations (and who were particularly concerned with prostitution, or "white slavery" as it was termed at the time). As John D'Emilio and Estelle Freedman explain, "The new drive against prostitution first surfaced in the form of a white slavery panic. Between 1908 and 1914, purity crusaders and others published dozens of sensationalistic tracts alleging a widespread traffic in women that sold young girls into virtual slavery. Replete with case histories, vivid illustrations, and strong advice to parents, these books described the subterfuges used by panderers to lure innocent victims to their fate."[94] The Mann Act, passed in 1910, made it illegal to "knowingly transport . . . any individual in interstate or foreign commerce, or in any Territory or Possession of the United States, with intent that such individual engage in prostitution, or in any sexual activity for which any person can be charged with a criminal offense."[95] The Justice Department obtained close to 2,200 convictions under the Mann Act in the eight years after its passage, and these arrests and convictions often attracted widespread attention in newspapers.[96] Thus the erroneous suggestion that Lisonbee was arrested in Los Angeles on a Mann Act charge for trafficking Stella Harper across state lines suggested to readers that their relationship was not the innocent partnership of two adventurous girls (as it had been depicted in the *Los Angeles Times* and United Press accounts), but rather a nefarious connection that threatened the sanctity of marriage. Indeed, the Mann Act was designed as a piece of legislation (like Wisconsin's Eugenic Marriage Law and Washington's Lazy Husband Law) that would regulate and protect marriage. In the AP account, Lisonbee's own voice was rarely present, and the only details provided were those that highlighted his violation of state and federal law. This framing suggested to readers that Lisonbee should be understood as a danger to the nation because he threated to destabilize marriages.

Although many newspapers around the nation published the AP newswire on Lisonbee's story, it was not the most widespread version to appear. In fact, reflecting the growing influence of syndicated features services, the most common way readers outside of Los Angeles encountered Lisonbee's story was not through a newspaper column but rather a photograph and caption syndicated by the Newspaper Enterprise Association. The NEA was a wire service owned by the Scripps-McRae Press Association that provided news features, comics, and photographs to hundreds of newspapers across the country.[97] The content was explicitly designed for small newspapers to reprint without editing, and thus the narratives circulated by the NEA were meant to appeal to the widest possible audience. Often this meant condensing meaning and appealing to exclusionary logics of social membership.[98]

This tendency can clearly be seen within the NEA's narration of Lisonbee's story. The only details that are produced as relevant are those that outline Lisonbee's violation of public space. As such, Lisonbee was treated as an idle curiosity, not an esteemed citizen. Appearing in at least fifteen newspapers nationwide, including Wisconsin's *Sheboygan Journal* and Missouri's *Jefferson City Post-Tribune*, the NEA's photo and caption distilled Lisonbee and Harper's story to one of adventure and deceit. The caption read, "For four years Catherine Wing and Stella Harper of Mammoth, Utah, successfully toured the United States, posing as man and wife, a ruse they adopted

GIRLS TRAVEL AS MAN AND WIFE

For four years Catherine Wing and Stella Harper of Mammoth, Utah, successfully toured the United States, posing as man and wife, a ruse they adopted when they set out as adventurers and found that they fared beter thus than as girl chums. Catherine, left, worked as a barber. Los Angeles authorities discovered their secret when they sought to lodge a suspicion of Mann act charges against them.

Figure 5.3. Photo and caption featuring Kenneth Lisonbee and Stella Harper, as they appeared in newspapers nationwide, distributed by the Newspaper Enterprise Association. Image reproduced with permission from Texas's *Borger News-Herald*.

when they set out as adventurers and found that they fared better thus than as girl chums. Catherine, left, worked as a barber. Los Angeles authorities discovered their secret when they sought to lodge a suspicion of Mann act charges against them."[99] Whereas in the *Los Angeles Times* Lisonbee explained his queer embodiment as motivated first by his desire to help his father on the family ranch and then by his drive to be economically productive, in the above caption Lisonbee's queer embodiment is explained as merely the means that facilitated the travel of two "adventurers." Lisonbee and Harper here appear as irresponsible and deceitful, eschewing family responsibilities and operating wholly outside the traditional family in the name of "adventure." Indeed, this framing is much different from the framing within the United Press account, where Lisonbee's queer embodiment was produced as facilitating the continuation of an innocent relationship that had originated on Lisonbee's "father's ranch." In contrast, the NEA narrative situated Lisonbee's queer embodiment as enabling the pair's departure from their familial homes. Indeed, they are situated as operating wholly outside of marriage, seemingly making a mockery of the institution.

The impropriety of their actions is again signaled in their photograph, wherein the faces of Lisonbee and Wing were cropped against a plain backdrop, creating an image reminiscent of a mug shot. This image was a modified version of a photograph published in the *Los Angeles Times* on January 12, 1929. The original version was a full-length image of Lisonbee standing next to a sitting Harper, who was shown holding Lisonbee's arm. The removal of the affectionate gesture between the pair had the effect of occluding the suggestion of same-sex desire, and yet it also made the pair seem more sinister. Indeed, when the image was originally published in the *Los Angeles Times*, it was accompanied by not only a caption but also a lengthy article in which the upright character of Lisonbee was established. The supportive stance of Lisonbee in the photograph thus seemed to verify the jail matron's assertion that Lisonbee's "attitude is that of the male protector toward the bewildered younger girl arrested with her. She watches over Miss Harper and looks after her wants solicitously."[100] Thus the photographic representation of Lisonbee in the *Times* helped to portray him as an exceptional citizen—an individual who was willing to sacrifice for his family, provide both emotional and financial support for the women in his life, and submit to the patriarchal authority of his father and, after arrest, the state. While the suggestion of same-sex intimacy is present, Lisonbee's positive characteristics were apparently enough to render them irrelevant to both the *Los Angeles Times* and Los Angeles District Attorney West.

In contrast, the NEA's "Girls Travel as Man and Life" photograph conveyed a much different message. Lisonbee and Harper were both presented as menaces to society because they were operating outside a heteronormative family unit, all the while ignoring the responsibilities of economic productivity. In this way they were rendered queer because they did not fulfill the expectations for proper behavior by young women, and instead pursued a life of selfish "adventures." As such, Lisonbee and Harper were produced in similar terms to the "hobos" and "tramps" who were becoming increasingly familiar figures within the mass-circulation press in the early twentieth century, and who, as Todd DePastino has argued, evoked public concern because they rejected the trappings of domestic life, home ownership, and the bosses' rule.[101] Significantly, as Margot Canaday has argued, "since at least the turn of the century, homosexuality was considered a defining characteristic of vagrants, tramps, and hoboes who 'promenade[d] unashamed on the public highways,' preferring 'rough-hewn male camaraderie' over a 'normal' life of work and family."[102] Although public conceptions of sexual deviance within hobo and vagrant communities were based largely in the assumption that such spaces were exclusively male, it seems likely that some readers would have transported these conceptions into their reading of Lisonbee and Harper's story as produced by the NEA.

On the whole, Kenneth Lisonbee's story was narrated in the press in contradictory ways. While local newspapers generally characterized Lisonbee's queer embodiment as emblematic of his identity as an exceptional citizen, this portrayal did not go uncontested. On the national scale Lisonbee's story similarly lacked coherence; while the NEA produced Lisonbee and Harper as pathological because their lives appeared to be organized outside of heteronormative family values, the UP wire dispatches celebrated Lisonbee's queer embodiment as emblematic of his identity as an exceptional citizen. However, throughout Lisonbee and Harper's time in the media spotlight, the connections among cross-dressing, same-sex love, and sexual deviance appeared to be rather loose. Nowhere were there any references to sexological theories of sexual inversion. Rather, the acceptability of Lisonbee's queer body was regulated just as the acceptability of trans men since the 1870s had—it relied on his performed and professed allegiance to normative male citizenship. In the positive descriptions of Lisonbee, newspapers made clear that he did not represent a threat to marriage or the public and that he should be understood instead as unexceptional—behaving not as a deviant but rather as every husband and son should.

Conclusion

Trans men pursued marriage consistently from the 1870s to the 1920s. It was a constant component of many of their lives, as it conferred respectability and allowed for them to legally claim male identities. However, marriage is also a central institution in American public life, and it became an increasingly contested one in these decades, with individual states and the federal government passing legislation that restricted access to the institution and/or regulated behavior once granted access to the institution. Given this increased anxiety around protecting the institution, one would expect that as time marched on, the response to trans husbands would become increasingly negative. And indeed, in this chapter, one thing that *is* evident is a growing trend toward pathology within the national mass-circulation press.

Increasingly, in the first decades of the twentieth century, national newspapers *could* pick up the story of a trans husband and utilize it to call for more eugenic marriage laws or to bemoan the practice of "white slavery." Indeed, such stories could be easily mobilized as morality tales because of the importance U.S. society and government placed on marriage in the early twentieth century. Marriage is an institution that confers substantial benefits, which is why some trans men desire access to it, and also why that access could be seen as scandalous by those who wanted to maintain marriage as an exclusionary institution. However, the fact that not all stories of trans husbands were met with indignation on the national (or local) scale illustrates that trans men—and trans husbands specifically—were not yet seen as a threat to the social order. Whereas other social figures were seen as dangerous enough to ban from marriage (the feeble-minded, underage, diseased, etc.), even in the early twentieth century—the heyday of marriage legislation— banning same-sex marriage was seemingly not on any legislator's radar. As the cases of Kerwineo, Gaffney, and Lisonbee reveal, in order to be rendered pathological, the actions of trans husbands had to violate the social order in some way *beyond* their gender deviance—for example, defying a eugenic marriage law or the Mann Act. The act of marrying a woman was not enough in and of itself to garner sensational coverage; the story had to fit within an established plotline of deviance and social disturbance.

Nonetheless, this chapter has also highlighted the importance of analyzing both the national discourse and the events on the ground. If one only looked at the coverage of Kenneth Lisonbee as articulated by the NEA, or Ralph Kerwineo in the *New York World*, one would assume that their purported deviance was met with swift justice at the hands of local authorities. However, nothing could be further from the truth. Both men were released from police custody without charge, local authorities having decided that their actions did not warrant legal punishment. This illustrates that changes in national discourse (in this case, the growing pathology of trans men in the national press) do not dictate local responses. Even as the eugenics movement was growing in power, and even as sexological thinking was increasingly influencing representations of nonbinary gender presentations, trans men still could (and did) receive support from their communities. This dynamic remained in place for white trans men into at least the 1940s, as an addendum to Kenneth Lisonbee's story reveals.

Conclusion

Kenneth Lisonbee's Eureka

After Kenneth Lisonbee's arrest in 1929, the *Los Angeles Times* reported that he was planning on "no more adventuring about the world, but a railroad ticket straight home to dad, who always said she was the best boy he ever had."[1] True to his word, Lisonbee returned to his parent's house in the rural outskirts of Eureka, Utah, shortly after his release from police custody. However, he did not return alone; the 1930 federal census lists both "Katherine R. Wing" (Lisonbee's legal name) *and* Estella Harper (the woman with whom he had been living in Los Angeles) as residing with Lisonbee's parents outside Eureka. His parents were aware of what had transpired in Los Angeles, as the Eureka press had covered the story. Lisonbee's father, Joseph Smith Wing, was even interviewed about the case by their local paper, the *Eureka Reporter*. He cast Kenneth's Los Angeles arrest in the most positive light possible, telling the paper that "his daughter is now back at work in the barber shop . . . and that her business had nearly doubled because of the advertising she had recently received."[2] Perhaps this was the case—in fact, perhaps Lisonbee's business was increased by trans men in the Los Angeles area who read about the revelation of Lisonbee's "true sex" in the local papers and sought out his particular expertise. Regardless of the veracity of Wing's explanation, or of the identities of the purported new clientele that Lisonbee was attracting, Wing's explanation to the *Eureka Reporter* indicated support for his son and helped to explain Lisonbee's cross-dressing as harmless.

The 1930 federal census and other local records indicate that Joseph Wing's support for his son went beyond simply providing sound bites to the local paper, however. Although the census counted Lisonbee as female in 1930, it's clear that Lisonbee's parents to some extent tolerated his male gender expression—the local papers reported that his parents had been aware that Kenneth had been dressing as man prior to his 1929 arrest. And while it's unclear whether Lisonbee ever publicly (or privately) claimed the identity of Kenneth while in Utah, by the mid-1930s he was once again living full-time as a man, with his parent's knowledge. By that point he had again relocated to southern California and taken up work at the same barbershop in Wilmar where he had worked prior to his 1929 arrest. This time, however, he returned to California not only with Stella Harper in tow, but with his parents as well. The foursome (Lisonbee, his parents, and Stella Harper) settled together in Alhambra, California, a city in the San Gabriel Valley, eight miles from central Los Angeles.[3]

Lisonbee's decision to relocate his family back to the San Gabriel Valley and to take up work at the very same barbershop where he worked prior to his 1929 arrest is intriguing in what it suggests about queer history. The San Gabriel Valley is over six hundred miles from Lisonbee's hometown of Eureka, Utah, and so it certainly would have been cheaper for the family to relocate to a city closer to home, perhaps Salt Lake City, or even Denver. However, they chose instead to move to Alhambra, California. Perhaps the connections that Lisonbee had established in the 1920s were an asset to the family. Perhaps the family was forced to leave Utah for financial reasons, and the fact that Lisonbee had once been a successful barber in Wilmar was the family's last hope—the mid-1930s was the height of the Great Depression, after all, and many families were forced out of Utah and migrated to California in hopes of finding economic opportunity in this period.[4]

On the surface, Lisonbee's decision to move back to the area could be explained by the fact that in the 1920s and 1930s Los Angeles was home to a dynamic queer community of lesbians, gay men, and sexually flexible, gender-variant individuals. The center of this world was Hollywood, where clubs such as B.B.B.'s Cellar and the Bali nightclub featured male and female impersonators and other performers who sang songs full of gay double entendres.[5] And while it's possible Lisonbee and Harper dabbled in that world, perhaps occasionally traveling the fourteen miles west to Hollywood, it seems likely that if it was a priority for them to be a part of that queer community they would have chosen to relocate closer to those renowned clubs and bars. However, it appears as though they did not need to live within a queer subculture in order to enjoy a supportive community. Indeed, when Lisonbee was arrested once again in 1940, the newspaper coverage indicates that the San Gabriel Valley was, in fact, an accommodating place for Lisonbee to work and live.

Lisonbee's 1940 arrest was prompted by a traffic stop, which resulted in police questioning the name provided on his driver's license.[6] The arrest was reported in newspapers across the country, and surprisingly this coverage was uniformly sympathetic. Whereas there had been a thread within the coverage of Lisonbee's 1929 arrest that cast his actions as nefarious and dangerous, in 1940 the coverage was overwhelmingly positive. Perhaps this distinction is due to the fact that the newspapers in 1940 made no mention of Lisonbee's previous marriage or romantic connections with women. He was simply Kenneth Lisonbee, barber—not Kenneth Lisonbee, fraudulent husband or Mann Act violator. Indeed, one of the surprising elements of the coverage of Lisonbee's 1940 arrest was that no mention was made of his prior arrest. Instead, newspapers reported that Lisonbee had been dressing as a man for fifteen years, and that this was revealed only by his recent arrest.[7] Lisonbee is quoted in the Los Angeles Times as saying, "Everybody knew I was a woman, but nobody ever busied himself or herself about my affairs before."[8] The local press apparently assumed this was the truth and did not look into Lisonbee's police record.

The fact that local newspapers did not mention Lisonbee's 1929 arrest is more than simply surprising—it reveals a great deal about how the local press viewed Lisonbee and his potential criminality. This presumption of innocence shows that the local press did not assume criminality when they encountered a white trans man (perhaps particularly when that trans man had no visible connection to a woman). Instead of presuming him guilty, newspapers were willing to entertain the notion that Lisonbee was an honest and law-abiding citizen, aside from his sartorial choices. The local press treatment of Lisonbee, therefore, reveals that even by 1940 the gender variance of a white individual in and of itself was not enough to provoke the assumption of criminality or of sexual deviance.

The local papers' assumption of innocence was mirrored by the judicial officials who were charged with determining Lisonbee's fate. As with his 1929 arrest, Judge Newell was sympathetic. As the Los Angeles Times reported, "Police Judge Kenneth Newell consulted the statutes. He consulted the police officers . . . Nowhere in the former could he find anything condemning women's donning of men's garments ... Nowhere among the latter could he find anything indicating that the barber shop was in any way unconventional except in the proprietor's predilection for men's attire."[9] Just as with the many cases described in this book, Lisonbee's acceptability was tied to his conventionality; he was able to convince Judge Newell that he was an acceptable citizen because he lived up to the expectations of being a "good man," despite his anatomy.

On the day of his hearing, Lisonbee came to the courtroom well prepared to prove his positive contributions to the community. He brought with him "a paper signed by the businessmen in the district about her shop which said, 'We wish to testify that we have known Katherine Wing for some time and are glad to testify to her honesty, sympathy, and modesty, and are only too pleased to hereby attest that she is a credit to any vicinity.'"[10] Of course, this statement might have been fabricated, but its inclusion in the *Los Angeles Times* coverage of the case is significant in that it helped to produce Lisonbee as a productive member of society, despite his queer embodiment. Furthermore, it helped to explain and validate Judge Newell's decision to dismiss the charges against Lisonbee. Indeed, it produced Lisonbee as someone with a great deal of social capital—someone who had the respect and loyalty of his neighbors and business associates, despite the dissonance between his anatomical sex and gender presentation.

Perhaps these statements of Lisonbee's status as a productive citizen were particularly important to include in the coverage of the case because he claimed to have no desire to return to women's clothes. The *Los Angeles Times* quoted him as saying, "I'm going to keep right on wearing these clothes ... everybody knows me as 'Ken' there and everybody has known for 10 years or more that I am a woman."[11] This statement reveals Lisonbee's steadfast desire to maintain his male gender presentation, but I would argue it also reveals an incredible amount of flexibility in southern Californian acceptance of queer forms of embodiment. Indeed, what Lisonbee is claiming here is that he had been able to gain acceptance as "Ken"—a "suave, white aproned barber who discussed sports, politics and business with customers in a straight-forward masculine voice"—even with female anatomy.[12] Even the inspectors at the State Board of Barber Examiners were accepting of Lisonbee's gender presentation; the *Los Angeles Times* reported that the inspectors "said they knew the Wilmar tonsorialist to be a woman, although the license was issued annually in a man's name. As far as they are concerned, it was said, that is all right."[13] It's worth reiterating that Lisonbee's barbershop was not in Hollywood or even Los Angeles, but rather the comparatively sleepier city of Wilmar, in the San Gabriel Valley, eight miles east of the center of LA.

Thus the lives of Kenneth Lisonbee/Wing and Stella Harper are incredibly provocative in what they suggest about the queer history of the United States. Their romance began in what would seem to be the most unlikely of places—the heart of Mormon Utah. What's more, once their queer relationship was discovered in Los Angeles, they sought refuge not in San Francisco or another large city; rather, they returned home to central Utah. As discussed above, it appears as though Lisonbee's parents accepted both his queer embodiment and his relationship with Harper. Thus the couple's eventual return to the Los Angeles area should not be thought of in the traditional rural-to-urban migration that has so dominated historical visions of queer history. Rather than traveling west to escape parental supervision, they moved west *with parents in tow*. And rather than traveling to California in order to join the queer subcultures of San Francisco or Hollywood, they chose to settle down in the San Gabriel Valley. None of these choices would appear likely given the existing urban-centered historiography of queer history.

However, as this book has illustrated over and over again, trans men in the late nineteenth and early twentieth centuries did not always abide by conventional wisdom established by the existing historiography. Kenneth Lisonbee's story suggests that trans men lived in the most unlikely of places (the heart of Mormon Utah) and could garner support for their gender deviance from unlikely sources (in his case, his parents, and the neighbors and business people surrounding his Wilmar, California, barbershop). His story is enticing in what it suggests about what we don't know. Indeed, Lisonbee's story implies that there were likely many more trans men in Mormon Utah and, therefore, throughout the nation. His story is only recoverable because his gender variance was revealed publicly and commented on in newspapers nationwide. However, there doubtless were many trans men who either passed successfully throughout their lives or whose communities never found it necessary to police the gender variant in their midst. Perhaps we don't know about more trans men from this period because the community support they enjoyed in their lifetimes renders them unrecoverable as "queer."

Of course, undergirding Lisonbee's ability to be seen as "sensible, serious, and sincere," as the judge charged with his case in 1929 referred to him, was his ability to conform to normative expectations of community membership—particularly whiteness and economic productivity. In a sense, his gender variance was allowable because he was seen as "just like us" by his community in every way aside from his gender. Because he was seen as a hardworking, successful entrepreneur, his clients were willing to go along with him when he asked to be called "Ken." In the process, all the dissenting qualities invoked in the term "queer" were rendered invisible, and Lisonbee gained acceptance as a normative citizen. Indeed Lisonbee, like many of the other subjects of this book, was able to lead a livable queer life because he articulated his acceptability according to the tropes of normative male citizenship, mainly whiteness, economic productivity, and heteronormativity. Clearly each of these categories are privileged ones, and thus by mobilizing these discourses the trans men of this book helped to reify their exclusionary logics. Articulating acceptability along these lines legitimated the discrimination and persecution of those trans men who were nonwhite, foreign, not economically productive, or sexually "deviant." In this way, Lisonbee's story (and the stories of many of the white trans men in this book) anticipate the politics of homonormativity, which suggests that acceptance is attainable only through conformity to the standards of normativity and respectability.

Despite the politics of homonormativity, there is one crucial way that the trans men in this book should undeniably be considered queer. As Susan Stryker has written, "People with trans identity could describe themselves as men and women too—or resist binary categorization altogether—but in doing either they queered the dominant relationship of sexed body and gendered subject."[14] The subjects of this book introduced their friends and neighbors to the idea that sex and gender were two distinct things. For example, Lisonbee's instance that his customers didn't make a fuss over calling him "Ken" while knowing that he was anatomically female underscores the idea that has been present in each of the preceding chapters: that Americans at the turn of the twentieth century had a far more nuanced understanding of sex, gender, and sexuality than previously has been acknowledged.

On the whole, then, this book has made several important interventions into the existing scholarship. First, it raises questions about the influence of sexologists in defining popular understandings of gender and sexuality by highlighting how sexological theories played a limited role in dictating local responses to trans men, even into the 1940s. On a related note, this book challenges the accepted geography of queer identity formation, wherein queerness and urban centers have been seen as having a particular (and exclusive) relationship. By deploying a methodology that prioritizes sources produced in local contexts and then tracking the ways narratives change as they circulated through the nation's emergent mass-circulation press, *True Sex* highlights the fact that previous studies that have only looked at the national level of discourse have missed much of the story, and that the history of gender and sexuality at the turn of the twentieth century is, in fact, much more complicated (and much more interesting) than previously thought.

Additionally, this book has provided new insight into the nature of U.S. citizenship. I have illustrated that trans men could (and did) mobilize the masculinist tropes of normative citizenship in order to legitimate their queer bodies and to render their seemingly strange lives understandable—and perhaps even laudable. However, as discussed above, this strategy did have its limits. For one, it was, generally, a strategy that could be used only by white individuals, or individuals (such as Jack Garland and Ralph Kerwineo) who were ethnically/racially ambiguous and could pass as white. Additionally, while this strategy was particularly effective in the historical context of the decades surrounding the turn of the twentieth century—a period in which the heterosexual/homosexual binary was yet to become completely hegemonic—it is important to note that it helped to reinforce emergent politics of heteronormativity by articulating acceptable forms of queer embodiment through their similarities to normative male citizenry. This last point highlights the need for historians to interrogate separately the histories of each group within the LGBT umbrella.

All too often the insights proffered from research on one group are believed to be transferrable to other groups referred to by the LGBT label. However, this book suggests that the main rubrics that have guided research on gay and lesbian history (namely, the search for "consciousness" and "community") do little to illuminate the particular histories of trans men in the decades around the turn of the twentieth century. Evidence discussed here suggests that many trans men did not seek out communities of similar individuals, nor did they all flock to urban centers to escape close-knit agrarian communities in the nation's interior. Indeed, the progressive narrative commonly embraced within queer history—which argues that queer identities emerged only after individuals moved to urban centers and escaped the confines of familial homes and agrarian economies—is challenged by the narratives of the trans men discussed in this book. *True Sex*, therefore, argues that American history—even in the most remote locations—is far queerer than previously understood.

This insight is particularly relevant in the current political moment, during which the mainstream media is increasingly portraying "rural" and "urban" America as diametrically opposed spaces with few shared values. Indeed, this rift was cracked wide open during the 2016 presidential election, after which the victory of Donald Trump was credited in part to the supposed fact that coastal elites lived in a "bubble" and were out of touch with the lives of rural Americans (or vice versa).[15] Often in such discourse, support for the rights of LGBT people is characterized as an elite, coastal value, whereas "real America" supports traditional family values. However, *True Sex* challenges that vision, and illustrates that "rural" and "urban" are not spaces with oppositional values. Instead, *True Sex* highlights that the United States has a rich and deep queer history that extends far beyond the "bubbles" of the East and West Coasts, and penetrates deep into the heartland of "real America."

ACKNOWLEDGMENTS

This book was a long time in the making, and its completion is due, in large part, to the support and encouragement from a broad range of mentors, family members, colleagues, friends, and librarians. Their backing has meant the world to me, and I am honored to be able to recognize them here.

My career as a historian began at Macalester College, where by pure luck I was assigned to Peter Rachleff's course "Historians and Race" during my first semester. That course transformed the way I thought about history, and Peter introduced me to the idea that scholarship could be a form of social justice work. I was lucky to be assigned Peter as my initial adviser at Macalester, but even more fortunate that he became my mentor, encouraging me through the years and helping me transform from an undisciplined-but-interested student into a serious historian. Another incredible professor I encountered at Macalester aided this transformation: Mary Wingerd. I am so grateful that I crossed paths with Mary, as she saw potential in me that I had yet to see in myself (in fact, she was the first one to suggest that I consider pursuing a PhD in history). She went above and beyond for me time and time again—meeting me in coffee shops to discuss my senior honors thesis, and then later, my graduate school applications—always offering me sterling advice and boosting my confidence. Additionally, my time at Macalester was made more enriching through my encounters and conversations with Scott Morgensen, Emily Smith-Rosenberg, and the late Teresita Martinez Vergne. They each, in their own way, supported me and urged me forward, and for that I will always be grateful.

At the University of Illinois, I had the excellent fortune of working with the singular Dave Roediger, who proved to be an excellent adviser— it is truly impossible to convey how much I learned from him, as an activist, teacher, and scholar. I was also incredibly privileged to be able to learn from another extraordinary individual at Illinois: Antoinette

Burton. Antoinette, through her sterling example of engaged scholarship, motivated me to work harder, think deeper, and disrupt more. I will never cease to be amazed at her productive capacity, which perhaps is matched only by her sparkling wit (or maybe her capacity to care for her students and colleagues). I have benefited tremendously from all these qualities, and I am overwhelmingly grateful for her continuing support and guidance. I have no doubt I am where I am today because of her. Additionally, I am also grateful that my time at Illinois allowed me to work closely with Kristin Hoganson, Fiona Ngô, and Siobhan Somerville. They each provided crucial guidance, asking hard questions, offering valuable advice, and more than anything helping me to imagine new lines of inquiry. I also benefited from conversations and course work with many other terrific faculty members, most notably Shefali Chandra, Kathryn Oberdeck, Jim Barrett, Craig Koslofsky, and Mark Micale. Lastly, my time at Illinois was deeply enriched by the incredible cohort of graduate students with whom I was immersed. Special thanks go to Myra Washington, Ian Hartman, Anna Kurhajec, Nathan Chio, Ryan Jones, Andy Eisen, and Kwame Holmes for creating an intellectual environment that was invigorating, challenging, and most of all, fun.

I completed *True Sex* while at Texas Tech University, and it has been shaped in profound ways by countless productive conversations I have had with colleagues and friends here. In particular, I would like to thank the following individuals, some of whom have moved on but have nonetheless enriched my experience here at Tech: Erin-Marie Legacey, Abby Swingen, Alan Barenberg, Aliza Wong, Stefano D'Amico, Karlos Hill, Barbara Hahn, Justin Hart, Patricia Pelley, Ron Milam, Miguel Levario, Sean Cunningham, Gretchen Adams, Ben Poole, Randy McBee, Julie Willett, Manu Vimalassery, Marta Tecedor, and Sarah Viren. Whether it was help in crafting my book proposal, developing syllabi, or simply sharing a meal or drinks, these people have helped sustain me— intellectually and emotionally—in the desert of West Texas. Particular thanks go to the participants of the Junior Faculty Writing Group— Jacob Baum, Christine Walker, Matt Johnson, Patrick Scharfe, Catharine Franklin, Sarah Keyes, Zach Brittsan, Paul Bjerk, and Angela Diaz—who read two different versions of chapter 3 and offered incredibly valuable feedback. The group has also served as a productive space of collegial conversations and intellectual exchange that has supported this project in indirect ways, for which I am very grateful. Additionally, big thanks go to the office staff of the Texas Tech History Department, past and present: Nina Pruitt, Mayela Guardiola, and Jackie Manz, each of whom have offered administrative assistance and generally helped make Holden Hall a pleasant place to work.

The completion of *True Sex* was made possible by the support of a number of institutions that have generously provided the funding necessary for me to research, write, and revise this book. While at the University of Illinois, I received financial support from the Graduate College, the Department of History, the Gender and Women's Studies Department, and the Unit for Criticism and Interpretive Theory. Additionally, I conducted much of the early research for this project on a trip to San Francisco, made possible by the Center for Lesbian and Gay Studies Joan Heller-Diane Bernard Fellowship. While at Texas Tech, I have received generous support from various entities on campus, including the Department of History, the Division of Institutional Diversity, Equity & Community Engagement, the Library, and the Humanities Center.

Additionally, while I conducted much of the research for this book within online databases, many brick-and-mortar libraries provided essential resources and support throughout this process. In particular, I would like to thank the staff at the interlibrary loan offices of both the University of Illinois and Texas Tech University. Additionally, I would like to thank the staff at the Denver Historical Society, the Bancroft Library at the University of California, Berkeley, San Francisco's GLBT Historical Society, the San Francisco History Center, the Los Angeles Public Library, the ONE National Archive, and the Lesbian Herstory Archive. Additionally, I would like to personally mention the following librarians and archivists for going far beyond the call of duty in helping me track down resources that have been particularly important to this project: David Matte and Craig Williams at the Idaho State Historical Society, Mary Jo Lanphear at the Ontario County Records and Archive Center, and Zack Wilske at the U.S. Citizenship and Immigration Services Historical Reference Library.

Many of this book's arguments have been tested out in front of audiences at conferences, workshops, and seminars, and I am grateful for the useful comments and probing questions I have received over the years. In particular, in 2008 I was incredibly lucky to be able to attend the

University College Dublin's Clinton Institute for American Studies Summer School, where I participated in Donald Pease's seminar "American Studies and the Question of Exceptionalism." The conversations from that week in Dublin had a profound impact on my thinking about this project when it was in its earliest stages, and I am so grateful to have had that experience, and to have gotten a chance to engage with an incredible cohort of other graduate students (Tanisha Ford, Cansu Özmen, and Britt Rusert foremost among them). Additionally, I am grateful for audience member questions and comments I have received at numerous conferences and workshops, including the Berkshire Conference of Women Historians as well as the annual meetings of the American Historical Association, the American Studies Association, and the National Women's Studies Association. Additionally, I had the good fortune of being accepted to present early an version of this research at Connexions: Histories of Race and Sex in North America, a working papers conference at New York University organized by Jennifer Morgan, Jennifer Brier, and Michelle Mitchell (special thanks to Jennifer Brier and Julian Carter for their transformative feedback). That conference paper eventually became the article "Ralph Kerwineo's Queer Body: Narrating the Scales of Social Membership in the Early Twentieth Century," which appeared in in GLQ in 2014, before transforming yet again to appear in chapters 4 and 5 of this book.

I am also tremendously grateful to the staff at New York University Press, each of whom has made the publication process as seamless as possible. My editor, Clara Platter, has been a dream to work with, always serving as an enthusiastic advocate for this book. Her assistant, Amy Klopfenstein, provided cheerful support as the manuscript neared completion, for which I am very thankful. And finally, I would like to extend heartfelt thanks to my anonymous reviewers, who offered me incredibly invaluable feedback and suggestions which I am confident helped improve and sharpen the book's arguments and analysis.

True Sex also would never have seen the light of day without the support of my family. My parents, Lemuel and Susan, have always encouraged me and supported my goals, no matter how far-fetched they seemed. In the final stretch of this process, they opened their home to me and mine during two summers, granting us not only a respite from the harsh Lubbock sun but also child care while I wrote in coffee shops and public libraries across Cape Cod. My sister, Sara, and her family (Tim, Nora, and Miles) have helped sustain me with love and light throughout this process as well. I completed my first draft of chapter 4 in Ellicott City, Maryland, alongside a tiny, newborn Nora, and several years later, the final edits of *True Sex* were joyfully interrupted by Face-Time calls with a newborn Miles. I love them all dearly and am so happy that they are still putting up with me after all these years.

Finally, my biggest thanks go to the ones closest to me: Jake, Frankie, and Thea. Jake has been my most steadfast supporter throughout this process, which at times seemed endless. I could not have done it without his unwavering confidence in me, or the daily inspiration he provides me through his incredible dedication to his own scholarship and teaching. More recently, our daughters, Frankie and Thea, have enriched my life in ways I never imagined and have brought us tremendous joy. This book is for them.

NOTES

INTRODUCTION

1 In this book, I have chosen to use male pronouns for subjects who expressed a male gender identity, regardless of their anatomy. A more detailed discussion of this choice and other terminology choices is provided later in this introduction.

2 "Woman in Man's Garb Voted Often," *New York World*, December 17, 1902.

3 "Ten Women Masquerade as Men," *Logansport (IN) Journal*, December 28, 1902. A similar report appeared in "Masquerading as Men," *Morning World-Herald* (Omaha, NE), December 22, 1902.

4 "Ten Women Masquerade as Men"

5 The term "cisgender" refers to individuals whose gender identity and sex that they were assigned at birth are the same.

6 See, for example, "She Was a Man for 20 Years," *Fort Worth Telegram*, December 19, 1903.

7 "Man-Girl Gets Out of Prison on $50 Bail," *Evening Wisconsin* (Milwaukee), May 5, 1914.

8 Jennifer Terry, "Anxious Slippages between 'Us' and 'Them': A Brief History of the Scientific Search for Homosexual Bodies," in *Deviant Bodies: Critical Perspectives on Difference in Science and Popular Culture*, ed. Jennifer Terry and Jacqueline Urla (Bloomington: Indiana University Press, 1995), 129–69.

9 George Chauncey, "From Sexual Inversion to Homosexuality: Medicalization and the Changing Conceptualization of Female Deviance," *Salmagundi* 58–59 (1982): 115.

10 Lisa Duggan, *Sapphic Slashers: Sex, Violence, and American Modernity* (Durham, NC: Duke University Press, 2001), 154.

11 "Prisoner Proves a Woman," *Chicago Daily Tribune*, November 26, 1899.

12 "Study of 'Ellis Glenn,'" *Chicago Daily Tribune*, November 29, 1899.

13 See, for example, "'Ellis Glenn' Again on Trial," *New York Times*, July 9, 1901; "Ellis Glenn on Trial," *St. Louis (MO) Post-Dispatch*, July 8, 1901; "Did Miss Ellis Glenn Masquerade as a Man?" *New York World*, July 8, 1901; "The Ellis-Glenn Case," *Anaconda (MT) Standard*, July 10, 1901; "Ellis Glenn Is on Trial," *Morning Herald* (Lexington, KY), July 9, 1901; "Ellis Glenn Arraigned," *Montgomery (AL) Advertiser*, July 9, 1901; "Ellis Glenn on Trial," *Fort Worth Register*, July 9, 1901; "Ellis Glenn Is on Trial," *Duluth (MN) News-Tribune*, July 9, 1901; "Woman Held for Forgery," *Columbus Enquirer-Sun*, July 9, 1901; "Glenn Case Is on Trial," *Washington Post*, July 9, 1901; "Ellis Glenn, Man-Woman, Is on Trial," *Daily*

News-Democrat (Belleville, IL), July 9, 1901; "Trial of the Mysterious Ellis Glenn Commenced," *Chicago Daily Tribune*, July 9, 1901.

14 See, for example, Elizabeth Lapovsky Kennedy and Madeline D. Davis, *Boots of Leather, Slippers of Gold: The History of a Lesbian Community* (New York: Routledge, 1993); Esther Newton, *Cherry Grove, Fire Island: Sixty Years in America's First Gay and Lesbian Town* (Boston: Beacon Press, 1993); George Chauncey, *Gay New York: Gender, Urban Culture, and the Making of the Gay Male World, 1890–1940* (New York: Basic Books, 1994); Marc Stein, *City of Sisterly and Brotherly Loves: Lesbian and Gay Philadelphia, 1945–1972* (Chicago: University of Chicago Press, 2004); Nan Alamilla Boyd, *Wide-Open Town: A History of Queer San Francisco to 1965* (Berkeley: University of California Press, 2003).

15 For an excellent discussion of the prevalence of community studies in queer history, see Marc Stein, "Theoretical Perspectives, Local Communities: The Making of U.S. LGBT Historiography," *GLQ* 11, no. 4 (2005): 605–25. For examples of work in queer studies that have looked beyond the city, see Mary Gray, *Out in the Country: Youth, Media, and Queer Visibility in Rural America* (New York: New York University Press, 2009); Scott Herring, *Another Country: Queer Anti-Urbanism* (New York: New York University Press, 2010); Karen Tongson, *Relocations: Queer Suburban Imaginaries* (New York: New York University Press, 2011); and Mary Gray, Colin Johnson, and Brian Gilley, eds., *Queering the Countryside: New Frontiers in Rural Queer Studies* (New York: New York University Press, 2015). For historical studies of nonurban queer life, see John Howard, *Men Like That: A Southern Queer History* (Chicago: University of Chicago Press, 1999); Brock Thompson, *The Unnatural State: Arkansas and the Queer South* (Fayetteville: University of Arkansas Press, 2010); E. Patrick Johnson, *Sweet Tea: Black Gay Men of the South* (Chapel Hill: University of North Carolina Press, 2011). Most of these historical works focus thematically on cisgender males and chronologically on the post–World War II period. For important exceptions to this trend, see Colin Johnson, *Just Queer Folks: Gender and Sexuality in Rural America* (Philadelphia: Temple University Press, 2013); Rachel Hope Cleves, *Charity and Sylvia: A Same-Sex Marriage in Early America* (New York: Oxford University Press, 2014); Peter Boag, *Re-dressing America's Frontier Past* (Berkeley: University of California Press, 2011).

16 Some other works that are not community studies include Peter Boag's *Redressing America's Frontier Past* and Nicholas Syrett's "A Busman's Holiday in the Not-So-Lonely Crowd: Business Culture, Epistolary Networks, and Itinerant Homosexuality in Mid-Twentieth-Century America," *Journal of the History of Sexuality* 21, no. 1 (2012): 121–40.

17 "Man-Girl Given Her Freedom," *Evening (Milwaukee) Wisconsin*, May 7, 1914. For a more detailed discussion of these narratives, see chapters 4 and 5.

18 Lisa Duggan, *Twilight for Equality? Neoliberalism, Cultural Politics, and the Attack on Democracy* (Boston: Beacon Press, 2004), 50.

19 Lisa Duggan's *Sapphic Slashers* focuses on the sensational press, while Clare Sears's *Arresting Dress: Cross-Dressing, Law, and Fascination in Nineteenth-*

Century San Francisco (Durham, NC: Duke University Press, 2014), focuses on San Francisco.

20 See, for example, Susan Stryker, "Transgender Studies: Queer Theory's Evil Twin," *GLQ* 10, no. 2 (2004): 212–15; and David Valentine, "The Categories Themselves," *GLQ* 10, no. 2, 215–20.

21 Scott Larson, " 'Indescribable Being': Theological Performances of Genderlessness in the Society of the Publick Universal Friend, 1776–1819," *Early American Studies* 12, no. 3 (2014): 583.

22 This view falls in line with what Genny Beemyn has written. Beemyn has argued that "the best that we as historians can do is acknowledge individuals whose actions would seem to indicate that they might be what we would call 'transgender' or 'transsexual' today without necessarily referring to them as such and to distinguish them from individuals who might have presented as a gender different from the one assigned to them at birth for reasons other than a sense of gender difference." Genny Beemyn, "A Presence in the Past: A Transgender History," *Journal of Women's History* 25, no. 4 (2013): 113. See also Genny Beemyn, "U.S. History," in *Trans Bodies, Trans Selves: A Resource for the Transgender Community*, ed. Laura Erickson-Schroth (New York: Oxford University Press, 2014), 501–36.

23 In addition to transgender studies, this project is also indebted to the insights offered by Jeanne Boydston in her great article "Gender as a Question of Historical Analysis," *Gender & History* 20, no. 3 (2008): 558–83.

24 Of course, the voices of the historical subjects discussed here are mediated through the sources they left behind, and thus recovering their "true" sense of self is impossible. However, I have done the best I could to prioritize their voices whenever possible while also acknowledging the always incomplete nature of such projects.

25 For examples of this debate, see Pat Califa, *Sex Changes: The Politics of Transgenderism* (San Francisco: Cleis Press, 1997); and Louis Sullivan, *From Female to Male: The Life of Jack Bee Garland* (Boston: Alyson Books, 1990). For a discussion of how other scholars have recently grappled with this debate, see Sears, *Arresting Dress*, 7–22; Peter Boag, "Go West Young Man, Go East Young Woman: Searching for the *Trans* in Western Gender History," *Western Historical Quarterly* 36, no. 4 (2005): 477–97; Erica Rand, *Ellis Island Snow Globe* (Durham, NC: Duke University Press, 2005), 80–92; and Larson, "Indescribable Being," 582–84. Additionally, for examples of the butch/trans debate, see Judith Halberstam, "Transgender Butch: Butch/FTM Border Wars and the Masculine Continuum," *GLQ: A Journal of Lesbian and Gay Studies* 4, no. 2 (1998): 237–310; and for an overview of how this debate boiled over during a recent conference, see Rachel Hope Cleves, "Lesbian Histories and Futures: A Dispatch from 'Gay American History @ 40,'" *NOTCHES*, May 18, 2016, available at http://notchesblog.com/.

26 "Suave, Trouser-Clad Barber Turns Out to Be Damsel," *Rocky Mountain News* (Denver), January 12, 1929; " 'Man Barber' a Girl; Also Acted Husband," *Daily News* (New York), January 13, 1929; "Sporty White-Aproned Barber Turns Out to

Be Pretty Girl," *Simpson's Leader-Times* (Kittanning, PA), January 14, 1929; "Posing as Man, Girl Weds Two," *Pointer* (Riverdale, IL), February 15, 1929; "Posing as Man, Girl Weds Two," *Dunkirk (NY) Observer*, February 25, 1929; "Trousered Tomboy Bleats in Bastille," *Helena (MT) Daily Independent*, January 12, 1929.

CHAPTER 1. THE LAST FEMALE HUSBAND

1 Waupun's population in 1883 was around 2,500.

2 The etymology of this term will be discussed later in this chapter.

3 The term "lesbian" was used by Dr. P. M. Wise in the article "A Case of Sexual Perversion," *Alienist and Neurologist: A Quarterly Journal of Scientific, Clinical, and Forensic Psychiatry and Neurology* 4, no. 1 (1882): 87–91. This article is often referred to as the first appearance of the term. See, for example, Jonathan Ned Katz, *Gay American History: Lesbians and Gay Men in the U.S.A.* (New York: Harper & Row, 1976), 221.

4 The scholarship on female same-sex relationships and cross-gender practices is well established. For examples of canonical texts in this field, see Carroll Smith-Rosenberg, "The Female World of Love and Ritual: Relations between Women in Nineteenth-Century America," *Signs: Journal of Women in Culture and Society* 1, no. 1 (1975): 1–29; Lillian Faderman, *Surpassing the Love of Men: Romantic Friendship and Love between Women from the Renaissance to the Present* (New York: Morrow, 1981); George Chauncey, "From Sexual Inversion to Homosexuality: Medicalization and the Changing Conceptualization of Female Deviance," *Salmagundi* 58–59 (1982): 114–46; Michel Foucault, *The History of Sexuality, Volume 1: An Introduction*, trans. Robert Hurley (1978; repr., New York: Vintage, 1990); J. Halberstam, *Female Masculinity* (Durham, NC: Duke University Press, 1998); Lisa Duggan, *Sapphic Slashers: Sex, Violence, and American Modernity* (Durham, NC: Duke University Press, 2000); Siobhan Somerville, *Queering the Color Line: Race and the Invention of Homosexuality in American Culture* (Durham, NC: Duke University Press, 2000).

5 Lillian Faderman, "The Morbidification of Love between Women by 19th-Century Sexologists," *Journal of Homosexuality* 4, no. 1 (1978): 73–90.

6 See Smith-Rosenberg, "Female World of Love and Ritual"; Chauncey, "From Sexual Inversion to Homosexuality."

7 Smith-Rosenberg, "Female World of Love and Ritual," 9.

8 Indeed, Cleves notes in the introduction to *Charity and Sylvia* that "early Americans did understand the potential for a sexual element within women's friendships." See Rachel Hope Cleves, *Charity and Sylvia: A Same-Sex Marriage in Early America* (New York: Oxford University Press, 2014), xviii. For another reexamination of perceptions of female sexuality in the nineteenth century, see April Haynes, *Riotous Flesh: Women, Physiology, and the Solitary Vice in Nineteenth-Century America* (Chicago: University of Chicago Press, 2015).

9 Lisa Duggan's *Sapphic Slashers* is one example of work that argues that the 1890s witnessed a decisive shift in the perception of female sexuality. Duggan writes,

"By the late nineteenth century, these textualizations of gender and sexuality increasingly worked to figure all such differences as simple and obvious deviance from conventional elite norms. Multiple variations and meanings were condensed into rigidly binary forms of either excess sexuality or inverted gender, 'primitive' or overcivilized masculinity or femininity." See Duggan, *Sapphic Slashers*, 26.

10 For a survey of this period, see Robert Weibe, *The Search for Order, 1877–1920* (New York: Hill and Wang, 1966); Jackson Lears, *Rebirth of a Nation: Making Modern America, 1877–1920* (New York: Harper Perennial, 2010). For more information about racial tension and the lynching epidemic in this period, see Steven Hahn, *A Nation under Our Feet: Black Political Struggles in the Rural South from Slavery to the Great Migration* (Cambridge, MA: Belknap Press of Harvard University Press, 2005); Karlos K. Hill, *Beyond the Rope: The Impact of Lynching on Black Culture and Memory* (New York: Cambridge University Press, 2016). For information about the anxiety surrounding the women's rights movement and the "New Woman" in particular, see Carroll Smith-Rosenberg, *Disorderly Conduct: Vision of Gender in Victorian America* (New York: Alfred A. Knopf, 1985); Laura L. Behling, *The Masculine Woman in America, 1890–1935* (Urbana: University of Illinois Press, 2001).

11 For more information about conflicts in the West during this period, see Patricia Limerick, *The Legacy of Conquest: The Unbroken Past of the American West* (New York: Norton, 1987). For more information on the Gilded Age / Progressive era, see Michael McGerr, *A Fierce Discontent: The Rise and Fall of the Progressive Movement in America, 1870–1920* (New York: Oxford University Press, 2005); Alan Trachtenberg, *The Incorporation of America: Culture and Society in the Gilded Age* (New York: Hill and Wang, 1982).

12 S. N. D. North, *The Newspaper and Periodical Press* (Washington, DC: Census Office, Department of the Interior, 1884), 73.

13 Carl F. Kaestle, "Seeing the Sites: Readers, Publishers, and Local Print Cultures in 1880," in *A History of the Book in America, Volume 4: Print in Motion: The Expansion of Publishing and Reading in the United States, 1880–1940*, ed. Carl F. Kaestle and Janice A. Radway (Chapel Hill: University of North Carolina Press, 2009), 29. See also Richard B. Kielbowicz and Linda Lawson, "Protecting the Small-Town Press: Community, Social Policy, and Postal Privileges, 1845–1970," *Canadian Review of American Studies* 19 (Spring 1988): 27.

14 Kaestle defines local print cultures as the "traditions, values, experiences, practices, infrastructures, and ideologies that provide common purposes and understandings within certain groups of print producers and readers." See Kaestle, "Seeing the Sites," 25.

15 The "Sentinel" referred to here is likely the *Milwaukee Sentinel*, as it appears that much of the information in this dispatch was based on an article printed in that paper. See "Disguised as a Man," *Milwaukee Sentinel*, October 30, 1883.

16 "Masquerading as a Man," *New York Times*, October 30, 1883; "Woman Married to Woman," *New York Herald*, October 30, 1883; "An Insane Freak," *Grand Forks*

(ND) Daily Herald, October 30, 1883; "Dressed in Man's Attire," *New Haven (CT) Evening Register,* October 30, 1883; "Woman Married to Woman," *Trenton (NJ) Times,* October 30, 1883; "No Title," *Daily Bacon* (Akron, OH), October 31, 1883; "A Truant Wife," *Helena (MT) Independent,* October 31, 1883; "Disguised in Masquerade," *Galveston (TX) Weekly News,* November 1, 1883. Also appeared as "A Female Husband," *Bismarck (ND) Tribune,* November 2, 1883; "Queer Taste," *Warren (PA) Ledger,* November 2, 1883; "A Disguised Wife," *Palo Alto Reporter* (Emmetsburg, IA), November 3, 1883; "A Woman Married to a Woman," *Sacramento (CA) Daily Record-Union,* October 30, 1883; "Strange Conduct," *Salt Lake (UT) Herald,* October 30, 1883; "One Woman Married to Another," *Breckenridge News* (Cloverport, KY), November 7, 1883; "No Title," *San Antonio Light,* October 30, 1883.

17 The *Milwaukee Sentinel* was a member of the Associated Press, and thus it stands to reason that this was the means through which the story was spread.

18 See, for example, "A Female Husband," *Public Ledger* (Memphis), November 5, 1883; "The Female Husband," *Little Falls (MN) Transcript,* November 5, 1883; "Female Husband Confesses," *Wisconsin State Journal (Madison),* November 6, 1883; "A Female Husband," *Weekly Wisconsin (Milwaukee),* November 7, 1883; "The Female Husband," *Worthington (MN) Advance,* November 8, 1883; The Female Husband," *Sioux County Herald* (Orange City, IA), November 8, 1883; "The Female Husband," *Salt Lake (UT) Daily Herald,* November 23, 1883; "A Female Husband," *Idaho Tri-Weekly Statesman (Boise),* November 24, 1883; "The Female Husbands," *Boston Daily Globe,* December 30, 1883.

19 Henry Fielding, *The female husband; or, The surprising history of Mrs. Mary, alias Mrs. George Hamilton, who was convicted of having married a young woman of Wells and lived with her as her husband. Taken from her own mouth since her confinement* (London, 1746).

20 For a further discussion of Fielding and his work, *The Female Husband,* see Terry Castle, "Matters Not Fit to Be Mentioned: Fielding's *The Female Husband,*" *ELH* 49, no. 3 (1982): 602–22; Halberstam, *Female Masculinity,* 50–53, 67; Susan Clayton, "Can Two and a Half Centuries of Female Husbands Inform (Trans)Gender History?" *Journal of Lesbian Studies* 14, no. 2 (2010): 288–302.

21 For a discussion of earlier references to "female husbands," see Halberstam, *Female Masculinity,* 65–73.

22 Jennifer Manion, "(Trans)gressing the Category of Woman in the Eighteenth Century," paper presented at the Society for Historians of the Early American Republic Conference, Baltimore, July 21, 2012.

23 Rachel Hope Cleves, "'What, Another Female Husband?': A Prehistory of Same-Sex Marriage in America," *Journal of American History* 101, no. 4 (2015): 1067. It is worth noting that the term "same-sex union" here might be taken with a grain of salt, as it is very possible that female husbands and their cisgender wives did not think of each other as two brides, but rather husband and wife. The term "female husband," however, flattened that distinction and normalized the gender of the female husband as *female.*

24 Clayton, "Can Two and a Half Centuries of Female Husbands Inform (Trans) Gender History?" 290.

25 "He Is a Woman," *Milwaukee Journal*, November 1, 1883.

26 Ibid.

27 See "A Vivid Imagination," *Milwaukee Sentinel*, November 3, 1883; "Dubious Dubois," *Waupun (WI) Times*, November 6, 1883.

28 "Frank Dubois," *Chicago Daily Tribune*, November 2, 1883; "Frank Dubois a Woman," *New York Times*, November 2, 1883; "Frank Dubois a Woman," *Boston Daily Globe*, November 3, 1883; "Mrs. Hudson's Freak," *Janesville (WI) Daily Gazette*, November 2, 1883; "Frank Dubois," *Decatur (IL) Review*, November 3, 1883; "Mrs. Hudson's Freak," *Atlantic (IA) Daily Telegram*, November 3, 1883.

29 See, for example, " 'Frank's' Stepmother, Living in Hyde Park, Settles the Question of 'His' Sex," *Chicago Daily Tribune*, November 6, 1883. An interview with Samuel Hudson was published in "The Dual Personage," *Milwaukee Sentinel*, November 2, 1883.

30 "Strange Stories," *Milwaukee Sentinel*, November 3, 1883.

31 "Found at Last," *Milwaukee Sentinel*, November 4, 1883; "The Waupun Couple," *Chicago Daily Tribune*, November 5, 1883; "She Is Sure He Is a Man," *Boston Daily Globe*, November 5, 1883.

32 "He Is a Woman."

33 "Romance and Reality," *Milwaukee Sentinel*, October 31, 1883.

34 "Strange Stories." The *Waupun Times* remarked, "There is no known or imaginable motive for such strange conduct if it be true." See "What Is It?" *Waupun (WI) Times*, October 30, 1883. The story would remain a mystery for almost a month, as it was not until law officials apprehended Dubois in late November 1883 that he finally confirmed his "true sex" and clarified the rationale behind his marriage. He stated that he had been hired to marry Fuller to save her from shame; as the *New York Times* described, "Miss Fuller was betrayed by some one and that the mock marriage was hatched up to cover the consequent disgrace." This explanation produced Dubois not as a deviant, but as an individual who was willing to sacrifice for another person. See "Mrs. Hudson's Wife," *New York Times*, December 3, 1883. This explanation also appeared in "Dubois in Custody," *Milwaukee Journal*, November 27, 1883; "Frank Dubois," *Kansas City (MO) Evening Star*, November 29, 1883; "Frank Dubois: 'He' Says 'His' Name Is Delia Smith and That 'He' Was Hired to Marry Gertie Fuller," *Chicago Daily Tribune*, December 1, 1883; "Frank Dubois Confesses to Being a Woman and Is Arrested," *National Republican* (Washington, DC), November 29, 1883. Significantly, as Gertrude Fuller refused to press charges against Dubois, and he was quickly released from custody. See "Quite a Mystery," *Milwaukee Sentinel*, December 2, 1883; "Dubois Is a Woman Again," *Waupun (WI) Times*, December 18, 1883.

35 The *Waupun Times* was only one of the two weekly newspapers published in Waupun in 1883, but it was the only paper that covered the story. Thus, even on the local level, the case was discussed in divergent ways. The circulation of these papers was about even (the *Times* had slightly higher numbers, with 800 subscrib-

ers, compared to the *Leader's* 720), and both of their editorial pages favored the Republican Party. However similar the papers were in terms of their popularity or general slant, the *Leader* did not cover the Dubois story, whereas the *Times* devoted a great deal of attention to it. See *N. W. Ayer & Son's American Newspaper Annual, 1883* (Philadelphia: N. W. Ayer & Son, 1884), 254.

36 "Dubious Dubois," *Waupun (WI) Times*, November 6, 1883.

37 Given the common practice within small newspapers such as the *Waupun Times* to reproduce articles that originally appeared in other (larger) newspapers, I assume that the "Case of Betty John" was one that originally appeared elsewhere; however, I have been unable to find the source or, for that matter, any information on the actual "Betty John" case.

38 "The Female Man," *Waupun (WI) Times*, November 13, 1883.

39 John Howard, "The Talk of the Country: Revisiting Accusation, Murder, and Mississippi, 1895," in *Queer Studies: An Interdisciplinary Reader*, ed. Robert Corber and Stephen Valocchi (Malden, MA: Blackwell, 2003), 147. Duggan also discussed analogues in *Sapphic Slashers*.

40 Jonathan Ned Katz, *Gay/Lesbian Almanac: A New Documentary* (New York: Carroll and Graf, 1983), 258–59.

41 Howard, "Talk of the Country," 147.

42 "Woman as Husbands," *Waupun (WI) Times*, November 27, 1883.

43 U.S. Bureau of the Census, *Seventh Census of the United States, 1850* (Washington, DC: U.S. Government Printing Office, 1850), Westerlo, New York, household number 532. In part because of the broad range of sources that Lobdell left behind, he has previously been the subject of the subject of several academic studies. Thus, rather than rehearse the details of his lived experiences, my discussion of Lobdell is focused on the significance of the ways in which his life was produced in the local, national, and sexological press in the late nineteenth century. For more information on Lobdell's life, see Bambi L. Lobdell, *"A Strange Sort of Being": The Transgender Life of Lucy Ann / Joseph Israel Lobdell, 1829–1912* (Jefferson, NC: McFarland, 2012), John M. Sloop, "Lucy Lobdell's Queer Circumstances," in *Queering Public Address: Sexualities in American Historical Discourse*, ed. Charles E. Morris III (Columbia: University of South Carolina Press, 2007), 149–72; Carolyn Dinshaw, "Born Too Soon, Born Too Late: The Female Hunter of Long Eddy, circa 1855," in *21st-Century Gay Culture*, ed. David A. Powell (Newcastle, UK: Cambridge Scholar Publishing, 2008), 1–12; Lillian Faderman, *Odd Girls and Twilight Lovers: A History of Lesbian Life in Twentieth-Century America* (New York: Columbia University Press, 1991), 43; Peter Boag, *Re-dressing America's Frontier Past* (Berkeley: University of California Press, 2011), chapter 5.

44 Dr. P. M. Wise's article, for example, suggests that the marriage was the result of family pressure.

45 Lucy Ann Lobdell, *The Narrative of the Female Hunter of Delaware County* (New York, 1855), 40–41. Lobdell wrote in the autobiography, "I made up my mind to dress in men's attire to seek labor, as I was used to men's work. And as I might

work harder at house-work, and get only a dollar per week, and I was capable of doing men's work, and getting men's wages, I resolved to try."

46 For a more detailed discussion of this period of Lobdell's life, see Lobdell, *Strange Sort of Being*, 59–89. See also A. C. Smith, "A Wild Woman's History: The Slayer of Hundreds of Bears and Wild Cast," in *History of Meeker County: A Historical Sketch of Meeker County, Minnesota from Its First Settlement to July 4th, 1876* (Litchfield, MN: Belfoy & Joubert, 1877), 98–111.

47 "Joe Lobdell and Wife: Their History, Etc.," *Jeffersonian* (Stroudsburg, PA), August 17, 1871.

48 "Romantic Paupers," *New York Herald-Tribune*, August 25, 1871. "Romantic Paupers," *Trenton (NJ) State Gazette*, September 8, 1871. The article also appeared as "A Strange Story," *Cambria Freeman* (Ebensburg, PA), September 7, 1871.

49 See, for example, "A Mountain Romance," *Millheim (PA) Journal*, May 31, 1877.

50 Quotations here from "A Curious Career: Remarkable Adventures of Lucy Ann Lobdell, an Eccentric Female Character Who Figured Successively as Hermit, Hunter, Music Teacher, Author, and 'Female Husband,'" *National Police Gazette* (New York), October 25, 1879.

51 Rachel Hope Cleves has written, "The closet is really an open secret. The ignorance that defines the closet is as likely to be a carefully constructed edifice as it is to be a total absence of knowledge. The closet depends on people strategically choosing to remain ignorant of inconvenient facts." See Cleves, *Charity and Sylvia*, xii. For further discussion of the closet as an open secret, see Eve Kosofsky Sedgwick, *Epistemology of the Closet* (Berkeley: University of California Press, 2008).

52 Testimony of John Lobdell, in "In the Matter of Lucy Ann Slater, a Supposed Lunatic," June 1880, Delaware County Clerk's Office, Delhi, New York.

53 Testimony of William W. Main, in ibid.

54 Testimony of Harry Walsh, in ibid.

55 See Christine Stansell, *City of Women: Sex and Class in New York, 1789–1860* (Urbana: University of Illinois Press, 1987). Bruce Dorsey also discusses this development in his work *Reforming Men and Women: Gender in the Antebellum City* (Ithaca, NY: Cornell University Press, 2002), 52.

56 Testimony of John Lobdell.

57 "A Strange Story," *New York Herald*, April 9, 1877.

58 "As Man and Wife," *New Haven (CT) Register*, November 3, 1883.

59 "A Strange Story."

60 Sarah Nicolazzo has made a similar argument about the importance of the category of "vagrant" in regulating the sexual and gender normativity within eighteenth-century British author Henry Fielding's *The Female Husband*. See Sarah Nicolazzo, "Henry Fielding's *The Female Husband* and the Sexuality of Vagrancy," *Eighteenth Century* 55, no. 4 (2014): 335–55.

61 See, for example, "Curious Career."

62 Richard von Krafft-Ebing, *Psychopathia Sexualis*, trans. Franklin S. Klaf (1886; repr., New York: Arcade Publishing, 1965).

63 Chauncey, "From Sexual Inversion to Homosexuality," 119.

64 See, for example, Jonathan Ned Katz, *Gay American History: Lesbians and Gay Men in the U.S.A.* (New York: Harper & Row, 1976), 221.

65 Wise, "Case of Sexual Perversion," 91.

66 Ibid., 88. This assertion of mental instability within Lobdell's family appears to be correct, as the Lobdell's mother, Sally, is listed as "insane" in the 1860 federal census. U.S. Bureau of the Census, *Eighth Census of the United States, 1860* (Washington. DC: U.S. Government Publishing Office, 1860), Hancock, New York, roll M653_744.

67 Wise, "Case of Sexual Perversion," 87–88.

68 Halberstam, *Female Masculinity*, 82.

69 Wise, "Case of Sexual Perversion," 89–90.

70 Ibid., 90.

71 As Siobhan Somerville has observed, "One of the most consistent medical characterizations of the anatomy of both African American women and lesbians was the myth of the unusually large clitoris." See Somerville, *Queering the Color Line*, 27. See also Valerie Traub, "The Psychomorphology of the Clitoris," *GLQ* 2, nos. 1–2 (1995): 81–113; and Margaret Gibson, "Clitoral Corruption: Body Metaphors and American Doctors' Constructions of Female Homosexuality, 1870–1900," in *Science and Homosexualities*, ed. Vernon Rosario (New York: Routledge, 1997), 108–32.

72 Lobdell was also mentioned in two other sexological articles in the late nineteenth century. See James G. Kiernan, "Original Communications. Insanity. Lecture XXVI: Sexual Perversion," *Detroit Lancet* 7, no. 2 (1884): 483. Kiernan also mentioned this story in his other article, "Psychological Aspects of the Sexual Appetite," *Alienist and Neurologist: A Quarterly Journal of Scientific, Clinical, and Forensic Psychiatry and Neurology* 12 (1891): 202–3.

73 Elizabeth Reis, *Bodies in Doubt: An American History of Intersex* (Baltimore: Johns Hopkins University Press, 2009), 24.

74 Ibid., 55–81.

75 See, for example, "Excitement as a Cholera Cure," *Daily Yellowstone Journal* (Miles City, MT), May 29, 1885; "Intoxication by Contagion," *Asheville (NC) Citizen*, January 29, 1887.

76 "Women as Husbands," *Waupun (WI) Times*, November 27, 1883.

77 Ibid.

78 "Dubois Is a Woman Again," *Waupun (WI) Times*, December 18, 1883.

79 "Female Husbands," *New York Times*, November 4, 1883.

80 Ibid.

81 Ibid.

82 *Peck's Sun* was the most widely circulated weekly in Milwaukee at the time and featured a series of fictional "bad boy" stories penned by Peck himself. This editorial went on to be republished in newspapers nationwide, including "The Female Husband," *Salt Lake (UT) Daily Herald*, November 23, 1883; "The Female Husbands," *Boston Daily Globe*, December 30, 1883.

83 For a discussion of the figure of the spinster in the American imagination, see Heather Love, "Gyn/Apology: Sarah Orne Jewett's Spinster Aesthetics," *ESQ: A Journal of the American Renaissance* 55, nos. 3–4 (2009): 305–34; Lee Virginia Chambers-Schiller, *Liberty, a Better Husband: Single Women in America: The Generation of 1780–1840* (New Haven, CT: Yale, 1984).

84 A search within the ProQuest online database of the *New York Times* from 1851 to 2006 (the most recent dates available as of this writing in January 2015) for "female husband" appeared three times: the first two references came in 1883 in articles related to Frank Dubois, and the third appeared in a 2005 review of the exhibit "Before Victoria: Extraordinary Women of the British Romantic Era" that was then on display at the New York Public Library. A similar search reveals that between 1849 and 1987, the *Chicago Tribune* published the term "female husband" twice, and each instance was prior to 1890. Additionally, the only instance of "female husband" appearing in the *National Police Gazette* in the period between 1845 and 1906 occurred in 1879 in an article about Joseph Lobdell. See "Frank Dubois Is a Woman," *New York Times*, November 2, 1883; "Female Husbands," *New York Times*, November 4, 183. See also Michael Frank, "Women Who Chafed at Society's Corset," *New York Times*, April 8, 2005; "Frank Dubois," *Chicago Daily Tribune*, November 2, 1883; "Her Husband Was a Woman," *Chicago Daily Tribune*, September 15, 1888; "A Curious Career," *National Police Gazette* (New York), October 25, 1879.

85 For more information of the growth of sensationalism within journalism in the 1890s, see, for example, John D. Stevens, *Sensationalism and the New York Press* (New York: Columbia University Press, 1991), 55–100; W. Joseph Campbell, *The Year That Defined American Journalism: 1897 and the Clash of Paradigms* (New York: Routledge, 2006).

86 Duggan herself acknowledges the limitations of her study, writing that "*Sapphic Slashers* centrally and specifically analyzes only one version of the cultural narratives of lesbian identity in the twentieth century . . . there were (and are) myriad other such narratives, circulating in relatively broad as well as narrowly constructed public arenas. Further research and interpretation will illuminate these and inevitably complicate and revise the accounts in *Sapphic Slashers*. The argument in these pages is thus offered provisionally, with an invitation to debate." See Duggan, *Sapphic Slashers*, 6.

CHAPTER 2. BEYOND COMMUNITY

1 Colin R. Johnson, *Just Queer Folks: Gender and Sexuality in Rural America* (Philadelphia: Temple University Press, 2013), 18.

2 This number includes only stories of individuals who had lived as men for a number of years. There were many more stories that appeared in newspapers in this period of adolescent girls who were caught dressing as a boy for various reasons—usually to escape home or to otherwise seek out adventure. While determining the "real" motivation behind the actions of these girls is impossible, these stories

nonetheless appear to be reporting a phenomenon distinct from individuals assigned female at birth but found to be living as male for a number of years. As such, stories within the "girl adventurer" genre are not included in the number here.

3 Glenn's life will be discussed in detail in chapter 3.

4 Martin Manalansan, *Global Divas: Filipino Gay Men in the Diaspora* (Durham, NC: Duke University Press, 2003), 21.

5 Brock Thompson, *The Un-natural State: Arkansas and the Queer South* (Fayetteville: University of Arkansas Press, 2010), 9.

6 Peter Boag, *Re-dressing America's Frontier Past* (Berkeley: University of California Press, 2011), 34–35.

7 Critiques of tolerance/acceptance within queer studies are long-standing. For a recent example of this work, see Suzanna Walters, *The Tolerance Trap: How God, Genes, and Good Intentions Are Sabotaging Gay Equality* (New York: New York University Press, 2014).

8 These are estimates based on census records. There is no immigration record for a "George Green" from this period, and thus it seems that Green may have emigrated as a women (but unfortunately his birth name is not known), or, if he emigrated as a man, he very well could have done so under another name.

9 See U.S. Bureau of the Census, *Tenth Census of the United States, 1880* (Washington, DC: National Archives and Records Administration, 1880), Swift Creek, North Carolina, series T9, roll 985, p. 31, household number 302, enumeration district no. 276.

10 See ibid.; U.S. Bureau of the Census, *Twelfth Census of the United States, 1900* (Washington, DC: National Archives and Records Administration, 1900), Swift Creek, North Carolina, series T623, roll 1221, p. 8A, household number 128, enumeration district no. 150.

11 The *Petersburg Daily Index-Appeal* reported that Mary's niece and her children lived in Petersburg, Virginia. See "A Sensation in Ettrick," *Petersburg (VA) Daily Index-Appeal*, March 22, 1902.

12 The village of Ettrick itself did not have any daily or weekly newspapers in 1904, and thus in this section the term "local newspapers" is used to refer to those published within twenty-five miles of Ettrick: Petersburg, Virginia's *Index-Appeal* and Richmond, Virginia's *Dispatch* and *Times*.

13 "A Sensation in Ettrick," *Petersburg (VA) Index-Appeal*, March 22, 1902.

14 "A Revealment Most Sensational," *Times* (Richmond, VA), March 22, 1902.

15 "All Ettrick Mystified," *Richmond Dispatch* (Richmond, VA), March 22, 1902; "Revealment Most Sensational."

16 "Mrs. Green's Secret, a Life Sacrifice," *Times* (Richmond, VA), March 23, 1902.

17 Ibid.

18 "The Funeral of George Green," *Petersburg (VA) Index-Appeal*, March 23, 1902. The staff at St. Joseph's Catholic Cemetery in Blandford, Virginia, has verified that Green is buried there.

19 See, for example, "Woman Who Lived as Man 35 Years and Had 'Wife' Dies," *Chicago Tribune*, March 22, 1902; "'George' Green Buried," *Philadelphia Inquirer*, March 23, 1902; "Husband and Wife Both Were Women," *New York World*, March 22, 1902; "Death Reveals Strange Secret," *San Francisco Call*, March 22, 1902; "She Masqueraded as Husband Until Death Revealed Her Secret," *Atlanta Constitution*, March 22, 1902.

20 John D'Emilio, "Capitalism and Gay Identity," in *The Lesbian and Gay Studies Reader*, ed. Henry Abelove, Michele Aina Barale, David Halperin (New York: Routledge, 1993), 468.

21 See, for example, the use of sexological writings in Waupun, Wisconsin, in the Frank Dubois case, discussed in previous chapter.

22 "Astounding Affair," *Ontario Repository-Messenger* (Canandaigua, NY), March 27, 1902.

23 U.S. Bureau of the Census, *Tenth Census of the United States, 1880*, Canandaigua, New York, p. 50; supervisor district no. 10, enumeration dist. no. 117. Copy in Alice/William Howard Vertical File, Ontario County Records and Archive Center, Canandaigua, New York (hereafter referred to as OCRAC).

24 "The Mystery of William Howard," *Democrat Chronicle* (Rochester, NY), March 23, 1902. Similar accounts appeared in "Masqueraded as a Man," *Utica (NY) Press*, n.d. (copy in Howard Vertical File, OCRAC); "Man-Woman Case Mystifies Canandaigua," *Evening Telegram* (Syracuse, NY), March 24, 1902.

25 "Man-Woman Case Mystifies Canandaigua."

26 "Howard Was a Woman," *Ontario County Journal* (Canandaigua, NY), March 28, 1902.

27 Ibid.

28 Newspaper reports published upon his death suggest that William Howard actually married twice—the first being a short-lived marriage to an unnamed woman in Hornellsville, and then his 1892 marriage to Edith Dyer. However, there is no official record of his first marriage.

29 "Howard Was a Woman." It is possible that Reverend Hubbell was relative of Howard's, as Hubbell was the last name of Howard's aunt and uncle (both of whom lived with Howard's immediate family in 1880).

30 An "Edith Dyer" is listed on the 1880 census in Hornellsville, New York. This is more than likely the woman whom Howard would later marry, as the *Ontario Repository-Messenger* reported that the pair met when Howard was working as a milk peddler in Hornellsville. However, most latter reports spell Howard's wife name as "Dwyer." See U.S. Bureau of the Census, *Tenth Census of the United States, 1880*, Hornellsville, New York, series T9, roll 908, p. 53, enumeration district 178.

31 "Howard Was a Woman."

32 "Astounding Affair."

33 "Howard Was a Woman."

34 Ibid.

35 "Man-Woman Case Mystifies Canandaigua."

36 The coroner's report ultimately proved that Howard's death was caused by "angina pectoris or paralysis of the heart," unrelated to poisoning. Coroner's decision, dated March 17, 1902, signed by O. J. Hallenbeck. Howard Vertical File, OCRAC.

37 Ibid., 7.

38 Ibid., 2–5.

39 "Mystery of William Howard." Similar accounts appeared in "Masqueraded as a Man"; "Man-Woman Case Mystifies Canandaigua."

40 "Mystery of William Howard."

41 See, for example, "Passed for a Man," *Sunday Oregonian* (Portland), March 23, 1902; "Supposed Man Proves to Be a Woman," *Anaconda (MT) Standard*, March 23, 1902; "Masqueraded as Man," *Columbus (GA) Enquirer-Sun*, March 23, 1902; "A Strange Story," *Victoria (TX) Weekly Advocate*, March 29, 1902; "Woman Husband," *Morning Herald* (Lexington, KY), March 23, 1902; "Masquerades as Man until Called by Death," *San Francisco Call*, March 23, 1902; "A Similar Case," *Times* (Richmond, VA), March 23, 1902; "Another Man Who Was a Woman, " *Macon (GA) Weekly Telegraph*, March 23, 1902; "Woman Posed as Man," *Montgomery (AL) Advertiser*, March 23, 1902; "Autopsy Revealed Secret," *Washington Post*, March 23, 1902; "Mysterious Death Comes to a Mysterious Woman," *Post-Standard* (Syracuse, NY), March 23, 1902.

42 "Woman Who Lived as Man 35 Years and Had 'Wife' Dies."

43 "Lived Her Life as a Man," *Chicago Tribune*, March 23, 1902.

44 "Aged Husband a Woman," *Washington Post*, March 22, 1902; "Autopsy Revealed Secret."

45 Papers that covered both of the stories were the *Washington Post, the Chicago Tribune, the Ontario Repository-Messenger* (Canandaigua, NY), the *Petersburg (VA) Index-Appeal*, the *Times* (Richmond, VA), the *San Francisco Call*, the *Morning Herald* (Lexington, KY), the *Macon (GA) Telegraph*, the *Boston Journal*, and the *Columbus (GA) Daily Enquirer-Sun*. Those that made no connection between the two cases (in addition to the *Chicago Tribune* and *Washington Post*) were the *Columbus (GA) Enquirer-Sun*, the *Boston Journal*, the *Morning Herald* (Lexington, KY), and the *San Francisco Call*.

The day after the *Petersburg Index-Appeal* of Petersburg, Virginia, reported Green's death, the paper published an article on the front page about Howard, titled "Another Man Turn to Woman," but the text of the article itself did not mention Green, or go into any detail about the similarities between the two cases. A very similar thing played out in Macon, Georgia's *Macon Weekly Telegraph*. See "Another Man Turn to Woman," *Petersburg (VA) Index-Appeal*, March 23, 1902; "Another Man Who Was a Woman," *Macon (GA) Weekly Telegraph*, March 23, 1902.

46 Peter Boag makes a similar point in his *Re-dressing America's Frontier Past*, arguing that the national press mobilized the trope of the "frontier" to symbolize a

pure national past in ways that purged representations of cross-dressers and other sexual/gender deviants.

47 "Howard Was a Woman."

48 As discussed above, census records indicate that Green moved from Erie, Pennsylvania, to Swift Creek, North Carolina, to Ettrick, Virginia, in the period between the 1860s and 1902, and it is likely that he moved previous to his appearance on the public record as "George Green," though those moves are lost to the historical record. For William Howard's part, he moved between the small towns of western New York, working in various itinerant positions, before settling down in the outskirts of Canandaigua.

49 U.S. Bureau of the Census, *Twelfth Census of the United States, 1900*, Prentiss, Mississippi, beat 1, roll T623_ 826, p. 12A, enumeration district 93; Prentiss County Historical Association, *History of Prentiss County, Mississippi* (Dallas: Curtis Media Corporation, 1984), 11.

50 "Dressed as a Man," *Evening Press* (Pawtucket, RI), July 23, 1903. Similar accounts appeared in "Supposed Man Really a Girl," *Chicago Daily Tribune*, July 23, 1903; "Masqueraded as a Man," *Columbus (GA) Ledger*, July 23, 1903; "Prefers Pants to Petticoats," *Atlanta Constitution*, July 23, 1903; "News Summary," *Idaho Falls Times*, July 24, 1903; "Poses as Man Eight Years," *Oxford Mirror* (Oxford Junction, IA), July 30, 1903.

51 "A Strange Case Reported," *Jackson (MS) Evening News*, July 13, 1903. This idea also appeared in newspapers throughout the country. See, for example, "Courted by the Girls Now Wears Petticoats," *Tucson Citizen*, July 17, 1903. "Mississippi Girls Are Badly Fooled," *St. Louis (MO) Post-Dispatch*, July 19, 1903; "Her Secret Found Out," *Salt Lake (UT) Tribune*, July 19, 1903.

52 Other scholars have explored the relationship between court cases regarding proper gender and sexual behavior and the press. See, for example, Lisa Duggan, *Sapphic Slashers: Sex, Violence, and American Modernity* (Durham, NC: Duke University Press, 2000); and more recently, Clare Sears, *Arresting Dress: Cross-Dressing, Law, and Fascination in Nineteenth-Century San Francisco* (Durham, NC: Duke University Press, 2014).

53 "No Title," *Daily Clarion-Ledger* (Jackson, MS), July 20, 1903.

54 Cities began passing laws prohibiting wearing the dress of the opposite sex in the mid-nineteenth century, although importantly, southern cities generally lagged behind their northern and western counterparts in passing such measures. In fact, the first two cities to pass such ordinances were Columbus, Ohio, and Chicago, Illinois (in 1848 and 1851, respectively). The first southern city to pass a cross-dressing ordinance was Charleston, South Carolina, in 1858, followed by Houston, Texas, in 1861.

55 "No Title," July 20, 1903.

56 "She Passed as Man," *Trenton (NJ) Times*, July 15, 1903; "Woman Passed as a Man for 8 Years," *New York World*, July 14, 1903; "Girl Masqueraded as a Man for Eight Years," *St. Louis (MO) Republic*, July 14, 1903; "Posed as Man Eight Years," *Atlanta*

Constitution, July 13, 1903; "Masquerades as Man," *Fort Worth Telegram*, July 17, 1903; "Girl Masqueraded as a Man," *Bisbee (AZ) Daily Review*, July 19, 1903.

57 Quote from "Courted by the Girls Now Wears Petticoats." For similar accounts, see "Mississippi Girls Are Badly Fooled"; "Her Secret Found Out."

58 William N. Eskridge Jr., *Gaylaw: Challenging the Apartheid of the Closet* (Cambridge, MA: Harvard University Press, 2002), 27.

59 U.S. Bureau of the Census, *1910 U.S. Federal Census* (Washington, DC: U.S. Government Printing Office, 1910), Prentiss, Mississippi, roll T624_756, p. 26A, enumeration district 106, image 1084; and Prentiss, Mississippi, roll T624_757, p. 24B, enumeration district 110, image 50.

60 Johnson, *Just Queer Folks*, 114.

61 Rachel Hope Cleves, *Charity and Sylvia: A Same-Sex Marriage in Early America* (New York: Oxford University Press, 2014), xiii.

62 Boag, *Re-dressing America's Frontier Past*, 1–2.

63 Monahan's life was the subject of Maggie Greenwood's 1993 film *The Ballad of Little Jo* and, more recently, an off-Broadway musical of the same name. For other scholarly interpretations of Monahan's life, see Tania Modleski, "A Woman's Gotta Do . . . What a Man's Gotta Do? Cross-Dressing in the Western," *Signs* 22, no. 3 (1997): 519–44; Yvonne Tasker, "Cowgirl Tales," in *Working Girls: Gender and Sexuality in Popular Cinema* (New York: Routledge, 1998), 49–64.

64 Historical sources spell Monahan's name is several different ways (often Monoghan or Monaghan), but in this chapter I have chosen to use to spelling that appears in 1870 and 1880 federal censuses.

65 U.S. Bureau of the Census, *1870 United States Federal Census* (Washington, DC: National Archives and Records Administration, 1870), Silver City, Idaho, household number 200. Copy in Josephine Monaghan Vertical File, Idaho State Historical Society Research Library, Boise, Idaho (hereafter referred to as ISHSRL).

66 "Joe Monaghan Was a Woman," *Idaho Daily Statesmen*, January 12, 1904; "Joe Monnahan's [*sic*] Strange Career," *Idaho Capital News*, January 14, 1904; "No Title," *Owyhee Avalanche* (Silver City, ID), January 15, 1904; "Concealed Her Sex for 40 years," *Silver City (ID) Nugget*, January 15, 1904.

67 The exact date of death is unclear, but Monahan's probate records state that he died "on or about the 5th day of January, 1904." See "In the Matter of the Estate of Johanna Monahan, Deceased," Owyhee County Probate Records, vol. 4, date January 26, 1904. Copy included in Monaghan Vertical File, ISHSRL.

68 "No Title," January 15, 1904.

69 Quotes taken from the "Local" section of the *Owyhee Avalanche*, January 15, 1904.

70 "Concealed Her Sex for 40 Years."

71 U.S. Bureau of the Census, *1880 United States Federal Census* (Washington, DC: National Archives and Records Administration, 1880), 1900 DeLamar Precinct, dwelling house number 227, enumeration district 29. Monaghan Vertical File, ISHSRL.

72 Peter Boag, "Go West Young Man, Go East Young Woman: Searching for the *Trans* in Western Gender History," *Western Historical Quarterly* 36, no. 4 (2005): 489.

73 "Masqueraded Many Years as a Cowboy, Death Disclosed Secret of Brave Woman Formerly of Buffalo," *Buffalo (NY) Evening News*, January 11, 1904.

74 Ibid.

75 Miranda Joseph, *Against the Romance of Community* (Minneapolis: University of Minnesota Press, 2002), vii.

CHAPTER 3. "THE TROUBLE THAT CLOTHES MAKE"

1 No doubt, acceptance and tolerance are two very different things. It seems clear from the evidence that rural neighbors tolerated their queer community members, in large part by not asking probing questions about their relationships or gender presentation. I see this working in a similar fashion to the distinctions Martha Hodes has made between toleration and tolerance in her work *White Women, Black Men: Illicit Sex in the Nineteenth-Century South* (New Haven, CT: Yale University Press, 1997), 3.

2 For an eloquent discussion of the ways that accusations of sexual misconduct prompted the lynching of black men, see Karlos K. Hill, *Beyond the Rope: The Impact of Lynching on Black Culture* (New York: Cambridge University Press, 2016), especially chapter 4.

3 Industrialization had eroded the scaffolding of previously dominant notions of male independence, which had been based on self-employment. Peter G. Filene estimates that in 1910, only about 37 percent of middle-class men were self-employed (a figure that had dropped from 67 percent just forty years earlier). See Filene, *Him/Her/Self: Sex Roles in Modern America* (Baltimore: Johns Hopkins University Press, 1986), 73. See also Richard Hofstadter, *The Age of Reform: From Bryan to FDR* (New York: Vintage, 1955), 218; Gail Bederman, *Manliness and Civilization: A Cultural History of Gender and Race in the United States, 1880–1917* (Chicago: University of Chicago Press, 1995), 12–18. For information regarding the women's rights movement, see Nancy F. Cott, *The Grounding of Modern Feminism* (New Haven, CT: Yale University Press, 1987). See also Jean V. Matthews, *The Rise of the New Woman: The Women's Movement in America, 1875–1930* (Chicago: Ivan R. Dee, 2003); Catherine Gourley, *Gibson Girls and Suffragists: Perceptions of Women from 1900 to 1918* (Minneapolis: Twenty-First Century Books, 2008).

4 For an example of this trope, see "Little Girl Would Be a Cowboy Bold," *New York Evening World*, January 29, 1904.

5 David Roediger, *How Race Survived U.S. History: From Settlement and Slavery to the Obama Phenomenon* (New York: Verso, 2008), 1.

6 Cheryl I. Harris, "Whiteness as Property," in *Critical Race Theory: The Key Writings That Formed the Movement*, ed. Kimberlé Crenshaw, Neil Gotanda, Gary Peller, and Kendall Thomas (New York: New Press, 1995), 277. My thinking on whiteness has also been profoundly shaped by David Roediger, *The Wages of*

Whiteness: Race and the Making of the Working Class (New York: Verso, 1991); and George Lipsitz, *Possessive Investment in Whiteness: How White People Profit from Identity Politics* (Philadelphia: Temple University Press, 1998).

7   Hannah Arendt, *The Origins of Totalitarianism* (New York: Harcourt Brace Jovanovich, 1973), 296; Lisa Caucho, *Social Death: Racialized Rightlessness and the Criminalization of the Unprotected* (New York: New York University Press, 2011), 6.

8   Khalil Muhammad, *Condemnation of Blackness: Race, Crime, and the Making of Modern America* (Cambridge, MA: Harvard University Press, 2010), 5.

9   Isabel Molina-Guzmán, "Gendering Latinidad through the Elián Discourse about Cuban Women," *Latino Studies* 3, no. 2 (2005): 182.

10 Ruby C. Tapia, "Un(di)ing Legacies: White Matters of Memory in Portraits of 'Our Princess,'" *Cultural Values* 5, no. 2 (2001): 263.

11 Leti Volpp discusses the ways the deviant behavior of racial minorities is often blamed on their racialized "culture," whereas the deviant behavior of whites is most often blamed on the individuals. See Volpp, "Blaming Culture for Bad Behavior," *Yale Journal of Law and the Humanities* 12, no. 1 (2000): 89–116.

12 Of course, sexology and race are not two disconnected categories. As Siobhan Somerville and Jennifer Terry have illustrated, sexological categories were deeply influenced by Darwinian logics. However, my point here is that sexological theories like sexual inversion were not embraced by the general public at this time. See Siobhan Somerville, *Queering the Color Line: Race and the Invention of Homosexuality in American Culture* (Durham, NC: Duke University Press, 2000); and Jennifer Terry, *An American Obsession: Science, Medicine, and Homosexuality in Modern Society* (Chicago: University of Chicago Press, 1999).

13 Certificate of marriage 5109, December 24, 1872, New York City Vital Records Collection, Municipal Archives. Celia was born in Fairfield, Maine, in 1844, and she remained in Maine into her twenties, where she worked as a schoolteacher. From the census records, it appears that she moved to New York between 1870 and 1880. U.S. Bureau of the Census, *Seventh Census of the United States* (Washington, DC: National Archives and Records Administration, 1850), Fairfield, Somerset, Maine, roll M432_269, p. 130A, image 255; U.S. Bureau of the Census, *Ninth Census of the United States* (Washington, DC: National Archives and Records Administration, 1870), Fairfield, Somerset, Maine, roll M593_558, p. 164B, image 335, Family History Library Film 552057.

14 "Murray Hall's Strange Life," *Boston Journal*, January 20, 1901.

15 "Murray Hall as a Juror," *Kansas City (MO) Star*, January 28, 1901.

16 U.S. Bureau of the Census, *Twelfth Census of the United States, 1900* (Washington, DC: National Archives and Records Administration, 1900), Manhattan, New York, roll 1085, p. 13B, enumeration district 101, FHL microfilm 1241085.

17 "Woman Who Lived Thirty Years as a Man," *San Francisco Chronicle*, January 18, 1901.

18 Ibid.

19 "Tammany Politician Proves to Be a Woman Masquerading as a Man," *Davenport (IA) Daily Leader*, January 20, 1901.

20 "Murray Hall's Sex Amazes Neighbors," *New York World*, January 19, 1901.

21 "Queer Verdict by Coroner's Jury Sitting over Murray Hall," *Daily Review* (Decatur, IL), January 29, 1901.

22 For a more detailed discussion of this, see Jane Hunter, *How Young Ladies Became Girls: The Victorian Origins of Girlhood* (New Haven, CT: Yale University Press, 2003).

23 For work on the woman suffrage movement, see, for example, Eleanor Flexner and Ellen Fitzpatrick, *Century of Struggle: The Woman's Rights Movement in the United States* (Cambridge, MA: Belknap Press of Harvard University Press, 1996); Ellen Dubois, *Woman Suffrage and Woman's Rights* (New York: New York University Press, 1998); and, more recently, Lisa Tetrault, *The Myth of Seneca Falls: Memory and the Women's Suffrage Movement, 1848–1898* (Chapel Hill: University of North Carolina Press, 2014); and Sally McMillen, *Lucy Stone: An Unapologetic Life* (New York: Oxford University Press, 2015).

24 See Laura L. Behling, "Unsightly Evidence: 'Female Inversion' and the U.S. Woman Suffrage Movement," in *The Masculine Woman in America, 1890–1935* (Urbana: University of Illinois Press, 2001), 21–59.

25 "Woman's Rights Convention," *New York Herald*, October 25, 1850.

26 "Murray Hall's Life," *Dallas Morning News*, May 5, 1901.

27 "Whiskers for Tammany Men," *New York Times*, January 20, 1901.

28 "Famous Cases in the Past Where Women Have Lived as Men, Reviewed by Cyrus Edson, M.D.," *New York World* (Sunday supplement), January 20, 1901.

29 Ibid.

30 The cases of women fighting as men in the Civil War have been well documented. See, for example, DeAnne Blanton and Lauren Cook, *They Fought Like Demons: Women Soldiers and the Civil War* (New York: Vintage, 2003).

31 "Famous Cases in the Past Where Women have Lived as Men, Reviewed by Cyrus Edson, M.D."

32 "Some Men-Women," *Boston Journal*, October 17, 1901.

33 "List or Manifest of Alien Passengers for the United States," *Passenger Lists of Vessels Arriving at New York, New York, 1897–1957*, Records of the U.S. Customs Service, Record Group 36, National Archives, Washington, DC, year 1908; microfilm serial T715, microfilm roll T715_1151, line 17.

34 "Record of Aliens Held for Special Inquiry," Passenger and Crew Lists of Vessels Arriving at New York, New York, 1897–1957, Records of the Immigration and Naturalization Service, National Archives at Washington, DC, microfilm serial T715, microfilm roll T715_1151, line 12. In explaining the decision, Robert Watchorn, Ellis Island commissioner of immigration, told the *New York Sun*, "The woman is able to earn her living and there was no reason for deporting her." See "Mustached Woman Free," *New York Sun*, October 6, 1908.

35 "Masquerades in Male Costume," *Los Angeles Times*, October 5, 1908.

36 "Lived 15 Years as a Man," *New York Tribune*, October 5, 1908. Similarly, the *New York Sun* reported, "She has been compelled to live up to her mustache, a disfigurement to her as a woman that prevented her from obtaining work except of the hardest kind on ranches in the West or farms elsewhere." See "Mustached, She Plays Man," *New York Sun*, October 5, 1908. Similar narratives appeared in newspapers nationwide, including the *Syracuse Herald* and the *San Francisco Call*. See, for example, "Left in Male Attire," *Syracuse (NY) Herald*, October 6, 1908; "Woman Masqueraded as Man for 15 Years," *San Francisco Call*, October 5, 1907; "Lived 15 Years as a Man"; "Woman Posed Long as Man," *Fort Worth Star-Telegram*, October 11, 1908; "Woman Admits She Is Ugly," *Alexandria (VA) Gazette*, October 6, 1908.

37 "Happy as a Man, Posed for 15 Years," *New York World*, October 5, 1908.

38 "Mustached, She Plays Man"; "For 15 Years," *Lowell (MA) Sun*, October 5, 1908.

39 Nancy Fraser and Linda Gordon, "A Genealogy of 'Dependency': Tracing a Keyword of the U.S. Welfare State," *Signs: Journal of Women and Culture in Society* 19, no. 2 (1994): 316.

40 *The Municipal Code of Chicago: Comprising the Laws of Illinois Relating to the City of Chicago, and the Ordinance of the City Council* (Chicago, 1881), law 1612, p. 377.

41 Clare Sears, "'A Dress Not Belonging to His or Her Sex': Cross-Dressing Law in San Francisco, 1860–1900" (PhD diss., University of California, Santa Cruz, 2005), 134.

42 Susan Schweik, *The Ugly Laws: Disability in Public* (New York: New York University Press, 2009), 165. Douglas Baynton has similarly argued, "When categories of citizenship were questioned, challenged, and disrupted, disability was called on to clarify and define who deserved, and who was deservedly excluded from, citizenship." See Baynton, "Disability and the Justification of Inequality in America," in *Race, Class, and Gender in the United States: An Integrated Study*, 7th ed., ed. Paula S. Rothenberg (New York: St. Martin's Press, 2007), 93.

43 Eli Clare, "Stolen Bodies, Reclaimed Bodies: Disability and Queerness," *Public Culture* 13, no. 3 (2001): 360.

44 "Mustached, She Plays Man."

45 By the early twentieth century, immigration into the United States was already limited by nation of origin: the 1882 Chinese Exclusion Act and the 1908 Gentlemen's Agreement made immigration from China and Japan extremely difficult. For information about Chinese immigration in this period, see Erica Lee, *At America's Gates: Chinese Immigration during the Exclusion Era, 1882–1943* (Chapel Hill: University of North Carolina Press, 2003). For information on the Gentlemen's Agreement, see Eithne Luibhéid, "Birthing a Nation: Race, Ethnicity, and Childbearing," in *Entry Denied: Controlling Sexuality at the Border* (Minneapolis: University of Minnesota Press, 2002), 55–76.

46 Martha Gardner, *The Qualities of a Citizen: Women, Immigration, and Citizenship, 1870–1965* (Princeton, NJ: Princeton University Press, 2005); Donna Gabaccia,

From the Other Side: Women, Gender, and Immigrant Life in the United States, 1820–1990 (Bloomington: Indiana University Press, 1994).

47 Eithne Luibhéid, "Introduction: Queering Migration and Citizenship," in *Queer Migrations: Sexuality, U.S. Citizenship, and Border Crossings*, ed. Eithne Luibhéid and Lionel Cantú Jr. (Minneapolis: University of Minnesota Press, 2005), xv.

48 "Left in Male Attire." The same article also appeared as "Woman Admits She Is Ugly"; "In Men's Clothes," *Hopkinsville Kentuckian*, October 8, 1908.

49 "Lived 15 Years as a Man."

50 Ibid. In Erica Rand's discussion of Woodhull's case, she argues that newspapers cast Woodhull as having a "humble economic status" because of references to Woodhull's occupation as a canvasser. Significantly, Rand's conclusions were based exclusively on a reading of the New York press, and considered only references to Woodhull's employment as indicative of his class status. However, newspapers generally placed more emphasis on Woodhull's capacity to be employable (through his queer embodiment) rather than his employment history. Additionally, newspapers on the local and national scale made frequent reference to Woodhull's strong moral fiber and respectability, two qualities that can be understood as implying middle-class standing. See Erica Rand, "Getting Dressed Up: The Displays of Frank Woodhull and the Policing of Gender," in *Ellis Island Snow Globe* (Durham, NC: Duke University Press, 2005), 67–106.

51 "Lives and Works 15 Years as Man," *Chicago Daily Tribune*, October 5, 1908; "Lived as Man," *Hutchinson (KS) News*, October 6, 1908.

52 "Mustached, She Plays Man."

53 "Woman in Male Garb Gains Her Freedom," *New York Times*, October 6, 1908.

54 "Lived 15 Years as a Man."

55 This article was attributed to the *New York World* and was syndicated nationally, including in the *Washington Post* and *Cleveland Plain Dealer*. See "The Trouble That Clothes Make," *Washington Post*, October 15, 1908; "The Trouble That Clothes Make and the Strange Adventure in Masquerade That Have Bothered," *Cleveland (OH) Plain Dealer*, October 18, 1908.

56 "The Trouble That Clothes Make."

57 Ibid.

58 Ibid.

59 On the "List or Manifest of Alien Passengers for the United States," Woodhull's nationality is listed as "Canada" and his "race or people" is listed as "English."

60 Luibhéid, *Entry Denied*, xv.

61 Elizabeth Yew, "Medical Inspection of the Immigrant at Ellis Island: 1891–1924," *Bulletin of the New York Academy of Medicine* 56, no. 5 (1980): 488–510.

62 Nayan Shah, *Contagious Divides: Epidemics and Race in San Francisco's Chinatown* (Berkeley: University of California Press, 2001), 184.

63 Michael Minch told the *Brooklyn Eagle*, "Since their [1886] marriage in County Kildare, Ireland, twenty years back, [they] have passed through the Immigration

bureau no less than half a dozen times without awakening the slightest suspicion in the officials." See "Twenty Years a Husband, but 'Michael' Is a Woman," *Brooklyn Eagle*, April 25, 1906. While this is likely an exaggeration, it appears to be not much of a stretch, as I have found Michael and Margaret Minch listed together on ship manifests twice in the years preceding their 1906 detention at Ellis Island: in 1890 and again in 1897. The pair would again successfully enter the United States (this time through Boston) in 1908. See "Passenger Lists of Vessels Arriving at New York, New York, 1820–1897," National Archives Microfilm Publication T715, 8892 rolls, year 1890, arrival New York, United States, microfilm serial M237, microfilm roll M237_544, line 31, list number 300; "List of Manifest," 1897 Passenger Lists of Vessels Arriving at New York, New York, 1820–1897, National Archives Microfilm Publication M237, 675 rolls, year 1897, microfilm serial 15, microfilm roll T715_1, line 15; "Passenger Lists of Vessels Arriving at Boston, Massachusetts, 1891–1943," National Archives and Records Administration, Washington, DC, microfilm serial T938, microfilm roll 127.

64 Margot Canaday, "'A New Species of Undesirable Immigrant': Perverse Aliens and the Limits of the Law, 1900–1924," in *The Straight State: Sexuality and Citizenship in Twentieth-Century America* (Princeton, NJ: Princeton University Press, 2009), 19–54.

65 U.S. Bureau of the Census, *Seventh Census of the United States, 1850*, Newtown, Fairfield, Connecticut, roll M432_37, p. 9, image 19; *Second Annual Catalogue of the Officers and Students of Vassar College (New York: John A. Green Printers, 1867)*, 11.

66 The official marriage record has been destroyed, but the marriage is referenced in local church record indices. See *Connecticut Church Records, State Library, Newtown—First Congregational Church, 1715–1946* (Hartford: Connecticut State Library, 1962), 25. De Forest references this marriage in newspaper interviews several decades later. See, for example, "'Potential Man' Belies Sex; Offers Problem," *Oakland (CA) Tribune*, September 2, 1915.

67 It appears that in 1880 Bradley was living in San Francisco with his mother, Julia, and a cousin, Ella. See U.S. Bureau of the Census, *Tenth Census of the United States, 1880* (Washington, DC: National Archives and Records Administration, 1880), San Francisco, California, roll T9_75, family history film 1254075, p. 356.1000, enumeration district 92, image 413.

68 "Newsboy's Home: Miss Eugenie De Forest to Appear for Its Benefit," *Morning Call* (San Francisco), October 1, 1893.

69 De Forest placed ads for his business in the *San Francisco Call*, and in July 1891 the address was listed as "Saratoga Hall, 814 Geary." In November 1903 the address was listed as "Eugene De Forest School of Acting. Saratoga Hall, 840 Geary St." See ads for education in the *San Francisco Call* of July 19, 1891, and November 18, 1903.

70 The final ad for De Forest's acting school appears in the *San Francisco Call* on November 18, 1909.

71 "Drama Prof. Proves to Be Woman," *Los Angeles Evening Herald*, September 1, 1915.

72 Caucho, *Social Death*, 2.

73 "Strange Story of Masquerade," *Los Angeles Times*, September 2, 1915.

74 See, for example, "Drama Prof. Proves to Be Woman"; "Prof. De Forest Is Free; Marriage Is Barred," *Los Angeles Evening Herald*, September 2, 1915.

75 "Strange Story of Masquerade."

76 "Drama Prof. Proves to be Woman"; " 'Man'-Woman Renounced by Fiancée," *Los Angeles Evening Herald*, September 1, 1915.

77 "Remarkable Story of a Los Angeles Woman Who Posed as Man 22 Years as a Result of Pre-natal Influence," *Washington Post*, September 19, 1915. Similar explanations appeared in newspapers nationwide, including "Woman Tells Own Story of Twenty-Five Years as a Man," *Los Angeles Evening Herald*, September 1, 1915; and "Strange Story of Masquerade." It's interesting to note that a similar explanation of the "pre-natal influence" is cited as influencing the sexual inversion the main character in Radclyffe Hall's *The Well of Loneliness*, first published in 1928.

78 "Wed, She Says, Both as Man and Woman," *New York World*, September 2, 1915. A similar explanation appears in "Pleads to Wear Male Attire," *Los Angeles Examiner*, September 2, 1915.

79 "Pleads to Wear Male Attire."

80 "Remarkable Story of a Los Angeles Woman Who Posed as Man 22 Years as a Result of Pre-natal Influence"; "Strange Story of Masquerade"; "Pleads to Wear Male Attire."

81 "Pleads to Wear Male Attire."

82 "Weds 'He' and 'She,' " *Washington Post*, September 2, 1915.

83 "Pleads to Wear Male Attire." See also " 'Potential Man' Belies Sex; Offers Problem," *Oakland (CA) Tribune*, September 2, 1915; "Weds 'He' and 'She.' "

84 "Pleads to Wear Male Attire."

85 "Remarkable Story of a Los Angeles Woman Who Posed as Man 22 Years as a Result of Pre-natal Influence"; "Prof. De Forest Can Wear Men's Clothes," *Evening News* (San Jose), September 3, 1915; " 'Potential Man' Belies Sex; Offers Problem," *Oakland (CA) Tribune*, September 2, 1915; "Wed, She Says, Both as Man And Woman," *New York World*, September 2, 1915; "Strange Story of Masquerade"; "Prof. De Forest Is Free; Marriage Is Barred."

86 "Prof. De Forest Can Wear Men's Clothes."

87 "Masqueraded in Man's Clothes," *Quincy (IL) Daily Whig*, November 28, 1899. Ellis Glenn has received scant attention by historians thus far, despite having been mentioned in Havelock Ellis's *Studies in the Psychology of Sex*. One notable exception is Kerry Segrave, "Various Frauds," in *Women Swindlers in America, 1860–1920* (Jefferson, NC: McFarland, 2007), 186–209.

88 "Ellis Glenn Is Not a Man," *St. Louis (MO) Post-Dispatch*, November 26, 1899.

89 "Identified," *Paducah (KY) Sun*, October 25, 1899; "Identified and Will Be Tried," *Daily Public Ledger* (Maysville, KY), October 26, 1899.

90 "Prisoner Proves a Woman," *Chicago Daily Tribune*, November 26, 1899. Initially, Glenn stated that the twin sister's name was Alice, but he later claimed that the sister's name was actually Ellis, and that the brother had assumed his sister's name in order to avoid prosecution on outstanding warrants.

91 "Study of 'Ellis Glenn,'" *Chicago Daily Tribune*, November 29, 1899.

92 Several recent books have grappled with the cultural logics of sensational trials. See, in particular, Robert A. Ferguson, *The Trial in American Life* (Chicago: University of Chicago Press, 2007). Additionally, several scholars have recently published works interrogating the ways gender affects court trials (and their coverage in the media). See, for example, Gordon Morris Bakken and Brenda Farrington, *Women Who Kill Men: California Courts, Gender, and the Press* (Lincoln: University of Nebraska Press, 2009).

93 "'Ellis Glenn' Again on Trial," *New York Times*, July 9, 1901. This statement is likely not an exaggeration, as I have found well over two hundred articles published on Glenn's case in the nation's dailies between 1899 and 1905.

94 See, for example, "Ellis Glenn, He, She or It?" *Post-Standard* (Syracuse, NY), November 26, 1899; "Engaged to a Woman," *Sunday World-Herald* (Omaha, NE), November 26, 1899; "Cut to the Core," *Sandusky (OH) Star*, November 27, 1899; "Their Prisoner Was a Woman," *Wellsboro (PA) Agitator*, November 29, 1899; "Is It Glenn or Rader?" *Waterloo (IA) Daily Courier*, December 1, 1899; "Ellis Glenn a Noted Forger," *Logansport (IN) Journal*, December 3, 1899; "Sets Aside Sentence," *Morning Olympian* (Olympia, WA), December 3, 1899; "A Woman," *Hopkinsville Kentuckian*, November 28, 1899; Ellis Glenn Case Now Ended," *Aurora (IL) Daily Express*, December 13, 1899; "Funny Mr. Glenn," *Daily Iowa Capital* (Des Moines), November 28, 1899.

95 See, for example, "'Ellis Glenn' Again on Trial"; "Ellis Glenn on Trial"; "Did Miss Ellis Glenn Masquerade as a Man?" *New York World*, July 8, 1901; "The Ellis-Glenn Case," *Anaconda (MT) Standard*, July 10, 1901; "Ellis Glenn Is on Trial," *Morning Herald* (Lexington, KY), July 9, 1901; "Ellis Glenn Arraigned," *Montgomery (AL) Advertiser*, July 9, 1901; "Ellis Glenn on Trial," *Fort Worth Register*, July 9, 1901; "Ellis Glenn Is on Trial," *Duluth (MN) News-Tribune*, July 9, 1901; "Woman Held for Forgery," *Columbus (OH) Enquirer-Sun*, July 9, 1901; "Glenn Case Is on Trial," *Washington Post*, July 9, 1901; "Ellis Glenn, Man-Woman, Is on Trial," *Daily News-Democrat* (Belleville, IL), July 9, 1901; "Trial of the Mysterious Ellis Glenn Commenced," *Chicago Daily Tribune*, July 9, 1901.

96 "Legal Tilt in Glenn Trial," *St. Louis (MO) Post-Dispatch*, July 21, 1901. While most papers covering the story published similar sentiments, a few other papers expressed doubts concerning the possibility of conviction. See "Tables Turned," *Paducah (KY) Sun*, July 20, 1901; "Prisoner Not Bert Glenn," *Washington Post*, July 20, 1901.

97 An Associated Press newswire that appeared widely reported that the final ballots resulted in seven jurors voting for conviction, with five voting for acquittal. See, for example, "Ellis Glenn Forgery Case," *New York Times*, July 31, 1901; "Glenn

Jury Dismissed," *Morning Herald* (Lexington, KY), July 31, 1901; "Glenn Case Closes," *Los Angeles Times*, July 31, 1901.

98 "Ellis Glenn Case to Be Re-Tried," *Morning Herald* (Lexington, KY), March 17, 1903.

99 "Ellis Glenn Freed," *Washington Post*, June 4, 1905.

100 "Ellen Glenn Reappears," *Chicago Daily Tribune*, August 26, 1905.

101 Ibid.

102 "Ellis Glenn Just Can't Be Good," *Paducah (KY) Sun*, August 28, 1905.

103 "Ellis Glenn in Again," *Baltimore Sun*, August 28, 1905. The same account appeared in "Ellis Glenn, the Man-Woman, in New Scrape," *New York World*, August 26, 1905; "Is Ellis Glenn in Police Toils?" *St. Louis (MO) Post-Dispatch*, August 27, 1905.

104 "Ellen Glenn Is Sentenced," *Logansport (IN) Journal*, November 23, 1905. See also "Ellen Glenn Sentenced," *Daily News* (Marshall, MI), December 1, 1905; "Sentenced to Three Years in Prison," *Detroit Free Press*, November 23, 1905; "Ellen Glenn Is Guilty," *Detroit Free Press*, November 17, 1905; "Ellen Glenn Guilty," *Daily News* (Marshall, MI), November 17, 1905. According to the register of the Detroit House of Corrections, Glenn ultimately only served about two and a half years and was paroled on February 21, 1908, on account of poor health. Romie Minor, an archivist at the Special Collections Department of the Detroit Public Library, provided this citation.

105 Among the many fictions in this account is Glenn's location; while Ellis references here that he came before the "public in Chicago," he is mistaken. He drew heavily from Chicago papers (especially the *Chicago Tribune*) in his writing, so it's likely that he confused the location of the source for the location of the subject. See Havelock Ellis, *Studies in the Psychology of Sex*, vol. 2: *Sexual Inversion*, 3rd ed. (1927; Charleston, SC: BiblioBooks, 2006), 295.

106 Significantly, however, this description of Glenn's body contradicts many of those published around Glenn's initial arrest in 1899. For example, in December 1899, both the *St. Paul Globe* and *Philadelphia Inquirer* described Glenn as being "about five feet tall, and will weigh not even 100 pounds." See "For a Brother's Guilt," *St. Paul (MN) Globe*, December 10, 1899; "The Romance of Ellis Green [sic]," *Philadelphia Inquirer*, December 10, 1899; "Study of 'Ellis Glenn." Various other descriptions of Glenn's body published over his lengthy tenure in the press suggested that he may have been taller—the *Chicago Tribune*, for example, reported in November 1899 that Glenn was five feet seven inches tall—but generally he was described as being rather short and slender. The records of the Detroit House of Corrections indicate that upon his release in 1908 he weighed 118 pounds. See Register of the Detroit House of Corrections, Detroit Public Library.

107 Ellis argued, "It is . . . noteworthy that a remarkably large portion of the cases in which homosexuality has led to crimes of violence, or otherwise come under medico-legal observation, has been among women. It is [well-known] that the part taken by women generally in open criminality, and especially in crimes of

violence, is small as compared with men. In the homosexual field, as we might have anticipated, the conditions are to some extant reversed . . . Inverted women, who may retain their feminine emotionality combined with some degree of infantile impulsiveness and masculine energy, present a favorable soil for the seeds of passional [sic] crime, under those conditions of jealousy and allied emotions which must so often enter into the invert's life." Ellis, *Studies in the Psychology of Sex*, 243.

108 Of course, there was still some disagreement within the sexological community regarding whether inversion should be considered a pathology. Havelock Ellis himself expressed some ambivalence about this issue, but from his perspective, ultimately, inverts were abnormal and prone to violence. Sexologists, then, were still far more uniform in their representations of inverts than the press was in this period.

109 Siobhan Somerville has discussed the ways sexologists in this era (including Havelock Ellis) utilized racial taxonomies and evolutionary theories in their work, and found anatomical similarities between (white) lesbians and African American women, evidence that both categories of women were "anomalous 'throwbacks' within a scheme of cultural and anatomical progress." See Somerville, *Queering the Color Line: Race and the Invention of Homosexuality in American Culture* (Durham, NC: Duke University Press, 2000), 29.

CHAPTER 4. GENDER TRANSGRESSIONS IN THE AGE OF U.S. EMPIRE

1 Many scholars have discussed the ways that official imperial discourse often legitimates imperialism through invocations of the aberrant gender and/or sexual formations within "backward" spaces. In the context of U.S. imperialism, see Warwick Anderson, *Colonial Pathologies: American Tropical Medicine, Race, and Hygiene in the Philippines* (Durham, NC: Duke University Press, 2006); Laura Briggs, *Reproducing Empire: Race, Sex, Science, and U.S. Imperialism in Puerto Rico* (Berkeley: University of California Press, 2002); Pablo Mitchell, *Coyote Nation: Sexuality, Race, and Conquest in Modernizing New Mexico, 1880–1920* (Chicago: University of Chicago Press, 2005); and Victor Román Mendoza, *Metroimperial Intimacies: Fantasy, Racial-Sexual Governance, and the Philippines in U.S. Imperialism, 1899–1913* (Durham, NC: Duke University Press, 2015). For an excellent discussion of how U.S. imperialism shaped domestic structures of race and sex, see Fiona Ngô, *Imperial Blues: Geographies of Race and Sex in Jazz Age New York* (Durham, NC: Duke University Press, 2014).

2 In this section, I will refer to Mugarrieta with male pronouns, as he lived the majority of his life as a man. Mugarrieta (or Jack Garland, the name he would later go by) has been discussed by several previous scholars, most notably Louis Sullivan, *From Female to Male: The Life of Jack Bee Garland* (Boston: Alyson Books, 1990); Nan Alamilla Boyd, "The Materiality of Gender: Looking for Lesbian Bodies in Transgender History," *Journal of Lesbian Studies* 3, no. 3 (1999): 73–81; Peter Boag, *Re-dressing America's Frontier Past* (Berkeley: University of California Press,

2011), 50–52; Linda Heidenreich, "Jack Mugarrieta Garland: A Queer Mestiz@ in the 'American West,'" *Lilith: A Feminist History Journal* 21 (August 2015): 65–77. Garland is also discussed in the 1979 documentary *She Even Chewed Tobacco* by the San Francisco Lesbian and Gay History Project.

3 Eliza Alice Mugarrieta, "Memorandum de la Senora Elisa A. De Mugarrieta, Referente a sus Trabajos y Luchas para Obtener Justicia del Gobierno de Mexico en la Reclamacion de su Fallecido Esposo el Comandante Jose Marcos Mugarrieta," Jose Marcos Murrieta Collection, 69/93m, Box 3, Folder "Mugarrieta, Eliza Alice," Bancroft Library at the University of California, Berkley.

4 For more information about Anglo attitudes toward Mexican Americans in this period, see Arnoldo De Leon, *They Called Them Greasers: Anglo Attitudes toward Mexicans in Texas, 1821–1900* (Austin: University of Texas Press, 1983).

5 "Was Dressed as a Boy, Pretty Miss Bean Travels around the World," *Stockton (CA) Daily Record*, August 23, 1897.

6 "Not Clara Garcia," *Stockton (CA) Daily Record*, September 29, 1897. For the original report, see "Babe Beam Is Clara Garcia," *Stockton (CA) Daily Record*, September 25, 1897.

7 "Wants Her for a Sister," *Stockton (CA) Daily Record*, September 11, 1897.

8 Many scholars have discussed the ways the state began to police gender and sexual normativity along racial and national lines at the turn of the twentieth century. See, for example, Margot Canaday, *The Straight State: Sexuality and Citizenship in Twentieth-Century America* (Princeton, NJ: Princeton University Press, 2009); Siobhan Somerville, *Queering the Color Line: Race and the Invention of Homosexuality in American Culture* (Durham, NC: Duke University Press, 2000); Nayan Shah, *Stranger Intimacy: Contesting Race, Sexuality, and the Law in the North American West* (Berkeley: University of California Press, 2012); Mendoza, *Metroimperial Intimacies*.

9 Bean did many things in order to seem less threatening than his gender deviance might initially suggest. For example, he expressed his support for heterosexual marriage and his opposition to "New Women," and consistently illustrated his knowledge of the legal codes surrounding dress, thereby displaying his desire to be a law-abiding citizen.

10 "Was Dressed as a Boy, Pretty Miss Bean Travels around the World." For a longer, more detailed description of Bean's time in Stockton, see Sullivan, *From Female to Male*.

11 For examples of Bean's articles, see "Babe Bean Hunts Bandits," *Stockton (CA) Evening Mail*, September 15, 1897; "Stockton's Men and Women," *Stockton (CA) Evening Mail*, September 28, 1897.

12 "Baby Bean a Bonny Boy," *Honolulu (HI) Evening Bulletin*, October 17, 1899.

13 Paul Kramer, *The Blood of Government: Race, Empire, the United States, and the Philippines* (Chapel Hill: University of North Carolina Press, 2006), 89–90.

14 "Was Jack Bee Garland on City of Para?" *San Francisco Chronicle*, September 24, 1936.

15 "Jack Goes to Japan," *Manila Freedom*, June 13, 1900. For additional newspaper coverage of Mugarrieta's time in Manila, see, for example, "'Babe' Bean the Stowaway," *San Francisco Chronicle*, November 2, 1899; "Girl Stowaway Reaches Manila," *San Francisco Chronicle*, December 12, 1899; "'Babe' Bean Is in Manila," *Stockton (CA) Evening Mail*, December 13, 1899; "Serious Accident," *Manila Freedom*, January 7, 1900; "Beebe Bean There," *Manila Freedom*, February 15, 1900; "Babe Bean Arrested in the City of Manila," *Stockton (CA) Evening Mail*, April 4, 1900; "Exploits of an Extraordinary Woman," *Stockton (CA) Evening Mail*, April 28, 1900; "Beebe Beam Back from the War," *San Francisco Examiner*, August 8, 1900.

16 Beebe Beam, "My Life as a Solider," *Sunday Examiner Magazine*, October 21, 1900.

17 Bean's mother, Eliza Alice Mugarrieta, describes her husband's military service in detail in a document titled "Memorandum de la Senora Elisa A. De Mugarrieta," Jose Marcos Murrieta Collection, 69/93m, Box 3, Folder "Mugarrieta, Eliza Alice," Bancroft Library at the University of California, Berkley.

18 "My Life as a Solider."

19 Significantly, this production was not without historical precedent. Many women served as men in the Civil War, and several of them even received pensions later in life in return for their service. For a discussion of these cases, see Lauren Cook Burgess, *An Uncommon Solider: The Civil War Letters of Sarah Wakeman, 153rd Regiment, New York State Volunteers, 1862–1864* (New York: Oxford University Press, 1996); De Anne Blanton and Lauren M. Cook, *They Fought Like Demons: Women Soldiers in the Civil War* (New York: Vintage, 2003).

20 Kristin Hoganson, *Fighting for American Manhood: How Gender Politics Provoked the Spanish-American and Philippine-American Wars* (New Haven, CT: Yale University Press, 1998), 142.

21 Garland's tattoo is described in "Military Rites Advocated for Jack Garland," *San Francisco Chronicle*, September 22, 1936. For another discussion of the performative impact of tattoos in terms of race, nation, and imperialism, see David Brody, *Visualizing Empire: Orientalism and Imperialism in the Philippines* (Chicago: University of Chicago Press, 2010), 15–18.

22 "Woman in Man's Clothes Arrested as Spy Suspect," *Los Angeles Times*, December 29, 1917.

23 It appears that upon arrest, once Garland's "true sex" was revealed by police, he once again claimed the identity of "Beebe Bean." However, evidence from Garland's time spent in Los Angeles suggests he was, in fact, living under the name Jack Garland prior to arrest, and thus I have chosen to refer to him as Garland in this section.

24 "Woman in Man's Clothes Arrested as Spy Suspect."

25 For a more in-depth discussion of the representation of the Boxer Rebellion in the U.S. imagination, see Paul A. Cohen, *History in Three Keys: The Boxers as Event, Experience, and Myth* (New York: Columbia University Press, 1997), 15.

26 "Bare History of Freed Man-Woman," *Los Angeles Times*, January 1, 1918. A letter by a friend of Garland's, dated February 11, 1918, suggests that upon release from

police custody, Garland was committed to St. Luke's Hospital in San Francisco, but this fact is not mentioned anywhere in the press coverage. See John to Sophie Treadwell, February 11, 1918, Bruce G. Shapiro Papers, GLBT Historical Society, San Francisco.

27 "Suspected as 'Mme. H.,'" *Washington Post*, December 30, 1917.

28 Ibid.; "Girl Dressed in Men's Togs Held in German Plot," *Chicago Daily Tribune*, December 30, 1917.

29 The first record of De Raylan in the United States is an ad he placed in the *New York Herald*, subletting an apartment on behalf of the "Imperial Russian Commissioner" in August 1893. The ad was placed in hopes of attracting visitors who planned to visit Chicago for the World's Fair. See "Advertisements," *New York Herald*, August 27, 1893. For examples of the theories about De Raylan's arrival in the United States see "No Title," *Tucson (AZ) Citizen*, December 22, 1906; "Death Bares Dual Life," *Chicago Daily Tribune*, December 20, 1906.

30 "Cut Marital Ties," *Chicago Daily*, June 14, 1903; "Illinois, Cook County Marriages, 1871–1920," Family History Library, Salt Lake City, Utah; Illinois Department of Public Health records, "Marriage Records, 1871–Present," Division of Vital Records, Springfield.

31 Nicolai De Raylan death certificate, De Raylan File, Chicago History Museum. The certificate indicates he was buried five days later in Greenwood Cemetery in Phoenix.

32 "Sex of Russian Diplomat of Chicago Bared by Death?" *Chicago Tribune*, December 19, 1906.

33 "Consul's Life a Big Enigma in Chicago," *Pittsburgh (PA) Press*, December 22, 1906.

34 This interview was published in newspapers nationwide. See, for example, "De Raylan Was Not a Faithful 'Husband,'" *Arizona Journal-Miner* (Prescott), January 11, 1907; "Wives Were Tricked by Smooth De Raylan," *Tucson (AZ) Daily Citizen*, January 4, 1907; "New Light on 'Mr.' De Raylan," *Baltimore American*, December 31, 1906.

35 See, for example: "De Raylan Case Clear," *Washington Post*, December 25, 1906; "De Raylan's Wives Clear Up Mystery of Woman Husband," *Evening Times* (Grand Forks, ND), December 26, 1906; "Woman Is Husband to Two Women," *San Francisco Call*, December 25, 1906; "Lived as Man for 15 Years," *Fort Worth Star-Telegram*, December 24, 1906; "She Wed a Woman," *Grand Rapids (MI) Press*, December 24, 1906; "'Wives' Acknowledge De Raylan's Real Sex," *Pawtucket (RI) Times*, December 24, 1906; "De Raylan Mystery Has Been Solved," *Tucson (AZ) Daily Citizen*, December 24, 1906; "Strange Mystery Solved," *Dallas Morning News*, December 25, 1906; "Remarkable Career of Chicago Man-Woman," *Montgomery (AL) Advertiser*, December 25, 1906.

36 "Death Bares Dual Life, " *Chicago Daily Tribune*, December 20, 1906.

37 "Body Will Be Disinterred," *Los Angeles Times*, May 28, 1907.

38 See, for example, the articles cited above, in note 34.

39 "De Raylan Case Clear."
40 "Wives Explain De Raylan Farce," *Chicago Daily Tribune*, December 24, 1906.
41 "Mystery Made Known," *Bryan (TX) Morning Eagle*, December 25, 1906.
42 See Canaday, *Straight State*.
43 "Thinks De Raylan Not Dead," *Chicago Daily News*, December 20, 1906. Anna De Raylan was so convinced that her husband was a man that she ordered that the body be exhumed and reevaluated in the spring of 1907. This may have been motivated by the fact that De Raylan's reported sex nullified their marriage, according to the Chicago courts, and as such Anna De Raylan lost the rights to her husband's estate (valued at over $6,000). However, the exhumed body proved to be anatomically female, and after some protest (claiming that perhaps De Raylan's head had been affixed to a female body), Anna De Raylan dropped her case and the estate ultimately was paid to De Raylan's mother back in Russia. See Notice, May 14, 1907, probate case P2–8482 (Probate File Copies: Anne De Raylan), Office of the Clerk of the Circuit Court of Cook Country, Chicago; "Consul Identified De Raylan," *Chicago Daily News*, May 29, 1907.
44 "Wives Say He Was a Man," *Kansas City (MO) Star*, December 20, 1906.
45 "Death Bares Dual Life," *Chicago Daily Tribune*, December 20, 1906.
46 "Thrice a Husband 'He' Is a Woman," *Pawtucket (RI) Times*, December 20, 1906.
47 Ibid.
48 "The Peculiar Mania Which Drives Some Women to Adopt the Clothes of Men," *Washington Post*, March 24, 1907.
49 Ibid.
50 An earlier version of this section appeared as Emily Skidmore, "Ralph Kerwineo's Queer Body: Narrating the Scales of Social Membership in the Early Twentieth Century," *GLQ: A Journal of Lesbian and Gay Studies* 20, no. 1 (2014): 141–66.
51 Kerwineo's racial background was described in numerous ways throughout his life. For example, the 1870 federal census lists all six members of Kerwineo's family (the Andersons) as "mulatto." On the 1880 census, they are each listed as "black." See U.S. Bureau of the Census, *Ninth Census of the United States, 1870* (Washington, DC: U.S. Government Printing Office, 1870), Kendallville Ward 2, Noble, Indiana, p. 9, lines 23–28; U.S. Bureau of the Census, "Census Reports Compiled from the Ninth Census," 1870, table 3, State of Indiana, p. 128; U.S. Bureau of the Census, *Tenth Census of the United States, 1880* (Washington, DC: U.S. Government Printing Office, 1882), City of Kendallville p. 32, line 38. However, Kerwineo's identity as part Native American is articulated by numerous parties and mentioned in Noble County Genealogical Society, *The Cemeteries of Noble County, Volume II* (Kendallville, IN: Modern Publishing, 1985), 11.
52 Chicago's city directory lists Cora Anderson and Mamie White as both living at 2714 Wabash Avenue and each working as nurses in 1904. See *Chicago City Directory* (Chicago: Chicago Directory Co., 1904), 181. The first time the pair appears in the Milwaukee city directory is in 1908. Kerwineo is listed as "Ralphero Kerwineo,

teacher." See *Wright's Directory of Milwaukee, 1908* (Milwaukee: Alfred G. Wright, 1908), 223, 1548.

53 Marriage certificate of Ralphero Kerwinies and Dorothy Kleinowski, March 24, 1914, by Edward J. Burke, Milwaukee Register of Deeds, v. 243.

54 By 1910, the city's population had swollen to 373,857, the vast majority of whom were either immigrants themselves or the children of immigrants. African Americans, on the other hand, were much smaller in number, comprising only 0.2% of the city's population—a percentage much lower than most other northern cities (and far smaller than Chicago's). Native Americans composed an even smaller portion of the city's population. See U.S. Bureau of the Census, *Thirteenth Census of the United States, Vol. 3: Population, 1910* (Washington, DC: U.S. Government Printing Office, 1913), 1101, 1075; Paula Lynagh, *Milwaukee's Negro Community* (Milwaukee: Citizen's Government Research Bureau, 1946), 4. Historian John Higham and scholar of religion Robert Orsi have usefully suggested that the new immigrants of eastern and southern Europe might be considered as "in-between peoples," as they often experienced racialization that was "in between" hard racism and full inclusion. See John Higham, *Strangers in the Land: Patterns of American Nativism, 1860–1925* (New York: Antheneum, 1974), 169; Robert Orsi, "The Religious Boundaries of an In-Between People: Street *Feste* and the Problem of the Dark-Skinned 'Other' in Italian Harlem, 1920–1990," *American Quarterly* 44 (September 1992): 313–47. For a discussion of the strategies and responses to racial passing in this era, see Gayle Wald, *Crossing the Line: Racial Passing in Twentieth-Century U.S. Literature and Culture* (Durham, NC: Duke University Press, 2000); Martha Sandweiss, *Passing Strange: A Gilded Age Tale of Love and Deception across the Color Line* (New York: Penguin, 2009).

55 U.S. Bureau of the Census, *Tenth Census of the United States, 1880*, City of Kendallville; U.S. Bureau of the Census, *Twelfth Census of the United States, 1900—Population* (Washington, DC: U.S. Government Printing Office, 1902), Chicago City, ward 4, p. 15, line 23; U.S. Bureau of the Census, *Thirteenth Census of the United States, Vol. 3: Population, 1910*, City of Milwaukee, p. 15, line 23. Kerwineo would again claim to have been born in South America on his 1914 marriage license. See marriage certificate of Ralphero Kerwinies and Dorothy Kleinowski.

56 Kerwineo and Mamie White lived for many years at 693 7th Avenue, and after their marriage, Kerwineo and Dorothy Kleinowski lived at 517 Cedar Avenue. For information regarding Milwaukee's spatial organization, see Joe Trotter, *Black Milwaukee: The Making of an Industrial Proletariat, 1915–1945* (Urbana: University of Illinois Press, 1985), 20–36. In 1900, 68 percent of black men and 73 percent of black women were employed as domestic servants (compared to 20.3 percent of foreign-born men and 41 percent of foreign-born women). For more information on employment, see U.S. Bureau of the Census, *Twelfth Census of the United States, 1900: Special Reports, Occupations* (Washington, DC: U.S. Government Printing Office, 1904), 608–12.

57 Christopher P. Wilson, "Plotting the Border: John Reed, Pancho Villa, and *Insurgent Mexico*," in *Cultures of United States Imperialism*, ed. Amy Kaplan and Donald E. Pease (Durham, NC: Duke University Press, 1993), 340–64.

58 As many scholars have noted, representations of Latino men in U.S. media have always been multifaceted, often vacillating from representations of effeminate men to dangerous Lotharios. However, in the particular historical moment discussed here, Latino men were figured in the press as dangerous, especially to white American women. See, for example, "American Girl's Murder Swiftly Avenged by United States Marines at Vera Cruz," *Washington Post*, May 3, 1914.

59 "They Are Now Writing the Last Chapter in Life of Ralph Kerwineo," *Milwaukee Journal*, May 4, 1914.

60 "The Girl Who 'Married' a Girl Has Created a Sensation throughout the United States," *Washington Post*, May 10, 1914. A similar narrative appeared in numerous papers nationwide. See "Bride Discovers Her Husband Is a Woman," *Frederick (MD) News-Post*, May 5, 1914; "Girl Gets License," *Daily Advocate* (Victoria, TX), May 8, 1914; "Posed as Man, Wed Twice," *New York Herald*, May 4, 1914.

61 "The Girl Who 'Married' a Girl Has Created a Sensation throughout the United States."

62 "Man-Girl Gets Out of Prison on $50 Bail," *Evening Wisconsin* (Milwaukee), May 5, 1914. For a reference of how Kerwineo was dressed after arrest, see "Girl Lives as Man and Weds," *Milwaukee Journal*, May 3, 1914.

63 Clare Sears has written about the connections between freak show displays and the enforcement of cross-dressing law. See Sears, "Electric Brilliancy: Cross-Dressing Law and Freak Show Displays in Nineteenth-Century San Francisco," in *The Transgender Studies Reader 2*, ed. Susan Stryker and Aren Z. Aizura (New York: Routledge, 2013), 554–64.

64 Ruth Wilson Gilmore, "Fatal Couplings of Power and Difference: Notes on Racism and Geography," *Professional Geographer* 54, no. 1 (2002): 19.

65 Significantly, Kleinowski's interviews in the national press are so different in content from how she was quoted in the local press that there is reason to believe at least some of what appeared on the national scale was exaggerated or fabricated.

66 Idah McGlone Gibson, "Cora Anderson Was a Good Man to Both Her Wives," *Day Book* (Chicago), May 14, 1914; "Amazing Double Life of Girl Who Lived for Years as a Man," *Day Book* (Chicago), May 13, 1914. This series also appeared in the *Des Moines Daily News*, *Pittsburgh Post-Gazette*, and *Wilkes-Barre Times-Leader*, among others.

67 Lisa Duggan, *Sapphic Slashers: Sex, Violence, and American Modernity* (Durham, NC: Duke University Press, 2000).

68 Gibson, "Cora Anderson Was Good Man to Both Her Wives."

69 Ibid.

70 Ibid.

71 Although ancient Rome was often thought to be an origin of modern whiteness (and claims of Egypt were increasingly made), these spaces were also frequently

produced as realms of sexual excess, a figuration that articulated these realms as "primitive" in relation to "modern" norms of sexuality. For a discussion of the various ways Egypt has been produced, for example, see Ella Shohat, "Disorienting Cleopatra: A Modern Trope of Identity," in *Taboo Memories, Diasporic Voices* (Durham, NC: Duke University Press, 2006), 166–200.

72 "Man Life of Woman Is Killed by Police," *Evening Wisconsin* (Milwaukee), May 4, 1914.

73 "They Are Now Writing the Last Chapter in Life of Ralph Kerwineo."

74 Somewhat surprisingly, the local press accepted this positioning, and maintained it even after Kerwineo's father's identity as a "negro barber" was revealed; discussions of Kerwineo's father consistently referred to him as either "colored" or "negro," but these words were never used to describe Kerwineo himself. See "Man-Girl Hypnotizes, Asserts Father at Kendallville, Ind.," *Milwaukee Journal*, May 5, 1914.

75 Mark Rifkin, "Romancing Kinship: A Queer Reading of Indian Education and Zitkala-Ŝa's *American Indian Stories*," *GLQ* 12, no. 1 (2006): 27–59. For another excellent discussion of the ways Native Americans have been figured as queer in U.S. history, see Scott Lauria Morgensen, *Spaces between Us: Settler Colonialism and Indigenous Decolonization* (Minneapolis: University of Minnesota Press, 2011).

76 Mark Rifkin, *When Did Indians Become Straight? Kinship, the History of Sexuality, and Native Sovereignty* (New York: Oxford University Press, 2011).

77 For a more detailed account of the ways in which Native Americans were depicted in this period, see Philip Deloria, *Playing Indian* (New Haven, CT: Yale University Press, 1999); Shari Hundorf, *Going Native: Indians in the American Cultural Imagination* (Ithaca, NY: Cornell University Press, 2001).

78 "They Are Now Writing the Last Chapter in Life of Ralph Kerwineo."

79 Sara Ahmed, *Queer Phenomenology: Orientations, Objects, Others* (Durham, NC: Duke University Press, 2006), 92, 94.

80 See, for example, "Women Who Figure in Astounding Drama in Which Girl Posed as Man Ten Years," *Milwaukee Sentinel*, May 5, 1914.

81 "Man-Girl Gets Out of Prison on $50 Bail."

82 "Would Like to Hire Cora Again," *Evening Wisconsin* (Milwaukee), May 5, 1914.

83 "Girl-Man Is Free; Judge Suspends Sentence in Court," *Milwaukee Sentinel*, May 7, 1914.

84 "Man-Girl Given Her Freedom," *Evening Wisconsin* (Milwaukee), May 7, 1914.

85 Canaday, *Straight State*, 22.

86 U.S. Bureau of the Census, *Thirteenth Census of the United States, Vol. 3: Population, 1910*, Borough of Manhattan, ward 18, enumeration district 982, household number 139.

87 Stratford's World War I draft registration card indicates that he was living in Hillsdale, New Jersey, and the 1920 federal census indicates that he was living as a boarder in the Nawn family home in that city. Peter Stratford draft registration

card, 21391, September 12, 1918, *World War I Registration Cards, 1917–1918*, National Archives, Washington, DC, Bergen County, New Jersey, roll 1711913; U.S. Bureau of the Census, *Fourteenth Census of the United States, 1920* (Washington, DC: U.S. Government Printing Office, 1920), Hillsdale, New Jersey, enumeration district 52, household number 90.

88 Personnel file of Peter Stratford, 1917–1919, National Personnel Records Center, St. Louis.

89 For information on the Unity movement, see Neal Vahle, *The Unity Movement: Its Evolution and Spiritual Teachings* (Philadelphia: Templeton Foundation Press, 2002). For information about the New Thought Movement more broadly, see Beryl Satter, *Each Mind a Kingdom: American Women, Sexual Purity, and the New Thought Movement, 1875–1920* (Berkeley: University of California Press, 2001); Gail M. Harley, *Emma Curtis Hopkins: Forgotten Founder of New Thought* (Syracuse, NY: Syracuse University Press, 2002).

90 Marriage license of Peter Stratford and Elizabeth Rowland, 19979, October 1, 1925, Jackson County, Missouri. *Missouri Marriage Records*, Missouri State Archives, Jefferson City.

91 Gisela Webb, "Third-Wave Sufism in America and the Bawa Muhaiyaddeen Fellowship," in *Sufism in the West*, ed. Jamal Malik and John Hinnells (New York: Routledge, 2006), 86–102. Interestingly, Sir Richard Burton—translator of the *Kama Sutra*—claimed to be a "Sufi master" in the late nineteenth century. See, for example, Edward Rice, *Captain Sir Richard Burton: A Biography* (Cambridge, MA: Da Capo Press, 1990), 206–8.

92 This framing of love letters as sources of "truth" was common in the early twentieth century. In fact, Gordon Morris Bakken and Brenda Farrington have argued that love letters were often featured prominently in the press and legal cases involving women on trial, as such evidence was assumed to provide unique insights into the accused. See Bakken and Farrington, *Women Who Kill Men: California Courts, Gender, and the Press* (Lincoln: University of Nebraska Press, 2009), 9–10.

93 "'Stratford's' Love Letters Discovered," *San Francisco Examiner*, May 3, 1929.

94 "Strange Life of Masquerader Told in Her Letter to Friends," *San Francisco Examiner*, May 4, 1929.

95 Robert Lee discusses in detail the content of such "yellow peril" stories that were popular in films in the early twentieth century. See Lee, "Inner Dikes and Barred Zones," in *Orientals: Asian Americans in Popular Culture* (Philadelphia: Temple University Press, 1999), 106–44. See also Marjorie Garber, "The Chic of Araby: Transvestism and the Erotics of Cultural Appropriation," in *Vested Interests: Cross-Dressing and Cultural Anxiety* (New York: Routledge, 1992), 304–53.

96 "Pauper Grave Final Chapter," *San Francisco Chronicle*, May 4, 1929.

97 "Invert Buried as Pauper," *Los Angeles Times*, May 5, 1929.

98 "Masquerader Was Member of S.F. Cult," *San Francisco Examiner*, May 3, 1929; "Death Reveals 'Husband' as Woman Writer Who Aided Literary Lights to

Success," *San Francisco Chronicle*, May 3, 1929; "Film Writer: 'Wife' of Strange Masquerader," *Modesto (CA) News-Herald*, May 3, 1929.

99 "6 Women Face Hoax Inquiry," *San Francisco Examiner*, May 4, 1929.

100 "Belief in Oriental Cult Led Woman to Pose as Husband," *New York American*, May 4, 1929. This article was credited to Universal Service.

101 "6 Women Face Hoax Inquiry."

102 " 'Wife' of Masquerader Flees to San Diego," *Los Angeles Examiner*, May 5, 1929.

103 "Masquerader Cult Hunted," *Los Angeles Examiner*, May 6, 1929, p. 7.

104 "Man-Woman Is Buried in Potter Field," *San Francisco Examiner*, May 5, 1929.

105 Philip Jenkins, *Mystics and Messiahs: Cults and New Religions in American History* (New York: Oxford University Press, 2000), 128–29.

106 "Death Reveals 'Husband' as Woman Writer Who Aided Literary Lights to Success."

107 "Lives as Wife 2 Years, Finds Mate Is Woman," *Chicago Tribune*, May 4, 1929.

108 Ibid.

109 "Potter's Field to Claim Woman Who Passed for Male," *Appleton (WI) Post-Crescent*, May 4, 1929; "Potters Field Grave Awaits 'Peter Stratford,' Who Posed as Man and Studied Sufism," *Galveston (TX) Daily News*, May 5, 1929; "Masquerades as Man and Is Unsuspected," *Daily Northwestern* (Oshkosh, WI), May 4, 1929; "Woman Reveals Secret of Sex Just before End," *Cumberland (MD) Evening Times*, May 4, 1929; "Woman Weds; Poses as Man," *Sioux City (IA) Journal*, May 5, 1929; "Pauper's Grave Yawns for Woman," *Abilene (TX) Morning Reporter-News*, May 5, 1929.

110 " 'Husband' Masked 4 Years as Man," *New York World*, May 4, 1929. Statement also made in "Woman Lived as Man, Wed to One of Her Sex," *New York Times*, May 4, 1929. A similar narrative is found in "Woman Weds; Poses as Man."

111 "Strange Triangle Is Revealed about Hoax," *Billings (MT) Gazette*, May 4, 1929.

112 " 'Stratford's' Body Remains Unclaimed," *New York Times*, May 5, 1929; "Woman Masqueraded as Man for Years; Was Married to Actress; Linked with Cult," *Davenport (IA) Democrat and Leader*, May 5, 1929; "Potters Field Grave Awaits 'Peter Stratford,' Who Posed as Man and Studied Sufism."

113 Lauren Berlant, *The Queen of America Goes to Washington City* (Durham, DC: Duke University Press, 1997), 195.

114 "Stratford Letters Reveal Many Loves," *Washington Post*, May 6, 1929.

115 Matthew 27:7, *The Holy Bible*, King James Version (New York: Gideons International, 1981), 1027.

116 "Man-Woman Is Buried in Potter Field"; "Grave Claims 'Hoax' Husband," *Oakland Tribune*, May 5, 1929.

117 "Potter's Field to Claim Woman Who Passed for Male"; "Potter's Field Grave Yawns for Woman Who Lived as Man," *Bismarck (ND) Tribune*, May 4, 1929; "Masquerades as Man and Is Unsuspected"; "Woman Masqueraded as Man for Years; Was Married to Actress; Linked with Cult"; "Potters Field Grave Awaits 'Peter Stratford,' Who Posed as Man and Studied Sufism"; "Woman Reveals Secret

of Sex Just before End"; "Woman Weds; Poses as Man"; "Masquerade of Woman Revealed," *Ada (OK) Evening News*, May 5, 1929; "Masquerades as Man Until Death," *Daily Globe* (Ironwood, MI), May 4, 1929; "Potter's Field Will Get Body," *Lima (OH) News*, May 5, 1929.

118 Lee Edelman, *No Future: Queer Theory and the Death Drive* (Durham, NC: Duke University Press, 2004), 4.

CHAPTER 5. TO HAVE AND TO HOLD

1 "Ethel Kimball Held in $200," *Boston Morning Journal*, June 14, 1911.

2 "Given Two Months," *Boston Daily Globe*, June 21, 1911.

3 Department of Public Health, Registry of Vital Records and Statistics, *Massachusetts Vital Records Index to Marriages, 1901–1955*, vol. 86, facsimile ed. (Boston: New England Historic Genealogical Society), 290.

4 "Ethel Kimball, Freed on One Charge, Is Rearrested," *Boston Daily Globe*, December 20, 1921.

5 "Denies She Wed Woman as Prank," *Trenton (NJ) Evening Times*, December 23, 1921. This AP wire story also appeared as "Girl Says Her Faith Was Whole in Wedding Impersonator," *Daily Herald* (Biloxi, MS), December 22, 1921; "Lived Two Weeks with Woman Ignorant of Prankish Sex Play," *Montgomery (AL) Advertiser*, December 22, 1921; "Denies Prank in Wedding," *Cleveland (OH) Plain Dealer*, December 22, 1921.

6 No divorce records exist (perhaps because the district judge assumed Hathaway's anatomy voided the initial marriage contract). However, it appears that Hathaway's bride moved on, relocating to Portland, Maine, and remarrying a man named Henry Fortune in 1930. See Maine State Archives, Maine Marriages, 1892–1996 (except 1967 to 1976), Augusta. Index obtained from Maine Department of the Secretary of State, Maine State Archives, http://www.state.me.us/.

7 " 'Man-Girl' Case Ends," *Baltimore Sun*, December 25, 1921.

8 "Ethel Kimball Sent to Psychopathic Hospital," *Boston Daily Globe*, May 24, 1922.

9 "Ethel Kimball Gets Five Months," *Boston Globe*, April 12, 1924.

10 "Ethel Kimball, 'Wife,' and Innkeeper Fined $25," *Boston Globe*, February 27, 1924.

11 "Ethel Kimball Lived as James A. Hathaway," *Boston Globe*, April 11, 1924.

12 After this arrest Pearl Davis disappears from the public record, but Hathaway's penchant for criminal activity ensured that his April 1924 arrest was not his last. In fact, two years later he was arrested again for passing bad checks. At that time he was in Manchester, New Hampshire, with a woman named Maude Allen, and the pair had registered at a hotel as "Mr. and Mrs. James Wilson." For coverage of this arrest, see "Boston Girls Posed as Man and Wife," *Boston Daily Globe*, August 11, 1926.

13 Of course, many cisgender Americans also married illegally in this period, and many more did not have access to documents verifying identity (birth certificates, for example, were not pervasive until the mid-twentieth century). However, despite how common it was for Americans to marry under false identities in the

early twentieth century, it was still a punishable offense, and the act of getting married itself nonetheless placed trans men under the type of state scrutiny that many presumably strove to avoid under normal circumstances. For more information on birth certificates in this period, see Susan Pearson, "'Age Ought to Be a Fact': The Campaign against Child Labor and the Rise of the Birth Certificate," *Journal of American History* 101, no. 4 (2015): 1144–65; Shane Landrum, "Registering Race, Policing Citizenship: Delayed Birth Registration and the Virginia Racial Integrity Act, 1924–1975," paper presented at the Public History Conference, Columbus, Ohio, June 3–6, 2010.

14 Nancy Cott, *Public Vows: A History of Marriage and the Nation* (Cambridge, MA: Harvard University Press, 2000), 4. For other discussions of marriage in U.S. history, see Michael Grossberg, *Governing the Hearth: Law and the Family in Nineteenth-Century America* (Chapel Hill: University of North Carolina Press, 1988); Joanna Grossman and Lawrence Friedman, eds., *Inside the Castle: Law and the Family in 20th Century America* (Princeton, NJ: Princeton University Press, 2014); Joanna Grossman, "Civil Rights: The Gay Marriage Controversy in Historical Perspective," in *Law, Society and History: Essays on Themes in the Legal History and Legal Sociology of Lawrence M. Friedman*, ed. Robert Gordon (Cambridge, UK: Cambridge University Press, 2011), 253–72; George Chauncey, *Why Marriage? The History Shaping Today's Debate over Gay Equality* (New York: Basic Books, 2004); Peggy Pascoe, *What Comes Naturally: Miscegenation Law and the Making of Race in America* (New York: Oxford University Press, 2009); Rachel Hope Cleves, "'What, Another Female Husband?': The Prehistory of Same-Sex Marriage," *Journal of American History* 101, no. 4 (2015): 1055–81.

15 Cott, *Public Vows*, 3.

16 Ibid., 37.

17 For a more detailed discussion of mobility in the nineteenth century, see Karen Halttunen, *Confidence Men and Painted Women: A Study of Middle-Class Culture in America, 1830–1870* (New Haven, CT: Yale University Press, 1986); David Henkin, *The Postal Age: The Emergence of Modern Communications in Nineteenth-Century America* (Chicago: University of Chicago Press, 2007); John Mark Faragher, *Women and Men on the Overland Trail* (New Haven, CT: Yale University Press, 1980).

18 "Girl Lives as Man and Weds," *Milwaukee Journal*, May 3, 1914.

19 Michael Grossberg, "Guarding the Altar: Physiological Restrictions and the Rise of State Intervention in Matrimony," *American Journal of Legal History* 26, no. 3 (1982): 197–226.

20 Other methods included immigration reform and birth control. For a more in-depth discussion of the eugenics movement in the United States, see Nancy Ordover, *American Eugenics: Race, Queer Anatomy, and the Science of Nationalism* (Minneapolis: University of Minnesota Press, 2003); Wendy Kline, *Building a Better Race: Gender, Sexuality, and Eugenics from the Turn of the Century to the Baby Boom* (Berkeley: University of California Press, 2005).

21 Cited in David F. Greenberg, *The Construction of Homosexuality* (Chicago: University of Chicago Press, 1988), 414.

22 Ordover, *American Eugenics*, 78–79.

23 Ibid., 79.

24 Washington State passed a similar law in 1909, but it was quickly struck down. Oregon and North Dakota passed similar laws around the same time that Wisconsin did, although the press paid closer attention to the controversy surrounding the Wisconsin law. See Fred S. Hall, *Medical Certification for Marriage: An Account of the Administration of the Wisconsin Marriage Law as It Relates to the Venereal Diseases* (New York: Russell Sage Foundation, 1925), 13.

25 "Wisconsin's Marriage Law," *Milwaukee Sentinel*, January 1, 1914.

26 Laws of 1913, chapter 738. Reprinted in Hall, *Medical Certification for Marriage*, 81.

27 The *Journal of the American Medical Association* reported in the *Milwaukee Sentinel* on January 1, 1914, that "the customary fee for a Wasserman test alone is from $10 to $25." See "Wisconsin's Marriage Law."

28 See, for example, "Eugenics Hits Snag," *Washington Post*, December 22, 1913; "Rush to Beat Eugenic Law," *New York Times*, January 1, 1914; "Defies Eugenic by Common Law," *Chicago Daily Tribune*, January 8, 1914; "Eugenic Woe Now Appears," *Los Angeles Times*, January 4, 1914; "Eugenics Puzzle Judge," *New York Times*, January 11, 1914; "Perils of Eugenic Laws," *Washington Post*, January 11, 1914. The local press covered the challenges, as well. See "Doctors Strike on Cupid's Test," *Milwaukee Journal*, December 14, 1913; "Eugenics Laws Are Sharply Attacked," *Milwaukee Sentinel*, December 20, 1913; "Cupid to Invoke Aid of Courts," *Milwaukee Journal*, January 2, 1914; "Medics Refuse a Health Test," *Milwaukee Journal*, January 3, 1914; "Stage Is Set for First Legal Test of New Eugenic Law," *Milwaukee Sentinel*, January 3, 1914; "War Is Started on Eugenics Law," *Milwaukee Sentinel*, January 4, 1914.

29 "Eugenic Marriage Plan Praised Here," *New York Times*, March 26, 1912.

30 Cathy Cohen, "Punks, Bulldaggers, and Welfare Queens: The Radical Potential of Queer Politics?" *GLQ* 3, no. 4 (1997): 453.

31 "Girl Gets Eugenic License as a Man; Then Weds a Girl," *New York World*, May 4, 1914; "Eugenic License to Girl as Man Ridicules Law," *New York World*, May 5, 1914; "'Husband' and Wife in Eugenic Marriage," *New York World*, May 7, 1914.

32 "Eugenic License to Girl as Man Ridicules Law." This article was reproduced throughout the country in the following days. See, for example, "Eugenic Statute," *Miami Herald Record*, May 12, 1914; "Eugenic Statute," *Montgomery (AL) Advertiser*, May 13, 1914; "Eugenic Statute Enforced in Wisconsin Is Shown to Be a Huge Joke," *Grand Forks (SD) Herald*, May 12, 1914; "Eugenic Law Absurd," *Washington Post*, May 6, 1914.

33 Ordover, *American Eugenics*, 70–118.

34 "'Husband' and Wife in Eugenic Marriage."

35 "Eugenic Law Absurd." For a similar narrative, see "Lived as a Man for Ten Years," *Boston Globe*, May 4, 1914; and "'Husband' Is a Girl," *Washington Post*, May 4, 1914.

36 Jennifer Terry, "Anxious Slippages between 'Us' and 'Them': A Brief History of the Scientific Search for Homosexual Bodies," in *Deviant Bodies: Critical Perspectives on Difference in Science and Popular Culture*, ed. Jennifer Terry and Jacqueline Urla (Bloomington: Indiana University Press, 1995), 138–39.

37 No legal records exist in either Wisconsin or Illinois related to Kerwineo and White's marriage, and White told reporters in 1914 that the pair simply proclaimed themselves man and wife upon their move away from Chicago, around 1908. See, for example, "Girl Lives as Man and Weds."

38 "Women Who Figure in Astounding Drama in Which Girl Posed as Man Ten Years," *Milwaukee Sentinel*, May 5, 1914.

39 Certificate of marriage 5109, December 24, 1872, New York City Vital Records Collection, Municipal Archives.

40 Wisconsin Department of Health and Family Services, *Wisconsin Vital Record Index, Pre-1907*, vol. 7 (Madison: Wisconsin Department of Health and Family Services Vital Records Division), 52.

41 "Howard Was a Woman," *Ontario County Journal* (Canandaigua, NY), March 28, 1902.

42 Official record of De Raylan's first marriage ceremony are difficult to find, but it certainly occurred, as there is a divorce case between De Raylan and his first wife on file in the Cook County Circuit Court, dated July 1, 1903 (case G240095 between Nicolai De Raylan and Eugenia De Raylan). For a record of De Raylan's second marriage, see "Marriage Certificate between Nicolai Deraylan [*sic*] and Anna Armstrong," August 4, 1903, Chicago, "Marriage Records, 1871–Present," Division of Vital Records, Springfield, Illinois.

43 "Louisa Has Her Say," *San Francisco Call*, January 29, 1895.

44 "Ellis Glenn Is Not a Man," *St. Louis (MO) Post-Dispatch*, November 26, 1899.

45 "3 De Forest Romances Bared," *Los Angeles Evening Herald*, September 1, 1915.

46 "Lazy Husbands Can't Be Lazy in Washington; State Won't Let Them," *Pittsburgh (PA) Press*, August 24, 1913; the article also appeared in *Milwaukee Journal* on August 9.

47 Ibid.

48 "Trying to Discredit Brown," *Seattle Star*, August 13, 1914.

49 "'Husband' Wedded Here Is a Woman," *Spokane (WA) Daily Chronicle*, February 18, 1916.

50 "'Robert' Gaffney Is Again a Woman," *New York Times*, February 20, 1916; "Woman Jailed as 'Lazy Husband' Given Freedom," *Philadelphia Inquirer*, February 27, 1916.

51 "'Robert' Gaffney Is Again a Woman."

52 "Convicted of Being a Lazy 'Husband': Posed as Man for the Last Twenty Years," *Daily News* (San Jose), February 19, 1916. The article also appeared as "Woman Convicted as Lazy Husband," *Iron County Register* (Ironton, MO), April 20, 1916; and "'Husband' a Woman, Hid Secret for Years," *Hopkinsville Kentuckian*, March 21, 1916 (this article was published without the image mentioned in the text).

53 Ibid.

54 When Margaret's children were mentioned, they were each attributed to her former husband, suggesting they were each born during her previous marriage. One solitary example to the contrary is an article published in the *Tacoma Times*, which mentioned that Margaret had an eleven-month-old baby but failed to hypothesize as to who the father was or under what circumstances the child was conceived. See "Find 'Lazy Husband" in Reality Is Woman," *Tacoma (WA) Times*, February 18, 1916.

55 "Convicted of Being a Lazy 'Husband'"; "Woman Convicted as Lazy Husband"; "'Husband' a Woman, Hid Secret for Years."

56 Marriage record between Margaret C. Jones and Clem R. Hart, Plainwell, Michigan, September 16, 1902, record 388, film 74, 1902 Calhoun–1902 Kalkaska, Michigan, Marriage Records, 1867–1952, Michigan Department of Community Health, Division for Vital Records and Health Statistics, Lansing. The highest level of education attained is referenced on the 1940 census. See U.S. Bureau of the Census, *1940 Federal Census* (Washington, DC: U.S. Government Printing Office, 1940), Seattle, roll T627_4380, p. 5A, enumeration district 40–224A.

57 Their divorce was mentioned in the *Daily News* of Marshall, Michigan, October 23, 1906. It is noted that the divorce was petitioned due to "non-support and wanton neglect," and that no defense was made because Clem Hart was "worthless financially."

58 There is no record of this birth, though the child died in January 1917 and his death record lists Margaret Jonas and Cline Hart as his parents. See James Urban Hart death certificate, January 3, 1917, Seattle, "Washington, Death Certificates, 1907–1960," film 1992505, cn. 21, Family History Library, Salt Lake City, Utah.

59 "Woman Tells of Her Remarkable Struggle to Bridge Sex Gulf," *Tacoma (WA) Times*, September 9, 1916.

60 Certificate of marriage between Robert A. Gaffney and Christine A. Hart, Spokane, Washington, September 25, 1911, license A12515, Washington State Archives, Olympia. It appears that after Margaret's marriage to Robert Gaffney, she and her first husband reconciled, as the pair are cited as living together with their two children in 1920. The 1920 census lists Clem and Margaret Hart as married, living in Seattle with their two children, Edward (age nine) and Mildred (age four). However, this reconciliation did not last long, and in 1922 Margaret married for a third time, this time to fifty-two-year-old Walter Bowie. Like each of her prior marriages, this one would also be short-lived, as Bowie would die just four short years later. U.S. Bureau of the Census, *Fourteenth Census of the United States, 1920* (Washington, DC: U.S. Government Printing Office, 1920), Seattle, roll T625_1928, p. 10B, enumeration district 204, image 526; Walter Plumer Bowie death certificate, December 3, 1926, film 2022318, reference IS3246, *Washington, Death Certificates, 1907–1960*, Family History Library, Salt Lake City, Utah.

61 Robert reappeared in the press briefly seven months after his initial arrest and provided a lengthy interview to Frank L. Boalt of the *Portland News*. This story,

which was subsequently reproduced in other newspapers in the Pacific Northwest, including the *Tacoma Times*, highlighted this angle of the story, and made
clear that Gaffney's motivation in marriage was that he was "touched by the
woman's helplessness." See Frank L. Boalt, "Woman Tells of Her Remarkable
Struggle to Bridge Sex Gulf."

62 "Babies Starve Because Commission Doesn't Act," *Tacoma (WA) Times*, January 7,
1915.

63 "Convicted of Being a Lazy 'Husband' "; "Woman Convicted as Lazy Husband";
and " 'Husband' a Woman, Hid Secret for Years."

64 In 1910 there were only thirteen newspaper chains operating in the United States,
and they were responsible for publishing sixty-two newspapers nationwide. By
1923, however, the number of chains had increased to thirty-one (with 153 dailies),
and by 1935 the number had risen to fifty-nine (with 329 dailies). See Alfred Mc-
Clung Lee, *The Daily Newspaper in America: The Evolution of a Social Instrument*
(New York: Octagon Books, 1973), 215; Edward E. Adams and Gerald J. Baldasty,
"Syndicated Service Dependence and a Lack of Commitment to Localism: Scripps
Newspapers and Market Subordination," *Journalism and Mass Communication
Quarterly* 78, no. 3 (2001): 519–32; Gerald Baldasty, "Expansion," in *E. W. Scripps
and the Business of Newspapers* (Urbana: University of Illinois Press, 1999), 19–32;
Paul Alfred Pratte, ". . . What sort of teeth . . . and who is it to bite?" in *Gods within
the Machine: A History of the American Society of Newspaper Editors, 1923–1993*
(Westport, CT: Praeger, 1995), 1–24; Ben Procter, *William Randolph Hearst: Final
Edition, 1911–1951* (New York: Oxford University Press, 2007), esp. 3–52.

65 The number of daily numbers in 1910 was 2,433, while it was only 2,027 in 1936.
See Lee, *Daily Newspaper in America*, 723.

66 As quoted in ibid., 537. For additional information on the United Press, see
Richard M. Harnett and Billy G. Ferguson, *Unipress: United Press International
Covering the 20th Century* (Golden, CO: Fulcrum, 2003).

67 Lisonbee's father was Joseph Smith Wing Jr., the son of Joseph Smith Wing and
Sarah Adelia Wright, Wing's fourth wife. See U.S. Bureau of the Census, *Ninth
Census of the United States, 1870* (Washington, DC: National Archives and Re-
cords Administration, 1870), roll M593_1612, p. 334, image 662.

68 Los Angeles City Directory, 1925, reel 23, p. 2024, Los Angeles City Directory
Microfilm Collection, Los Angeles Public Library.

69 Marriage license for Kenneth Wing and Eileen Garnett, no. 18195, Orange County,
Santa Ana, California. Copy in author's possession.

70 Lisonbee explained his marriage to Garnett in "Woman-'Husband' in Jail," *Los
Angeles Times*, January 11, 1929.

71 Kenneth appears in the Los Angeles City Directory in 1925 and 1926 as "Kenneth
Wing." No "Kenneth Wing" appears in the city directory after 1926, but "Kenneth
Lisonbee" first appears in 1927. See Los Angeles City Directory, 1926, reel 25,
p. 2112; 1927, reel 26, p. 1272; 1928, reel 27, p. 1352. Los Angeles City Directory
Microfilm Collection, Los Angeles Public Library.

72 "Eureka Girl Posing as Man Arrested on Coast," *Eureka (UT) Reporter*, January 17, 1929; "Woman-'Husband' in Jail."

73 The reason Lisonbee and Harper were taken into police custody is not entirely clear. Lisonbee told the *Los Angeles Times* that they were brought to police attention because "some neighbor women began to talk," but no details are given about the gossip. See "Woman-'Husband' in Jail."

74 Here I am using the term "heterosexual" to refer to a relationship between a cisgender man and a cisgender woman.

75 Population statistics for 1920 taken from U.S. Bureau of the Census, "Table 15: Population of the 100 Largest Urban Places, 1920," available at http://www.census.gov/. Population statistics for 1930 taken from U.S. Bureau of the Census, "Table 16: Population of the 100 Largest Urban Places, 1930," available at http://www.census.gov/.

76 The *Evening Herald* was more popular during the week than the *Examiner* was (selling an average of 229,159 issues daily versus the *Examiner*'s 204,245), but it did not have a Sunday edition. Sunday editions of the *Los Angeles Examiner* sold an estimated 446,526 copies a week. The *Los Angeles Times*, on the other hand, was less popular: its weekday circulation was 162,959, and its Sunday circulation 246,453. N. W. Ayer & Sons, *N. W. Ayer & Son's Directory of Newspapers and Periodicals, 1930* (Philadelphia: N. W. Ayer & Sons, 1930), 91–95. For information regarding Hearst's Los Angeles newspapers, see Procter, *William Randolph Hearst*, 129–52.

77 "Arrest Bares Her Disguise," *Los Angeles Examiner*, January 11, 1929.

78 "Ranch Tomboy in Legal Mess," *Los Angeles Times*, January 12, 1929.

79 In 1929, stories of the mythic frontier were very popular, and often heralded its promise (juxtaposed to the purportedly suffocating nature of modern life). For a more detailed discussion of representations of the frontier in this period, see Richard Slotkin, "From Open Range to Mean Streets: Myth and Formula Fiction, 1910–1940," in *Gunfighter Nation: The Myth of the Frontier in Twentieth-Century America* (Norman: University of Oklahoma Press, 1998), 194–230.

80 "Ranch Tomboy in Legal Mess."

81 The 1910 federal census lists five children in the Wing household, including Joseph (age twenty-five), Irvin (eighteen), Mabel (fourteen), Catherine (six), and Theodore (one). The following federal census indicates that by 1920 Wing's older siblings had left, leaving Catherine (age sixteen) and Ted (age eleven). U.S. Bureau of the Census, *Thirteenth Census of the United States, 1910* (Washington, DC: U.S. Government Printing Office, 1910), Springville, Utah; enumeration district 201, household number 203; U.S. Bureau of the Census, *Fourteenth Census of the United States, 1920*, Springville City, Utah, enumeration district 224, household number 77.

82 "Woman-'Husband' In Jail."

83 Ibid.

84 "Ranch Tomboy in Legal Mess."

85 "Girl-'Husband' Gets Liberty," *Los Angeles Times*, January 15, 1929; "Woman Posing as 'Husband' to Go Free," *Los Angeles Evening Herald*, January 15, 1929.

86 Ibid. Emphasis added.

87 Ibid.

88 Ibid.

89 "Suave, Trouser-Clad Barber Turns Out to Be Damsel," *Rocky Mountain News* (Denver), January 12, 1929; " 'Man Barber' a Girl; Also Acted Husband," *Daily News* (New York), January 13, 1929; "Sporty White-Aproned Barber Turns Out to Be Pretty Girl," *Simpson's Leader-Times* (Kittanning, PA), January 14, 1929; "Posing as Man, Girl Weds Two," *Pointer* (Riverdale, IL), February 15, 1929; "Posing as Man, Girl Weds Two," *Dunkirk (NY) Observer*, February 25, 1929.

90 Ibid. Significantly, the rationale behind Lisonbee's marriage was removed from the article published in New York's *Daily News*.

91 Ibid.

92 Ibid.

93 The full text of this account read as follows:

> LOS ANGELES, Cal. Jan 10—(AP)—Katherine Wing, who yesterday frustrated officer's attempt to prosecute her on Mann act charges when she revealed that she was a woman posing as a man, faced the possibility of another court action today when she admitted having been married to Eileen Garnet.
>
> The girl, who was raised on a ranch in Titnic, Utah, said that she has always worn men's clothing. Two years ago, she said, she met Miss Garnet in Los Angeles and married her. She said the ceremony was performed by a justice of the peace in Santa Ana, Cal. The marriage was happy, Miss Wing said, and finally was broken off because Miss Garnet's parents and other relatives came to live with them. She then returned to Utah. She came here three months ago, bringing Stella Harper with her. Miss Wing posed as a man and was employed as a barber. A Mann act charge was filed against her when it was discovered that she was not married to the girl.
>
> Officers say that it is a felony under California law to take part in such a marriage as that Miss Wing described in Santa Ana. The girl is being held for Santa Ana officers.

This account appeared in numerous papers nationwide. See, for example, "Girl-Man Free under Mann Act in Jail Again," *Fresno (CA) Bee*, January 11, 1929; "Trousered Tomboy Bleats in Bastille," *Helena (MT) Daily Independent*, January 12, 1929; "Utah Woman Held in Jail," *Salt Lake (UT) Tribune*, January 12, 1929; "Katherine Wing Sent to Jail in Adventure Case," *Montana Standard* (Butte), January 12, 1929; "Girl, Posing as Husband, Goes to Jail," *Galveston (TX) Daily News*, January 12, 1929.

94 John D'Emilio and Estelle B. Freedman, *Intimate Matters: A History of Sexuality in America* (New York: Harper & Row, 1988), 208.

95 David Langum, *Crossing the Line: Legislating Morality and the Mann Act* (Chicago: University of Chicago Press, 1994). For a broader discussion of the efforts of Progressive Era vice reformers, see, for example, Mary E. Odem, *Delinquent Daughters: Protecting and Policing Adolescent Female Sexuality in the United States, 1885–1920* (Chapel Hill: University of North Carolina Press, 1995); Kevin Mumford, *Interzones: Black/White Sex Districts in New York and Chicago in the Early Twentieth Century* (New York: Columbia University Press, 1997); Mara L. Keire, *For Business and Pleasure: Red-Light Districts and the Regulation of Vice in the United States, 1890–1933* (Baltimore: Johns Hopkins University Press, 2010).

96 Statistic given in D'Emilio and Freedman, *Intimate Matters*, 208.

97 Baldasty, *E. W. Scripps and the Business of Newspapers*, 43–56; Lee, *Daily Newspaper in America*, 576–602.

98 Adams and Baldasty, "Syndicated Service Dependence and a Lack of Commitment to Localism."

99 "Girls Travel as Man and Wife," *Sheboygan (WI) Journal*, January 16, 1929; "Girls Travel as Man and Wife," *Zanesville (OH) Signal*, January 16, 1929; 'Girls Travel as Man and Wife," *Syracuse (NY) Herald*, January 16, 1929; "Girls Travel as Man and Wife," *Decatur (IL) Daily Review*, January 17, 1929; "Girls Travel as Man and Wife," *Edwardsville (IL) Intelligencer*, January 17, 1929; "Girls Travel as Man and Wife," *Jefferson City (MO) Post-Tribune*, January 18, 1929; "Girls Travel as Man and Wife," *Portsmouth (OH) Daily Times*, January 18, 1929; "Girls Travel as Man and Wife," *Lima (OH) News*, January 18, 1929; "Girls Travel as Man and Wife," *Wisconsin Rapids (WI) Daily Tribune*, January 18, 1929; "'Man and Wife' Just Two Maids," *Independent* (Helena, MT), January 19, 1929; "Girls Travel as Man and Wife," *Olean (NY) Times*, January 19, 1929; "Girls Travel as Man and Wife," *Bismarck (ND) Tribune*, January 22, 1929; "Girls Travel as Man and Wife," *News-Palladium* (Benton Harbor, MI), January 23, 1929; "Girls Travel as Man and Wife," *Ironwood (MI) Daily Globe*, January 25, 1929; "Girls Travel as Man and Wife," *Lancaster (OH) Daily Gazette*, January 15, 1929. In at least one case—"Finis Written in Their Adventure," *The Bee* (Danville, VA), January 16, 1929—the photo is credited to "International Newsreels" (the newsreel company created by William Randolph Hearst in 1929), seeming to indicate that Lisonbee's story also circulated via newsreel, wherein the narrative was likely similar to the one issued by the NEA described here. Unfortunately, archival holdings of early newsreels are spotty, and neither the UCLA Film and Television Archives nor the National Archives have any record of the story.

100 "Ranch Tomboy in Legal Mess."

101 Todd DePastino, *Citizen Hobo: How a Century of Homelessness Shaped America* (Chicago: University of Chicago Press, 2003). See also Frank Tobias Higbie, *Indispensable Outcasts: Hobo Workers and Community in the American Midwest, 1880–1930* (Urbana: University of Illinois Press, 2003); Mark Wyman, *Hoboes: Bindlestiffs, Fruit Tramps, and the Harvesting of the West* (Boston: Hill and Wang, 2010).

102 Margot Canaday, *The Straight State: Sexuality and Citizenship in Twentieth-Century America* (Princeton, NJ: Princeton University Press, 2009), 99. Quotation from P. R. Vessie, "The Wanderlust Impulse," *Medical Journal and Record* 120 (July–December 1924): 20.

CONCLUSION

1 "Ranch Tomboy in Legal Mess," *Los Angeles Times*, January 12, 1929.

2 "Charges are Dismissed against Katherine Wing," *Eureka (UT) Reporter*, January 24, 1929.

3 The 1937 city directory for Alhambra, California, lists Kenneth Lisonbee, "barber," as living at the same address as his parents, Joseph and Adelaide Wing. Although Stella Harper is nowhere listed in that year's directory, two years later she is listed at the same address as the Lisonbee/Wings: 2750 New Avenue. See *Polk's Alhambra City Directory* (Los Angeles: R. L. Polk & Co., 1937), 832, 856; *Polk's Alhambra City Directory* (Los Angeles: R. L. Polk & Co., 1939), 869.

4 However, it appears that Lisonbee's parents were not destitute, as the 1940 census lists them as owning their home at 2750 New Avenue in Alhambra, and Joseph Wing claimed an income of $1,000. See U.S. Bureau of the Census, *Sixteenth Census of the United States, 1940* (Washington, DC: National Archives and Records Administration, 1940), roll T627_253, p. 66A, enumeration district 19–690.

5 For more information on Hollywood and queer life in this period, see Lillian Faderman and Stuart Timmons, *Gay L.A.: A History of Sexual Outlaws, Power Politics, and Lipstick Lesbians* (New York: Basic Books, 2006), 39–70.

6 State-sponsored identification documents, like driver's licenses, have of course been challenging for trans people to access, as they require multiple pieces of proof of identity, which may or may not correspond with one's chosen name or gender presentation. This is a topic explored at some length within trans studies. See, for example. Toby Beauchamp, "Artful Concealment and Strategic Visibility: Transgender Bodies and U.S. State Surveillance after 9/11," in *The Transgender Studies Reader 2*, ed. Aren Aizura and Susan Stryker (New York: Routledge, 2013), 46–55.

7 Several newspapers around the country published an AP wire about Lisonbee's arrest titled "Fifteen Year Masquerade Revealed." See " 'Fifteen Year Masquerade Revealed," *Moberly (MO) Monitor-Index*, April 29, 1940; "Fifteen Year Masquerade Revealed," *Charleston (WV) Gazette*, April 28, 1940.

8 "Barber Working Years under Man's Name Revealed as Woman," *Los Angeles Times*, April 27, 1940.

9 Ibid.

10 "Woman Barber Wins Leniency," *Los Angeles Times*, May 1, 1940.

11 Ibid.

12 Quote from " 'Man Barber' a Girl; Also Acted Husband," *Daily News* (New York), January 13, 1929.

13 "Woman Barber Wins Leniency." It appears that after his 1940 arrest, Lisonbee
returned to using his legal last name (Wing). Additionally, it seems that at some
point Stella Harper assumed the last name of Wing as well; when she died on
January 17, 1973, the name listed in the *California Death Index* was Estella A.
Wing. Lisonbee lived until December 22, 1991, and his death is registered under
two names: both Katherine and Kennie. See State of California, *California Death
Index, 1940–1997* (Sacramento: State of California Department of Health Services,
Center for Health Statistics).

14 Susan Stryker, "Transgender History, Homonormativity, and Disciplinarily," *Radical History Review* 100 (Winter 2008): 147.

15 For examples of this, see J. D. Vance, "Life outside the Liberal Bubble," *New York
Times*, November 9, 2016; Richard Cohen, " 'Real America' Is Its Own Bubble,"
Washington Post, December 12, 2016.

SELECTED BIBLIOGRAPHY

MANUSCRIPT AND ARCHIVAL SOURCES

De Raylan Nicolai, File. Chicago History Museum.

Howard, Alice/William, Vertical File. Ontario County Records and Archive Center, Canandaigua, New York.

Los Angeles City Directory Microfilm Collection. Los Angeles Public Library.

Monaghan, Josephine, Vertical File. Idaho State Historical Society Research Library, Boise.

Mugarrieta, Eliza Alice, Papers. Jose Marcos Murrieta Collection, Bancroft Library, University of California, Berkley.

Shapiro, Bruce G., Papers. GLBT Historical Society, San Francisco.

Stratford, Peter, Personnel File, 1917–1919. Civilian Personnel Records, National Personnel Records Center, St. Louis.

Sullivan, Louis, Collection. GLBT Historical Society, San Francisco.

COURT CASES

"In the Matter of Lucy Ann Slater, a Supposed Lunatic," June 1880. Delaware County Clerk's Office, Delhi, New York.

Probate Case P2–8482. Probate File Copies: Anne De Raylan. Office of the Clerk of the Circuit Court of Cook Country, Chicago.

PRIMARY AND SECONDARY SOURCES

Adams, Edward E., and Gerald J. Baldasty. "Syndicated Service Dependence and a Lack of Commitment to Localism: Scripps Newspapers and Market Subordination." *Journalism and Mass Communication Quarterly* 78, no. 3 (2001): 519–32.

Ahmed, Sarah. *Queer Phenomenology: Orientations, Objects, Others.* Durham, NC: Duke University Press, 2006.

Anderson, Warwick. *Colonial Pathologies: American Tropical Medicine, Race, and Hygiene in the Philippines.* Durham, NC: Duke University Press, 2006.

Arendt, Hannah. *The Origins of Totalitarianism.* New York: Harcourt Brace Jovanovich, 1973.

Ayer, N. W. *N. W. Ayer & Son's American Newspaper Annual, 1883.* Philadelphia: N. W. Ayer & Son, 1884.

———. *N. W. Ayer & Son's American Newspaper Annual, 1902.* Philadelphia: N. W. Ayer & Son, 1903.

———. *N. W. Ayers & Son's American Newspaper Annual, 1904*. Philadelphia: N. W. Ayer & Son, 1905.

———. *N. W. Ayers & Son's American Newspaper Annual, 1907*. Philadelphia: N. W. Ayer & Son, 1908.

———. *N. W. Ayers & Son's American Newspaper Annual and Directory, 1914*. New York: N. W. Ayer & Son, 1915.

———. *N. W. Ayer & Son's Directory of Newspapers and Periodicals, 1930*. Philadelphia: N. W. Ayer & Sons, 1930.

Bakken, Gordon Morris, and Brenda Farrington. *Women Who Kill Men: California Courts, Gender, and the Press*. Lincoln: University of Nebraska Press, 2009.

Baldasty, Gerald. *E. W. Scripps and the Business of Newspapers*. Urbana: University of Illinois Press, 1999.

Baltich, Frances. *Search for Safety: The Founding of Stockton's Black Community*. Sacramento: Cottage Creations, 1982.

Baynton, Douglas. "Disability and the Justification of Inequality in America." In *Race, Class, and Gender in the United States: An Integrated Study*, 7th ed., edited by Paula S. Rothenberg, 92–101. New York: St. Martin's Press, 2007.

Beauchamp, Toby. "Artful Concealment and Strategic Visibility: Transgender Bodies and U.S. State Surveillance after 9/11." In *The Transgender Studies Reader 2*, edited by Aren Aizura and Susan Stryker, 46–55. New York: Routledge, 2013.

Bederman, Gail. *Manliness and Civilization: A Cultural History of Gender and Race in the United States, 1880–1917*. Chicago: University of Chicago Press, 1995.

Beemyn, Genny. "A Presence in the Past: A Transgender History." *Journal of Women's History* 25, no. 4 (2013): 113–21.

———. "U.S. History." In *Trans Bodies, Trans Selves: A Resource for the Transgender Community*, edited by Laura Erickson-Schroth, 501–36. New York: Oxford University Press, 2014.

Behling, Laura L. *The Masculine Woman in America, 1890–1935*. Urbana: University of Illinois Press, 2001.

Berlant, Lauren. *The Queen of America Goes to Washington City*. Durham, NC: Duke University Press, 1997.

Blanton, DeAnne, and Lauren Cook. *They Fought Like Demons: Women Soldiers and the Civil War*. New York: Vintage, 2003.

Boag, Peter. "Go West Young Man, Go East Young Woman: Searching for the *Trans* in Western Gender History." *Western Historical Quarterly* 36, no. 4 (2005): 477–97.

———. *Re-dressing America's Frontier Past*. Berkeley: University of California Press, 2011.

———. *Same-Sex Affairs: Constructing and Controlling Sexuality in the Pacific Northwest*. Berkeley: University of California Press, 2005.

Bosniak, Linda. "Universal Citizenship and the Problem of Alienage." *Northwestern Law Review* 94 (Spring 2000): 964–65.

Boyd, Nan Alamilla. "The Materiality of Gender: Looking for Lesbian Bodies in Transgender History." *Journal of Lesbian Studies* 3, no. 3 (1999): 73–81.

———. *Wide-Open Town: A History of Queer San Francisco to 1965*. Berkeley: University of California Press, 2003.

Boydston, Jeanne. "Gender as a Question of Historical Analysis." *Gender & History* 20, no. 3 (2008): 558–83.

———. *Home and Work: Housework, Wages, and the Ideology of Labor in the Early Republic*. New York: Oxford University Press, 1990.

Briggs, Laura. *Reproducing Empire: Race, Sex, Science, and U.S. Imperialism in Puerto Rico*. Berkeley: University of California Press, 2002.

Brody, David. *Visualizing Empire: Orientalism and Imperialism in the Philippines*. Chicago: University of Chicago Press, 2010.

Bruyneel, Kevin. *The Third Space of Sovereignty: The Postcolonial Politics of U.S.-Indigenous Relations*. Minneapolis: University of Minnesota Press, 2007.

Buchanan, Thomas R. "Black Milwaukee, 1890–1915." Master's thesis, University of Wisconsin–Milwaukee, 1974.

Burgess, Lauren Cook. *An Uncommon Solider: The Civil War Letters of Sarah Wakeman, 153rd Regiment, New York State Volunteers, 1862–1864*. New York: Oxford University Press, 1996.

Butler, Judith. *Gender Trouble: Feminism and the Subversion of Identity*. New York: Routledge, 1990.

Cahn, Naomi R. "Faithless Wives and Lazy Husbands: Gender Norms in Nineteenth Century Divorce Laws." *University of Illinois Law Review* 3 (2002): 651–98.

Califa, Pat. *Sex Changes: The Politics of Transgenderism*. San Francisco: Cleis Press, 1997.

Campbell, W. Joseph. *The Year That Defined American Journalism: 1897 and the Clash of Paradigms*. New York: Routledge, 2006.

Canaday, Margot. *The Straight State: Sexuality and Citizenship in Twentieth-Century America*. Princeton, NJ: Princeton University Press, 2009.

Carter, Julian. *The Heart of Whiteness: Normal Sexuality and Race in America, 1880–1940*. Durham, NC: Duke University Press, 2007.

Castle, Terry. "Matters Not Fit to Be Mentioned: Fielding's *The Female Husband.*" *ELH* 49, no. 3 (1982): 602–22.

Caucho, Lisa. *Social Death: Racialized Rightlessness and the Criminalization of the Unprotected*. New York: New York University Press, 2011.

Chambers-Schiller, Lee Virginia. *Liberty, a Better Husband: Single Women in America: The Generation of 1780–1840*. New Haven, CT: Yale, 1984.

Chauncey, George. "From Sexual Inversion to Homosexuality: Medicine and the Changing Conceptualization of Female Deviance." *Salmagundi* 58–59 (1982): 114–46.

———. *Gay New York: Gender, Urban Culture, and the Making of the Gay Male World, 1890–1940*. New York: Basic Books, 1994.

————. *Why Marriage? The History Shaping Today's Debate over Gay Equality.* New York: Basic Books, 2004.

Chen, Constance M. *"The Sex Side of Life": Mary Ware Dennett's Pioneering Battle for Birth Control and Sex Education.* New York: New Press, 1996.

Clare, Eli. "Stolen Bodies, Reclaimed Bodies: Disability and Queerness." *Public Culture* 13, no. 3 (2001): 359–65.

Clayton, Susan. "Can Two and a Half Centuries of Female Husbands Inform (Trans) History?" *Journal of Lesbian Studies* 14, no. 2 (2010): 288–302.

Cleves, Rachel Hope. "Beyond the Binaries in Early America: Special Issue Introduction." *Early American Studies* 12, no. 3 (2014): 459–68.

————. *Charity and Sylvia: A Same-Sex Marriage in Early America.* New York: Oxford University Press, 2014.

————. " 'What, Another Female Husband?': A Prehistory of Same-Sex Marriage in America." *Journal of American History* 101, no. 4 (2015): 1055–81.

Cohen, Cathy. "Punks, Bulldaggers, and Welfare Queens: The Radical Potential of Queer Politics?" *GLQ* 3, no. 4 (1997): 440–53.

Cohen, Paul A. *History in Three Keys: The Boxers as Event, Experience, and Myth.* New York: Columbia University Press, 1997.

Cott, Nancy. *Public Vows: A History of Marriage and the Nation.* Cambridge, MA: Harvard University Press, 2000.

————. *The Grounding of Modern Feminism.* New Haven, CT: Yale University Press, 1987.

Cromwell, Jason. "Passing Women and Female-Bodied Men: (Re)claiming FTM History." In *Reclaiming Genders: Transsexual Grammars at the Fin de Siècle*, edited by Kate More and Steven Whittle, 34–61. London: Continuum, 1999.

————. *Transmen and FTMs: Identities, Bodies, Genders, and Sexualities.* Urbana: University of Illinois Press, 1999.

D'Emilio, John. "Capitalism and Gay Identity." In *The Lesbian and Gay Studies Reader*, edited by Henry Abelove, Michele Aina Barale, and David Halperin, 467–78. New York: Routledge, 1993.

————. *Sexual Politics, Sexual Communities: The Making of a Homosexual Minority in the United States, 1940–1970.* Chicago: University of Chicago Press, 1983.

D'Emilio, John, and Estelle B. Freedman. *Intimate Matters: A History of Sexuality in America.* New York: Harper & Row, 1988.

De la Croix, St. Sukie. *Chicago Whispers: A History of LGBT Chicago before Stonewall.* Madison: University of Wisconsin Press, 2012.

Deloria, Philip. *Playing Indian.* New Haven, CT: Yale University Press, 1999.

De Lauretis, Teresa. *The Practice of Love.* Bloomington: Indiana University Press, 1994.

DePastino, Todd. *Citizen Hobo: How a Century of Homelessness Shaped America.* Chicago: University of Chicago Press, 2003.

De Leon, Arnoldo. *They Called Them Greasers: Anglo Attitudes toward Mexicans in Texas, 1821–1900.* Austin: University of Texas Press, 1983.

Dinshaw, Carolyn. "Born Too Soon, Born Too Late: The Female Hunter of Long Eddy, circa 1855." In *21st-Century Gay Culture*, edited by David A. Powell, 1–12. Newcastle, UK: Cambridge Scholar Publishing, 2008.

Dorsey, Bruce. *Reforming Men and Women: Gender in the Antebellum City*. Ithaca, NY: Cornell University Press, 2002.

Dubbert, Joe L. "Progressivism and the Masculinity Crisis." In *The American Man*, edited by Elizabeth H. Pleck and Joseph H. Pleck, 303–20. Englewood Cliffs, NJ: Prentice Hall, 1980.

Duberman, Martin. " 'She Even Chewed Tobacco': A Pictorial Narrative of Passing Women in America." In *Hidden from History: Reclaiming the Gay and Lesbian Past*, edited by Martin B. Duberman, Martha Vicinus, and George Chauncey, 183–204. New York: New American Library, 1989.

Dubois, Ellen. *Woman Suffrage and Woman's Rights*. New York: New York University Press, 1998.

Duggan, Lisa. *Sapphic Slashers: Sex, Violence, and American Modernity*. Durham, NC: Duke University Press, 2000.

———. *Twilight for Equality? Neoliberalism, Cultural Politics, and the Attack on Democracy*. Boston: Beacon Press, 2004.

Edelman, Lee. *No Future: Queer Theory and the Death Drive*. Durham, NC: Duke University Press, 2004.

Edwards, Holly, ed. *Noble Dreams, Wicked Pleasures: Orientalism in America, 1870–1930*. Princeton, NJ: Princeton University Press, 2000.

Ellis, Havelock. *Studies in the Psychology of Sex*. Vol. 2: *Sexual Inversion*. 3rd ed. 1927. Reprint, Charleston, SC: BiblioBazaar, 2006.

Eskridge, William N. *Gaylaw: Challenging the Apartheid of the Closet*. Cambridge, MA: Harvard University Press, 2002.

———. "Law and the Construction of the Closet: American Regulation of Same-Sex Intimacy, 1880–1946." *Iowa Law Review* 82, no. 4 (1997): 1036–37.

Ethington, Philip J. *The Public City: The Political Construction of Urban Life in San Francisco, 1850–1890*. Berkeley: University of California Press, 1994.

Faderman, Lillian. *Odd Girls and Twilight Lovers: A History of Lesbian Life in Twentieth-Century America*. New York: Columbia University Press, 1991.

———. *Surpassing the Love of Men: Romantic Friendship and Love between Women from the Renaissance to the Present*. New York: Morrow, 1981.

———. "The Morbidification of Love between Women by 19th-Century Sexologists." *Journal of Homosexuality* 4, no. 1 (1978): 73–90.

Faderman, Lillian, and Stuart Timmons. *Gay L.A.: A History of Sexual Outlaws, Power Politics, and Lipstick Lesbians*. New York: Basic Books, 2006.

Faragher, John Mark. *Women and Men on the Overland Trail*. New Haven, CT: Yale University Press, 1980.

Fielding, Henry. *The female husband; or, The surprising history of Mrs. Mary, alias Mrs. George Hamilton, who was convicted of having married a young woman of Wells and lived with her as her husband. Taken from her own mouth since her confinement.* London, 1746.

Filene, Peter G. *Him/Her/Self: Sex Roles in Modern America.* Baltimore: Johns Hopkins University Press, 1986.

Flexner, Eleanor, and Ellen Fitzpatrick. *Century of Struggle: The Woman's Rights Movement in the United States.* Cambridge, MA: Belknap Press of Harvard University Press, 1996.

Foucault, Michel. *The History of Sexuality, Volume 1: An Introduction.* Translated by Robert Hurley. 1978. Reprint, New York: Vintage, 1990.

Fraser, Nancy, and Linda Gordon. "A Genealogy of Dependency: Tracing a Keyword of the U.S. Welfare State." *Signs: Journal of Women and Culture in Society* 19, no. 2 (1994): 309–36.

Ferguson, Robert A. *The Trial in American Life.* Chicago: University of Chicago Press, 2007.

Gabaccia, Donna. *From the Other Side: Women, Gender, and Immigrant Life in the United States, 1820–1990.* Bloomington: Indiana University Press, 1994.

Garber, Marjorie. *Vested Interests: Cross-Dressing and Cultural Anxiety.* New York: Harper Perennial, 1992.

Gardner, Martha. *The Qualities of a Citizen: Women, Immigration, and Citizenship, 1870–1965.* Princeton, NJ: Princeton University Press, 2005.

Gibson, Margaret. "Clitoral Corruption: Body Metaphors and American Doctors' Constructions of Female Homosexuality, 1870–1900." In *Science and Homosexualities,* edited by Vernon Rosario, 108–32. New York: Routledge, 1997.

Gilmore, Ruth Wilson. "Fatal Couplings of Power and Difference: Notes on Racism and Geography." *Professional Geographer* 54, no. 1 (2002): 15–24.

Gourley, Catherine. *Gibson Girls and Suffragists: Perceptions of Women from 1900 to 1918.* Minneapolis: Twenty-First Century Books, 2008.

Gray, Mary. *Out in the Country: Youth, Media, and Queer Visibility in Rural America.* New York: New York University Press, 2009.

Gray, Mary, Colin Johnson, and Brian Gilley, eds. *Queering the Countryside: New Frontiers in Rural Queer Studies.* New York: New York University Press, 2016.

Greenberg, David F. *The Construction of Homosexuality.* Chicago: University of Chicago Press, 1988.

Grossberg, Michael. *Governing the Hearth: Law and the Family in Nineteenth-Century America.* Chapel Hill: University of North Carolina Press, 1988.

———. "Guarding the Altar: Physiological Restrictions and the Rise of State Intervention in Matrimony." *American Journal of Legal History* 26, no. 3 (1982): 197–226.

Grossman, Joanna. "Civil Rights: The Gay Marriage Controversy in Historical Perspective." In *Law, Society and History: Essays on Themes in the Legal History and Legal Sociology of Lawrence M. Friedman,* edited by Robert Gordon, 253–72. Cambridge, UK: Cambridge University Press, 2011.

Grossman, Joanna, and Lawrence Friedman, eds. *Inside the Castle: Law and the Family in 20th Century America.* Princeton, NJ: Princeton University Press, 2014.

Hahn, Steven. *A Nation under Our Feet: Black Political Struggles in the Rural South from Slavery to the Great Migration*. Cambridge, MA: Belknap Press of Harvard University Press, 2005.

Halberstam, J. *Female Masculinity*. Durham, NC: Duke University Press, 1998.

———. *In a Queer Time and Place: Transgender Bodies, Subcultural Lives*. Durham, NC: Duke University Press, 2005.

———. "Telling Tales, Brandon Teena, Billy Tipton, and Transgender Biography." *a/b: Auto/Biography Studies* 15, no. 1 (2000): 62–81.

Hale, Grace Elizabeth. *Making Whiteness: The Culture of Segregation in the South, 1890–1940*. New York: Pantheon Books, 1998.

Hall, Fred S. *Medical Certification for Marriage: An Account of the Administration of the Wisconsin Marriage Law as It Relates to the Venereal Diseases*. New York: Russell Sage Foundation, 1925.

Halttunen, Karen. *Confidence Men and Painted Women: A Study of Middle-Class Culture in America, 1830–1870*. New Haven, CT: Yale University Press, 1986.

Harley, Gail M. *Emma Curtis Hopkins: Forgotten Founder of New Thought*. Syracuse, NY: Syracuse University Press, 2002.

Harnett, Richard M., and Billy G. Ferguson. *Unipress: United Press International Covering the 20th Century*. Golden, CO: Fulcrum, 2003.

Harris, Cheryl I. "Whiteness as Property." In *Critical Race Theory: The Key Writings That Formed the Movement*, edited by Kimberlé Crenshaw, Neil Gotanda, Gary Peller, and Kendall Thomas, 276–91. New York: New Press, 1995.

Haynes, April. *Riotous Flesh: Women, Physiology, and the Solitary Vice in Nineteenth-Century America*. Chicago: University of Chicago Press, 2015.

Heidenreich, Linda. "Jack Mugarrieta Garland: A Queer Mestiz@ in the 'American West.'" *Lilith: A Feminist History Journal* 21 (August 2015): 65–77.

Henkin, David. *The Postal Age: The Emergence of Modern Communications in Nineteenth-Century America*. Chicago: University of Chicago Press, 2007.

Herring, Scott. *Another Country: Queer Anti-Urbanism*. New York: New York University Press, 2010.

Higbie, Frank Tobias. *Indispensable Outcasts: Hobo Workers and Community in the American Midwest, 1880–1930*. Urbana: University of Illinois Press, 2003.

Higham, John. *Strangers in the Land: Patterns of American Nativism, 1860–1925*. New York: Atheneum, 1974.

Hill, Karlos K. *Beyond the Rope: The Impact of Lynching on Black Culture and Memory*. New York: Cambridge University Press, 2016.

Hodes, Martha. *White Women: Black Men: Illicit Sex in the Nineteenth-Century South*. New Haven, CT: Yale University Press, 1997.

Hofstadter, Richard. *The Age of Reform: From Bryan to FDR*. New York: Vintage, 1955.

Hoganson, Kristin. *Fighting for American Manhood: How Gender Politics Provoked the Spanish-American and Philippine-American Wars*. New Haven, CT: Yale University Press, 1998.

Horsman, Reginald. *Race and Manifest Destiny: The Origins of American Racial Anglo-Saxonism*. Cambridge, MA: Harvard University Press, 1981.

Howard, John. *Men Like That: A Southern Queer History*. Chicago: University of Chicago Press, 1999.

———. "The Talk of the Country: Revisiting Accusation, Murder, and Mississippi, 1895." In *Queer Studies: An Interdisciplinary Reader*, edited by Robert Corber and Stephen Valocchi, 142–58. Malden, MA: Blackwell, 2003.

Hundorf, Shari. *Going Native: Indians in the American Cultural Imagination*. Ithaca, NY: Cornell University Press, 2001.

Hunter, Jane. *How Young Ladies Became Girls: The Victorian Origins of American Girlhood*. New Haven, CT: Yale University Press, 2003.

Hurewitz, Daniel. *Bohemian Los Angeles and the Making of Modern Politics*. Berkeley: University of California Press, 2007.

Jacobson, Mathew Frye. *Barbarian Virtues: The United States Encounters Foreign Peoples at Home and Abroad, 1876–1917*. New York: Hill and Wang, 2000.

James, Ernest C., ed. *Narrative and Publications Relating to Lucy Ann Lobdell, the Female Hunter of Delaware and Sullivan Counties, New York*. Sacramento: E. C. James, 1996.

Jenkins, Philip. *Mystics and Messiahs: Cults and New Religions in American History*. New York: Oxford University Press, 2000.

Johnson, Colin. *Just Queer Folks: Gender and Sexuality in Rural America*. Philadelphia: Temple University Press, 2013.

Johnson, E. Patrick. *Sweet Tea: Black Gay Men of the South*. Chapel Hill: University of North Carolina Press, 2011.

Joseph, Miranda. *Against the Romance of Community*. Minneapolis: University of Minnesota Press, 2002.

Kaestle, Carl F. "Seeing the Sites: Readers, Publishers, and Local Print Cultures in 1880." In *A History of the Book in America, Volume 4: Print in Motion: The Expansion of Publishing and Reading in the United States, 1880–1940*, edited by Carl F. Kaestle and Janice A. Radway, 22–48. Chapel Hill: University of North Carolina Press, 2009.

Kaplan, Richard. "From Partisanship to Professionalism: The Transformation of the Daily Press." In *Print in Motion: The Expansion of Publishing and Reading in the United States, 1880–1940*, edited by Carl F. Kaestle and Janice A. Radway, 116–39. Chapel Hill: University of North Carolina Press, 2009.

Katz, Jonathan Ned. *Gay American History: Lesbians and Gay Men in the U.S.A.* New York: Harper & Row, 1976.

———. *Gay/Lesbian Almanac: A New Documentary*. New York: Carroll and Graf, 1983.

Keire, Mara L. *For Business and Pleasure: Red-Light Districts and the Regulation of Vice in the United States, 1890–1933*. Baltimore: Johns Hopkins University Press, 2010.

Kennedy, Elizabeth Lapovsky, and Madeline D. Davis. *Boots of Leather, Slippers of Gold: The History of a Lesbian Community*. New York: Routledge, 1993.

Kielbowicz, Richard B., and Linda Lawson. "Protecting the Small-Town Press: Community, Social Policy, and Postal Privileges, 1845–1970." *Canadian Review of American Studies* 19 (Spring 1988): 23–45.

Kiernan, James G. "Invert Marriages." *Urologic and Cutaneous Review* 18 (1914): 550.

———. "Original Communications. Insanity. Lecture XXVI: Sexual Perversion." *Detroit Lancet* 7 (1884): 482–83.

Kimmel, Michael. "The Contemporary 'Crisis' in Masculinity in Historical Perspective." In *The Making of Masculinities*, edited by Harry Brod, 121–54. Boston: Allen and Unwin, 1987.

Kline, Wendy. *Building a Better Race: Gender, Sexuality, and Eugenics from the Turn of the Century to the Baby Boom*. Berkeley: University of California Press, 2005.

Krafft-Ebing, Richard von. *Psychopathia Sexualis*. Translated by Franklin S. Klaf. 1886. New York: Arcade Publishing, 1965.

Kramer, Paul. *The Blood of Government: Race, Empire, the United States, and the Philippines*. Chapel Hill: University of North Carolina Press, 2006.

Kunzel, Regina. *Criminal Intimacy: Prison and the Uneven History of Modern American Sexuality*. Chicago: University of Chicago Press, 2008.

Landrum, Shane. "Registering Race, Policing Citizenship: Delayed Birth Registration and the Virginia Racial Integrity Act, 1924–1975." Paper presented at the Public History Conference, Columbus, Ohio, June 3–6, 2010.

Langum, David. *Crossing the Line: Legislating Morality and the Mann Act*. Chicago: University of Chicago Press, 1994.

Larson, Scott. "'Indescribable Being': Theological Performances of Genderlessness in the Society of the Publick Universal Friend, 1776–1819." *Early American Studies* 12, no. 3 (2014): 576–600.

Lears, T. J. Jackson. *No Place of Grace*. New York: Pantheon Books, 1981.

———. *Rebirth of a Nation: Making Modern America, 1877–1920*. New York: Harper Perennial, 2010.

Lee, Alfred McClung. *The Daily Newspaper in America: The Evolution of a Social Instrument*. New York: Octagon Books, 1973.

Lee, Erica. *At America's Gates: Chinese Immigration during the Exclusion Era, 1882–1943*. Chapel Hill: University of North Carolina Press, 2003.

Lee, Robert. *Orientals: Asian Americans in Popular Culture*. Philadelphia: Temple University Press, 1999.

Limerick, Patricia. *The Legacy of Conquest: The Unbroken Past of the American West*. New York: Norton, 1987.

Lipsitz, George. *Possessive Investment in Whiteness: How White People Profit from Identity Politics*. Philadelphia: Temple University Press, 1998.

Lobdell, Bambi L. *"A Strange Sort of Being": The Transgender Life of Lucy Ann / Joseph Israel Lobdell, 1829–1912*. Jefferson, NC: McFarland, 2012.

Lobdell, Lucy Ann. *The Narrative of the Female Hunter of Delaware County*. New York, 1855.

Love, Heather. *Feeling Backward: Loss and the Politics of Queer History*. Durham, NC: Duke University Press, 2007.

———. "Gyn/Apology: Sarah Orne Jewett's Spinster Aesthetics." *ESQ: A Journal of the American Renaissance* 55, nos. 3–4 (2009): 305–34.

Luibhéid, Eithne. *Entry Denied: Controlling Sexuality at the Border*. Minneapolis: University of Minnesota Press, 2002.

Luibhéid, Eithne, and Lionel Cantú Jr., eds. *Queer Migrations: Sexuality, U.S. Citizenship, and Border Crossings*. Minneapolis: University of Minnesota Press, 2005.

Lynagh, Paula. *Milwaukee's Negro Community*. Milwaukee: Citizen's Government Research Bureau, 1946.

Manalansan, Martin. "Diasporic Deviants/Divas: How Filipino Gay Transmigrants 'Play with the World.'" In *Queer Diasporas*, edited by Cindy Patton and Benigno Sánchez-Eppler, 183–203. Durham, NC: Duke University Press, 2000.

———. *Global Divas: Filipino Gay Men in the Diaspora*. Durham, NC: Duke University Press, 2003.

Manion, Jennifer. "(Trans)gressing the Category of Woman in the Eighteenth Century." Paper presented at the Society for Historians of the Early American Republic Conference, Baltimore, July 21, 2012.

"Marriages between Women." *Alienist and Neurologist: A Quarterly Journal of Scientific, Clinical and Forensic Psychiatry and Neurology* 23 (1902): 497–99.

Matthews, Jean V. *The Rise of the New Woman: The Women's Movement in America, 1875–1930*. Chicago: Ivan R. Dee, 2003.

McGerr, Michael. *A Fierce Discontent: The Rise and Fall of the Progressive Movement in America, 1870–1920*. New York: Oxford University Press, 2005.

McMillen, Sally. *Lucy Stone: An Unapologetic Life*. New York: Oxford University Press, 2015.

Mead, Rebecca J. *How the Vote Was Won: Woman Suffrage in the Western United States, 1868–1914*. New York: New York University Press, 2004.

Mendoza, Victor Román. *Metroimperial Intimacies: Fantasy, Racial-Sexual Governance, and the Philippines in U.S. Imperialism, 1899–1913*. Durham, NC: Duke University Press, 2015.

Miles, Tiya. "'His Kingdom for a Kiss': Indians and Intimacy in the Narrative of John Murrant." In *Haunted by Empire: Geographies of Intimacy in North American History*, edited by Laura Stoler, 163–90. Durham, NC: Duke University Press, 2006.

Minnick, Sylvia Sun. *Samfow: The San Joaquin Chinese Legacy*. Fresno, CA: Panorama West, 1988.

———. *The Chinese Community of Stockton*. Chicago: Arcadia, 2002.

Mitchell, Pablo. *Coyote Nation: Sexuality, Race, and Conquest in Modernizing New Mexico, 1880–1920*. Chicago: University of Chicago Press, 2005.

Modleski, Tania. "A Woman's Gotta Do . . . What a Man's Gotta Do? Cross-Dressing in the Western." *Signs* 22, no. 3 (1997): 519–44.

Molina, Natalia. *Fit to Be Citizens? Public Health and Race in Los Angeles, 1879–1939*. Berkeley: University of California Press, 2006.

Molina-Guzmán, Isabel. "Gendering Latinidad through the Elián Discourse about Cuban Women." *Latino Studies* 3, no. 2 (2005): 179–204.

Morgensen, Scott Lauria. *Spaces between Us: Settler Colonialism and Indigenous Decolonization*. Minneapolis: University of Minnesota Press, 2011.

Morison, Elting, ed. *Letters of Theodore Roosevelt, Volume 3*. Cambridge, MA: Harvard University Press, 1951.

Muhammad, Khalil. *Condemnation of Blackness: Race, Crime, and the Making of Modern America*. Cambridge, MA: Harvard University Press, 2010.

Mumford, Kevin. *Interzones: Black/White Sex Districts in New York and Chicago in the Early Twentieth Century*. New York: Columbia University Press, 1997.

Newton, Ester. *Cherry Grove, Fire Island: Sixty Years in America's First Gay and Lesbian Town*. Boston: Beacon Press, 1993.

———. "The Mythic Mannish Lesbian: Radclyffe Hall and the New Woman." *Signs* 9, no. 4 (1984): 557–75.

Ngai, Mae. *Impossible Subjects: Illegal Aliens and the Making of Modern America*. Princeton, NJ: Princeton University Press, 2004.

Ngô, Fiona. *Imperial Blues: Geographies of Race and Sex in Jazz Age New York*. Durham, NC: Duke University Press, 2014.

Nicolazzo, Sarah. "Henry Fielding's *The Female Husband* and the Sexuality of Vagrancy." *Eighteenth Century* 55, no. 4 (2014): 335–55.

Niven, Francis L. *Manhattan Omnibus: Stories of Historical Interest of Manhattan and Its Surrounding Communities*. Bozeman, MT: F. L. Niven, 1989.

Noble County Genealogical Society. *The Cemeteries of Noble County, Volume II*. Kendallville, IN: Modern Publishing, 1985.

North, S. N. D. *The Newspaper and Periodical Press*. Washington, DC: Census Office, Department of the Interior, 1884.

Odem, Mary E. *Delinquent Daughters: Protecting and Policing Adolescent Female Sexuality in the United States, 1885–1920*. Chapel Hill: University of North Carolina Press, 1995.

Ordover, Nancy. *American Eugenics: Race, Queer Anatomy, and the Science of Nationalism*. Minneapolis: University of Minnesota Press, 2003.

Orsi, Robert. "The Religious Boundaries of an In-Between People: Street *Feste* and the Problem of the Dark-Skinned 'Other' in Italian Harlem, 1920–1990." *American Quarterly* 44 (September 1992): 313–47.

Pascoe, Peggy. *Relations of Rescue: The Search for Female Moral Authority in the American West, 1874–1939*. New York: Oxford University Press, 1993.

———. *What Comes Naturally: Miscegenation Law and the Making of Race in America*. New York: Oxford University Press, 2009.

Pearson, Susan. "'Age Ought to Be a Fact': The Campaign against Child Labor and the Rise of the Birth Certificate." *Journal of American History* 101, no. 4 (2015): 1144–65.

Pratte, Paul Alfred. *Gods within the Machine: A History of the American Society of Newspaper Editors, 1923–1993*. Westport, CT: Praeger, 1995.

Procter, Ben. *William Randolph Hearst: Final Edition, 1911–1951*. New York: Oxford University Press, 2007.

Puar, Jasbir K. "Queer Times, Queer Assemblages." *Social Text* 23, nos. 2–4 (2005): 121–39.

———. *Terrorist Assemblages: Homonationalism in Queer Times*. Durham, NC: Duke University Press, 2007.

Rand, Erica. *Ellis Island Snow Globe*. Durham, NC: Duke University Press, 2005.

Reis, Elizabeth. *Bodies in Doubt: An American History of Intersex*. Baltimore: Johns Hopkins University Press, 2009.

Rice, Edward. *Captain Sir Richard Burton: A Biography*. Cambridge, MA: Da Capo Press, 1990.

Rifkin, Mark. "Romancing Kinship: A Queer Reading of Indian Education and Zitkala-Ša's *American Indian Stories*." *GLQ* 12, no. 1 (2006): 27–59.

———. *When Did Indians Become Straight? Kinship, the History of Sexuality, and Native Sovereignty*. New York: Oxford University Press, 2011.

Roediger, David. *How Race Survived U.S. History: From Settlement and Slavery to the Obama Phenomenon*. New York: Verso, 2008.

———. *The Wages of Whiteness: Race and the Making of the American Working Class*. New York: Verso, 1991.

———. *Working towards Whiteness: How America's Immigrants Became White*. New York: Basic Books, 2005.

Rofel, Lisa. "Qualities of Desire: Imagining Gay Identities in China." *GLQ* 5, no. 4 (1999): 451–74.

Rotundo, E. Anthony. *American Manhood: Transformations in Masculinity from the Revolution to the Modern Era*. New York: Basic Books, 1993.

Rowell, George, ed. *Geo. P. Rowell and Co.'s American Newspaper Directory*. New York: Geo. P. Rowell & Co., 1877.

Rupp, Leila. *A Desired Past: A Shot History of Same-Sex Love in America*. Chicago: University of Chicago Press, 1999.

Russo, Daniel J. "The Origins of Local News in the U.S. Country Press, 1940s–1870s." *Journalism Monographs* 65 (1980): 1–43.

San Francisco Lesbian and Gay History Project. *She Even Chewed Tobacco*. Documentary film, 1979.

Sánchez-Eppler, Benigno, and Cindy Patton. "Introduction: With a Passport out of Eden." In *Queer Diasporas*, edited by Cindy Patton and Benigno Sánchez-Eppler, 1–14. Durham, NC: Duke University Press, 2000.

Sandweiss, Martha. *Passing Strange: A Gilded Age Tale of Love and Deception across the Color Line*. New York: Penguin, 2009.

Satter, Beryl. *Each Mind a Kingdom: American Women, Sexual Purity, and the New Thought Movement, 1875–1920*. Berkeley: University of California Press, 2001.

Schlatter, Evelyn A. "Drag's a Life: Women, Gender, and Cross-Dressing in the Nineteenth Century West." In *Writing the Range: Race, Class, and Culture in the Women's West*, edited by Elizabeth Jameson and Susan Lodge Armitage, 334–48. Norman: University of Oklahoma Press, 1997.

Schweik, Susan. *The Ugly Laws: Disability in Public*. New York: New York University Press, 2009.

Segrave, Kerry. *Women Swindlers in America, 1860–1920*. Jefferson, NC: McFarland, 2007.

Sears, Clare. "'A Dress Not Belonging to His or Her Sex': Cross-Dressing Law in San Francisco, 1860–1900." PhD diss., University of California, Santa Cruz, 2005.

———. *Arresting Dress: Cross-Dressing, Law, and Fascination in Nineteenth-Century San Francisco*. Durham, NC: Duke University Press, 2014.

———. "Electric Brilliancy: Cross-Dressing Law and Freak Show Displays in Nineteenth-Century San Francisco." *WSQ: Women's Studies Quarterly* 36, no. 3 (2008): 170–87.

Schirmer, Daniel B., and Stephen Rosskamm Shalom, eds. *The Philippines Reader: A History of Colonialism, Neocolonialism, Dictatorship, and Resistance*. Boston: South End Press, 1987.

Sedgwick, Eve Kosofsky. *Epistemology of the Closet*. Berkeley: University of California Press, 2008.

Shah, Nayan. "Between 'Oriental Depravity' and 'Natural Degenerates': Spatial Border-lands and the Making of Ordinary Americans." *American Quarterly* 57, no. 3 (2005): 703–25.

———. *Contagious Divides: Epidemics and Race in San Francisco's Chinatown*. Berkeley: University of California Press, 2001.

Shohat, Ella. "Gender in Hollywood's Orient." *Middle East Report* 162 (January–February 1990): 40–42.

———. *Taboo Memories, Diasporic Voices*. Durham: Duke University Press, 2006.

Skidmore, Emily. "Ralph Kerwineo's Queer Body: Narrating the Scales of Social Membership in the Early Twentieth Century." *GLQ: A Journal of Lesbian and Gay Studies* 20, no. 1 (2014): 141–66.

Sloop, John M. "Lucy Lobdell's Queer Circumstances." In *Queering Public Address: Sexualities in American Historical Discourse*, edited by Charles E. Morris III, 149–72. Columbia: University of South Carolina Press, 2007.

Slotkin, Richard. *Gunfighter Nation: The Myth of the Frontier in Twentieth-Century America*. Norman: University of Oklahoma Press, 1998.

———. *Regeneration through Violence: The Mythology of the American Frontier*. Middleton, CT: Wesleyan University Press, 1973.

Smith, A. C. *History of Meeker County: A Historical Sketch of Meeker County, Minnesota from Its First Settlement to July 4th, 1876*. Litchfield, MN: Belfoy & Joubert, 1877.

Smith-Rosenberg, Carroll. *Disorderly Conduct: Visions of Gender in Victorian America*. New York: Alfred A. Knopf, 1985.

———. "The Female World of Love and Ritual: Relations between Women in Nineteenth-Century America." *Signs: Journal of Women in Culture and Society* 1, no. 1 (1975): 1–29.

Somerville, Siobhan. *Queering the Color Line: Race and the Invention of Homosexuality in American Culture*. Durham, NC: Duke University Press, 2000.

Stansell, Christine. *City of Women: Sex and Class in New York, 1789–1860*. Urbana: University of Illinois Press, 1987.

Stein, Marc. *City of Sisterly and Brotherly Loves: Lesbian and Gay Philadelphia*. Chicago: University of Chicago Press, 2000.

———. "Theoretical Perspectives, Local Communities: The Making of U.S. LGBT Historiography." *GLQ* 11, no. 4 (2005): 605–25.

Stern, Alexandra. *Eugenic Nation: Faults and Frontiers of Better Breeding in Modern America* Berkeley: University of California Press, 2005.

Stevens, John D. *Sensationalism and the New York Press*. New York: Columbia University Press, 1991.

Stryker, Susan. *Transgender History*. Berkeley, CA: Seal Press, 2008.

———. "Transgender History, Homonormativity, and Disciplinarily." *Radical History Review* 100 (Winter 2008): 145–57.

———. "Transgender Studies: Queer Theory's Evil Twin." *GLQ* 10, no. 2 (2004): 212–15.

Sullivan, Louis. *From Female to Male: The Life of Jack Bee Garland*. Boston: Alyson Books, 1990.

Syrett, Nicholas L. "A Busman's Holiday in the Not-So-Lonely Crowd: Business Culture, Epistolary Networks, and Itinerant Homosexuality in Mid-Twentieth-Century America." *Journal of the History of Sexuality* 21, no. 1 (2012): 121–40.

———. "The Boys of Beaver Meadow: A Homosexual Community at 1920s Dartmouth College." *American Studies* 48, no. 2 (2007): 9–18.

Tapia, Ruby C. "Un(di)ing Legacies: White Matters of Memory in Portraits of 'Our Princess.'" *Cultural Values* 5, no. 2 (2001): 261–87.

Tasker, Yvonne. *Working Girls: Gender and Sexuality in Popular Cinema*. New York: Routledge, 1998.

Teo, Hsu-Ming. "Orientalism and Mass Market Romance Novels in the Twentieth Century." In *Edward Said: The Legacy of a Public Intellectual*, edited by Ned Curthoys and Debjani Ganguly, 241–62. Melbourne: Melbourne University Press, 2007.

Terry, Jennifer. *An American Obsession: Science, Medicine, and Homosexuality in Modern Society*. Chicago: University of Chicago Press, 1999.

———. "Anxious Slippages between 'Us' and 'Them': A Brief History of the Scientific Search for Homosexual Bodies." In *Deviant Bodies: Critical Perspectives on Difference in Science and Popular Culture*, edited by Jennifer Terry and Jacqueline Urla, 129–69. Bloomington: Indiana University Press, 1995.

Tetrault, Lisa. *The Myth of Seneca Falls: Memory and the Women's Suffrage Movement, 1848–1898*. Chapel Hill: University of North Carolina Press, 2014.

The Commercial Advertiser Directory for the City of Buffalo. Buffalo, NY: E. R. Jewett, 1859.

The Commercial Advertiser Directory for the City of Buffalo. Buffalo, NY: E. R. Jewett, 1860.

Thompson, Brock. *The Un-natural State: Arkansas and the Queer South*. Fayetteville: University of Arkansas Press, 2010.

Tong, Benson. *Unsubmissive Women: Chinese Prostitutes in Nineteenth-Century San Francisco*. Norman: University of Oklahoma Press, 1994.

Tongson, Karen. *Relocations: Queer Suburban Imaginaries*. New York: New York University Press, 2011.

Trachtenberg, Alan. *The Incorporation of America: Culture and Society in the Gilded Age*. New York: Hill and Wang, 1982.

Traub, Valerie. "The Psychomorphology of the Clitoris." *GLQ* 2, nos. 1–2 (1995): 81–113.

Trotter, Joe William. *Black Milwaukee: The Making of an Industrial Proletariat, 1915–1945*. 2nd ed. Urbana: University of Illinois Press, 2007.

Vahle, Neal. *The Unity Movement: Its Evolution and Spiritual Teachings*. Philadelphia: Templeton Foundation Press, 2002.

Valentine, David. "The Categories Themselves." *GLQ* 10, no. 2 (2004): 215–20.

Volpp, Leti. "Blaming Culture for Bad Behavior." *Yale Journal of Law and the Humanities* 12, no. 1 (2000): 89–116.

Wald, Gayle. *Crossing the Line: Racial Passing in Twentieth-Century U.S. Literature and Culture*. Durham, NC: Duke University Press, 2000.

Walters, Suzanna. *The Tolerance Trap: How God, Genes, and Good Intentions Are Sabotaging Gay Equality*. New York: New York University Press, 2014.

Webb, Gisela. "Third-Wave Sufism in America and the Bawa Muhaiyaddeen Fellowship." In *Sufism in the West*, edited by Jamal Malik and John Hinnells, 86–102. New York: Routledge, 2006.

Weibe, Robert. *The Search for Order, 1877–1920*. New York: Hill and Wang, 1966.

Welter, Barbara. "The Cult of True Womanhood: 1820–1860." *American Quarterly* 18, no. 2, pt. 1 (1966): 151–74.

White, Richard. "Frederick Jackson Turner and Buffalo Bill." In *The Frontier in American Culture*, edited by Richard White and Patricia Nelson Limerick, 6–65. Berkeley: University of California Press, 1994.

Wilson, Angela R. "Getting Your Kicks on Route 66: Stories of Gay and Lesbian Life in Rural America, c. 1950s–1970s." In *De-centering Sexualities: Politics and Representations Beyond the Metropolis*, edited by Richard Phillips, David Shuttleton, and Diane Watt, 199–216. New York: Routledge, 2000.

Wilson, Christopher P. "Plotting the Border: John Reed, Pancho Villa, and *Insurgent Mexico*." In *Cultures of United States Imperialism*, edited by Amy Kaplan and Donald E. Pease, 340–64. Durham, NC: Duke University Press, 1993.

Wingerd, Mary Lethert. *Claiming the City: Politics, Faith, and the Power of Place in St. Paul*. Ithaca, NY: Cornell University Press, 2001.

Wise, P. M. "A Case of Sexual Perversion." *Alienist and Neurologist: A Quarterly Journal of Scientific, Clinical, and Forensic Psychiatry and Neurology* 4, no. 1 (1883): 87–91.

Wyman, Mark. *Hoboes: Bindlestiffs, Fruit Tramps, and the Harvesting of the West*. Boston: Hill and Wang, 2010.

Yew, Elizabeth. "Medical Inspection of the Immigrant at Ellis Island: 1891–1924." *Bulletin of the New York Academy of Medicine* 56, no. 5 (1980): 488–510.

INDEX

ABOUT THE AUTHOR

Emily Skidmore is Assistant Professor of History at Texas Tech University, specializing in the history of gender and sexuality in the United States. She lives in Lubbock, Texas.

CPSIA information can be obtained
at www.ICGtesting.com
Printed in the USA
LVHW091303150419
614214LV00004B/14/P